Computer Communications and Networks

Series editor
A.J. Sammes, Centre for Forensic Computing, Cranfield University, Shrivenham Campus, Swindon, UK

The **Computer Communications and Networks** series is a range of textbooks, monographs and handbooks. It sets out to provide students, researchers, and non-specialists alike with a sure grounding in current knowledge, together with comprehensible access to the latest developments in computer communications and networking.

Emphasis is placed on clear and explanatory styles that support a tutorial approach, so that even the most complex of topics is presented in a lucid and intelligible manner.

More information about this series at http://www.springer.com/series/4198

Shao Ying Zhu • Richard Hill
Marcello Trovati
Editors

Guide to Security Assurance for Cloud Computing

Editors
Shao Ying Zhu
Department of Computing and Mathematics
College of Engineering and Technology
University of Derby
Derby, UK

Richard Hill
Department of Computing and Mathematics
College of Engineering and Technology
University of Derby
Derby, UK

Marcello Trovati
Department of Computing and Mathematics
College of Engineering and Technology
University of Derby
Derby, UK

ISSN 1617-7975 ISSN 2197-8433 (electronic)
Computer Communications and Networks
ISBN 978-3-319-25986-4 ISBN 978-3-319-25988-8 (eBook)
DOI 10.1007/978-3-319-25988-8

Library of Congress Control Number: 2015959475

Springer Cham Heidelberg New York Dordrecht London

Printed on acid-free paper

Springer International Publishing AG Switzerland is part of Springer Science+Business Media (www.springer.com)

Foreword

The potential benefits of cloud computing are often heralded and acknowledged, notably the lower cost and better fit of on-demand computing resources to most users' requirements as opposed to the relatively high cost of ownership and maintenance of equipment and software. Data centres are thriving, multiple types of service are now available, and registering as a cloud customer only takes a few minutes and a credit card. Yet, there is still a great reluctance evident in many organisations to trust the cloud with critical operating data and processes, which often encompass personal information. This inhibiting factor has been repeatedly identified as a serious barrier to moving to the type of IT infrastructure that is often regarded as crucial to business success in a modern economy. The key issue is one of trust and that is why the theme of this book – assurance – is of such topical significance. The editors have brought together a set of varied but complimentary and informative papers on the topics of governance, compliance and methodologies with reference to the emerging standards for cloud computing security. This comprehensive coverage is augmented by studies of particular issues including denial of service attacks, the growing role of the cloud in mobile device applications such as vehicular networks and the importance of rigorous proof systems in building trust. The book's value lies in providing a single point of reference in the form of a collection of highly relevant information and insights into the theme of security assurance in the cloud.

University of St Andrews, St Andrews, UK
August 2015 Dr. Colin Allison

Preface

Overview and Goals

The rapid adoption of cloud computing has created massive opportunity both for existing businesses and for emerging business models that would not have been possible without 'the cloud'. Much of the opportunity created by cloud computing has come about as a result of the proliferation of mobile computing devices, such as smartphones, tablets and wearable computing. Such devices enable users to interact and therefore collaborate in uncontrolled environments, as they are no longer shackled to enterprise-constrained desktop architectures.

Whilst such a shift in architecture does enable new ways of doing business, it also presents opportunities for costly mistakes via system vulnerabilities or nefarious activities. The opportunities to 'break into' systems are correspondingly increased as software becomes more distributed.

However, there are also arguments to the contrary in relation to cloud computing. Data centres have far greater physical security than most enterprises utilise, and it is likely that the system security is more comprehensive also. It follows that if an enterprise has a need to adopt a cloud architecture (which in many cases is becoming inevitable), it needs to understand how to exploit the opportunities offered by cloud architectures, whilst protecting against the introduction of system vulnerabilities that could harm the business.

Guide to Security Assurance for Cloud Computing presents a series of leading edge articles that discuss and explore the concepts and principles, tools, techniques and deployment models in the context of secure cloud computing.

Key objectives for this book include:

- Coverage of pertinent issues in relation to challenges that prevent organisations from moving to cloud architectures
- Providing relevant theoretical frameworks and the latest empirical research findings
- Discussing real-world vulnerabilities of cloud-based software in order to address the challenges of securing distributed software
- Advancing understanding of the practicalities of cloud security and how applications can assure and comply with legislation

Organisation and Features

This book is organised into two parts:

- Part I describes the important general concepts and principles of security assurance in cloud-based environments.
- Part II discusses applications and approaches to cloud security that illustrate the current state of the art.

Target Audiences

We have written this book to support a number of potential audiences. *Enterprise architects* and *business analysts* will both have a need to understand the implications of assuring cloud security, in terms of the issues to be considered when integrating information architectures across and within cloud environments.

Business leaders, strategists and *IT infrastructure managers* will have a desire to appreciate how security can be assured as architectures become more distributed, especially when there is a need to migrate legacy applications to the cloud.

Cloud security engineers and *consultants* will have a broad range of interests, from the engineering of secure solutions through to performance assessment, auditing and evaluation. Those involved in system design and implementation as *application developers* will observe how potential system vulnerabilities can be prevented now and in future iterations of relevant systems.

Finally, as a collection of the latest theoretical, practical and evaluative work in the field of cloud security assurance, we anticipate that this book will be of direct interest to *researchers* and also *university instructors* for adoption as a course textbook.

Suggested Uses

Guide to Security Assurance for Cloud Computing can be used as an introduction to the topic of secure cloud computing, and as such the reader is advised to consult Part I for a thorough overview of the fundamental principles and relevant concepts.

Part II illustrates implementation of the various concepts, using real-world implementations of scenarios that have considered security in the context of cloud computing.

Readers can use the book as a 'primer' if they have no prior knowledge and then consult individual chapters at will as a reference text. Alternatively, for *university instructors*, we suggest the following programme of study for a 12-week semester format:

- Week 1: Introduction
- Weeks 2–7: Part I

- Weeks 8–11: Part II
- Week 12: Assessment

Instructors are encouraged to make use of the various case studies within the book to provide the starting point for seminar or tutorial discussions and as a means of summatively assessing learners at the end of the course.

Derby, UK

Shao Ying Zhu
Richard Hill
Marcello Trovati

Acknowledgements

The editors acknowledge the support of the following colleagues during the review and editing phases of this book:

Colin Allison (University of St Andrew, UK)
Marco Anisetti (Università degli Studi di Milano, Italy)
David Evans (University of Derby, UK)
Filippo Gaudenzi (Università degli Studi di Milano, Italy)
Lu Liu (University of Derby, UK)
John Panneerselvam (University of Derby, UK)
Bo Yuan (University of Derby, UK)

The editors acknowledge the efforts of the authors of the individual chapters; without whose work, this book would not have been possible.

Department of Computing and Mathematics
College of Engineering and Technology
University of Derby, Derby, UK
August 2015

Shao Ying Zhu
Richard Hill
Marcello Trovati

Contents

Contributors

Asma Adnane Department of Computing and Mathematics, College of Engineering and Technology, University of Derby, Derby, UK

Farhan Ahmad Department of Computing and Mathematics, College of Engineering and Technology, University of Derby, Derby, UK

James Alderman Information Security Group, Royal Holloway, University of London, Egham, UK

Marco Anisetti DI – Università degli Studi di Milano, Milano, Italy

Claudio A. Ardagna DI – Università degli Studi di Milano, Milano, Italy

Jason Crampton Information Security Group, Royal Holloway, University of London, Egham, UK

Kevin Curran Faculty of Computing and Engineering, School of Computing and Intelligent Systems, Ulster University, Londonderry, UK

Ernesto Damiani DI – Università degli Studi di Milano, Milano, Italy

Edward Devlin Logistics Department of General Motors, Limerick, Ireland

Rhonda L. Farrell Booz Allen Hamilton, Annapolis Junction, MD, USA

Manoj Singh Gaur Department of Computer Science and Engineering, Malaviya National Institute of Technology, Jaipur, India

Benny Gordon Letterkenny Institute of Technology, Co. Donegal, Ireland

Thomas Holding Department of Engineering and Technology, University of Derby, Derby, UK

Kenneth Johnston Letterkenny Institute of Technology, Co. Donegal, Ireland

Muhammad Kazim Department of Computing and Mathematics, College of Engineering and Technology, University of Derby, Derby, UK

Hristo Koshutanski University of Malaga, Malaga, Spain

Lu Liu Department of Engineering and Technology, University of Derby, Derby, UK

Jesus Luna Cloud Security Alliance, Scotland, UK

Antonio Mãna University of Malaga, Malaga, Spain

Keith M. Martin Information Security Group, Royal Holloway, University of London, Egham, UK

Nigel McKelvey School of Computing, Letterkenny Institute of Technology, Letterkenny, Co. Donegal, Ireland

Chris Mitchell Information Security Group, Royal Holloway, University of London, Egham, UK

John Panneerselvam Department of Engineering and Technology, University of Derby, Derby, UK

Siani Pearson Security and Manageability Lab, Hewlett Packard Labs, Bristol, UK

Luca Pino City University of London, London, UK

Christoph Reich Furtwangen University, Furtwangen, Germany

Sushmita Ruj Indian Statistical Institute, Kolkata, India

Shweta Saharan Computer Engineering Department, Indian Institute of Information Technology, Kota, India

Dheeraj Sanghi Computer Science and Engineering, Indian Institute of Technology, Kanpur, India

Binanda Sengupta Indian Statistical Institute, Kolkata, India

Gaurav Somani Department of Computer Science and Engineering, Central University of Rajasthan, Ajmer, Rajasthan, India

George Spanoudakis City University of London, London, UK

Shao Ying Zhu Department of Computing and Mathematics, College of Engineering and Technology, University of Derby, Derby, UK

About the Editors

The editors are all members of the Department of Computing and Mathematics at the University of Derby, UK, where **Dr. Richard Hill** is a Professor and Head of Department, **Dr. Shao Ying Zhu** is a Senior Lecturer in Computing and **Dr. Marcello Trovati** serves as a Senior Lecturer in Mathematics. The other publications of the editors include the Springer titles *Big-Data Analytics and Cloud Computing*, *Guide to Cloud Computing* and *Cloud Computing for Enterprise Architectures*.

Dr. Shao Ying Zhu
s.y.zhu@derby.ac.uk
Work:
Room E514
University of Derby
Kedleston Road
Derby
Derbyshire
DE22 1GB

Prof Richard Hill
r.hill@derby.ac.uk
Work:
Room E516
University of Derby
Kedleston Road
Derby
Derbyshire
DE22 1GB

Dr. Marcello Trovati
M.Trovati@derby.ac.uk
Work:
Room E317
University of Derby
Kedleston Road
Derby
Derbyshire
DE22 1GB

Part I

Key Concepts

Privacy, Compliance and the Cloud

1

Chris Mitchell

Abstract

Use of the cloud clearly brings with it major privacy concerns. Whilst a range of technical solutions, including use of one of the many variants of homomorphic encryption, potentially enable these concerns to be addressed, in practice such complex privacy enhancing technologies are not widely used. Instead, cloud users, including both individuals and organisations, rely in practice on contractual agreements to help ensure that personally identifiable information (PII) stored in the cloud is handled appropriately. This contractual approach builds on *compliance*, a widely used notion in information security. Specifically, cloud service providers obtain certification of compliance to appropriate security standards and guidelines, notably the ISO/IEC 27000 series, to prove they provide a secure service. To provide privacy guarantees, a standard, ISO/IEC 27018:2014, has recently been published specifically aimed at enabling cloud service vendors to show compliance with regulations and laws governing the handling of PII. This is just the first in an emerging series of standards providing guidelines on cloud security and privacy, as well as more general PII handling in IT systems. This paper reviews the state of the art in such standards and also looks forward to areas where further standards and guidelines are needed, including discussing the issues that they need to address.

Keywords

Privacy • Conformance • Security standards • Cloud privacy

C. Mitchell (✉)
Information Security Group, Royal Holloway, University of London, Egham TW20 0EX, UK
e-mail: me@chrismitchell.net

S.Y. Zhu et al. (eds.), *Guide to Security Assurance for Cloud Computing*,
Computer Communications and Networks, DOI 10.1007/978-3-319-25988-8_1

1.1 Introduction

Almost by definition storing and processing data in the cloud bring with it major security and privacy concerns, over and above those that apply in any environment where sensitive data is processed. That is, except in the case of a private cloud, owned and operated by the data owner, use of the cloud involves passing control over that data to the organisation providing the cloud service.

From the privacy perspective, a key issue is how PII is handled by the cloud service provider. Indeed, in many jurisdictions the client of the cloud service will have legal responsibilities governing the handling of PII, and these responsibilities will extend to ensuring that the PII is handled appropriately by any cloud service provider.

To make the nature of these responsibilities a little clearer, we introduce some terminology (all taken from ISO/IEC 29100 [1]). *Personally identifiable information (PII)* is 'any information that (a) can be used to identify the PII principal to whom such information relates or (b) is or might be directly or indirectly linked to a PII principal'. A *PII principal* is a 'natural person to whom the personally identifiable information (PII) relates'. A *PII controller* is a 'privacy stakeholder (or privacy stakeholders) that determines the purposes and means for processing PII other than natural persons who use data for personal purposes'. A *PII processor* is a 'privacy stakeholder that processes PII on behalf of and in accordance with the instructions of a PII controller'. Using this terminology, the PII controller has legal responsibilities governing the processing of the PII it controls, and these extend to ensuring that any PII processors it appoints (such as cloud service providers) process PII in accordance with the law.

There is a range of ways in which a PII controller could try to meet its obligations regarding the protection of PII. One approach would be to avoid any use of the cloud and retain control of all PII storage and processing 'in-house'. However, as has been widely discussed, many advantages arise from the use of the cloud, and so we take it as read for the purposes of this chapter that the PII controller wishes to transfer PII to a cloud provider for storage and processing. In this context, one approach would be to encrypt all PII before transfer to the cloud and to only decrypt it when it is retrieved from the cloud. However, with conventional encryption techniques, this would prevent the cloud provider doing anything but storing the data, which again limits the usefulness of the cloud. A more sophisticated encryption technique known as *homomorphic encryption* seeks to solve this problem (see, e.g. [2]). An encryption technique that is homomorphic with respect to the operator $^\circ$ is one which has the property that, for a given key K, the encryption function E satisfies $E(x^\circ y) = E(x)^\circ E(y)$ for all x and y. Schemes have been devised that are homomorphic for a range of operation types, the goal being to find a scheme which is homomorphic with respect to a set of operations capturing the types of processing likely to be required of a cloud provider. This would then enable the cloud provider to process the data in encrypted form, i.e. so that the cloud provider is able to process data but learns nothing about the data being processed. However, despite huge progress in developing schemes of this type in recent years, the available algorithms remain too computationally complex for routine deployment. This means that, in practice, we must find nontechnical means to protect remotely processed PII, which leads to the compliance approach, i.e. where the PII controller seeks to be assured about the deployed security measures and privacy practices of the cloud PII processor.

In this chapter we look at how standards are being developed covering the potentially complex relationship between the PII controller and the PII processor. More specifically, how can PII controllers know whether or not PII processors will handle PII appropriately, how can PII processors ensure that they meet their obligations to PII controllers and how can standards help with this?

The remainder of the chapter is organised as follows. In the next section, we review the compliance approach and existing standards directed specifically at PII processing issues. This is followed by an examination of standards currently being developed in this area. Before concluding we look briefly at possible future topics for standardisation in this key area.

1.2 Compliance: The State of the Art

We start by discussing what we mean here by compliance. This necessitates taking a somewhat broader perspective of security management before we return to looking at cloud security and privacy issues in particular. The compliance approach we refer to here is essentially an approach to security management that involves setting up a standards-compliant security management system and then being audited against compliance with the standards. If the audit is successful, the resulting certification can be used to give third parties confidence that security management is being performed in accordance with accepted norms and practices and, of course, give the organisation itself confidence that its security management is in accordance with the state of the art.

Such a compliance approach is widely adopted across industry, commerce and government. The main advantage of such an approach is that it disseminates good practice and encourages the universal adoption of an agreed baseline for IT security. The main disadvantage, as has been widely documented in the literature (see, e.g. [3, 4]), is that it encourages a slavish box-ticking approach to security, where minimal safeguards are put in place without appropriate ongoing management and organisation-wide buy-in. However, it could be argued that most of the criticisms are not of the approach itself but of the way it is implemented and that organisations which do not implement the standardised approach well would not implement any other approach to security very well either. It is certainly the case that without careful and considered adoption, any approach to IT security will fail, whether it is the compliance-led approach or some other ad hoc scheme. In any event, to a first approximation, the compliance approach is the only show in town: it is what we have and it is what is being implemented, and hence, it is worth taking very seriously (and enhancing, wherever possible).

The leading contender for such a standard-based approach is based on the ISO/IEC 27000 series of standards. According to ISO/IEC 27000 [5], an *information security management system (ISMS)* consists of the policies, procedures, guidelines and associated resources and activities, collectively managed by an organisation, in the pursuit of protecting its information assets. An ISMS is a systematic approach for establishing, implementing, operating, monitoring, reviewing, maintaining and improving an organisation's information security to achieve business objectives. It is based upon a risk assessment and the organisation's risk acceptance levels designed to effectively treat and manage risks. Analysing requirements for the protection of information assets and applying appropriate controls to ensure the protection of these information assets, as required, contribute to the successful implementation of an ISMS. As well as defining the concept of an ISMS, ISO/IEC 27000 [5] provides a comprehensive set of related terminology.

In doing so, ISO/IEC 27000 provides the foundation for ISO/IEC 27001 [6], the heart of the ISO/IEC 27000 series. According to its scope statement, ISO/IEC 27001 'specifies the requirements for establishing, implementing, maintaining and continually improving an ISMS within the context of the organisation. ... [It] also includes requirements for the assessment and treatment of information security risks tailored to the needs of the organisation. The requirements ... are generic and are intended to be applicable to all organisations, regardless of type, size or nature'. In other words, ISO/IEC 27001 describes what is needed to create and operate an ISMS.

Application of ISO/IEC 27001 is supported by perhaps the best known of these standards, namely, ISO/IEC 27002 [7]. ISO/IEC 27002 provides a catalogue of *security controls*, i.e. measures that can be implemented by an organisation to address identified security risks and associated implementation guidance. This comprehensive set of controls has a long history and has been revised and expanded over time – with origins in a British standard (BS 7799 [8] which became BS 7799-1 [9]) first published in the mid-1990s. In passing we note that ISO/IEC 27001 is also derived from a British standard, namely, BS 7799-2 [10, 11].

The controls in ISO/IEC 27002 are organised into 14 categories, covering topics such as information security policies (clause 5), human resource security (clause 7), asset management (clause 8), access control (clause 9), supplier relationships (clause 15) and compliance (clause 18). Within each clause a number of control objectives are defined; there are a total of 35 such objectives. For example, clause 18.1, entitled *Compliance with legal and contractual requirements*, gives the objective 'To avoid breaches of legal, statutory, regulatory or contractual obligations related to information security objectives'. Under each objective are one or more detailed controls, typically with extensive accompanying implementation guidance, which can be deployed to help meet the objective. There are over 100 such controls, ranging from *monitoring and review of supplier services* ('Organisations should regularly monitor, review and audit supplier service delivery': clause 15.1.2) to *regulation of cryptographic controls* ('Cryptographic controls should be used in compliance with all relevant agreements, legislation and regulations': clause 18.1.5).

The set of controls in ISO/IEC 27002 is intended as a guide to the designers of an ISMS. That is, it is certainly not mandated for any organisation using the ISO/IEC 27001 approach to adopt all the controls given in ISO/IEC 27002; indeed the intention is that the risk analysis performed as part of setting up the ISMS should consider the appropriateness of the controls in the catalogue and adopt (only) those that are necessary to address the identified risks. Nevertheless, many of the controls are so fundamental that it is hard to imagine IT systems which do not need their adoption to ensure reasonable levels of security.

Returning to the focus on privacy, it merits note that one of the controls in ISO/IEC 27002 (in clause 18.1.4) is entitled *Privacy and protection of personally identifiable information* and specifies that 'Privacy and protection of personally identifiable information should be ensured as required in relevant legislation and regulation where applicable'. The associated implementation guidance is very general, starting by stating that 'An organization's data policy for privacy and protection of personally identifiable information should be developed and implemented. This policy should be communicated to all persons involved in the processing of personally identifiable information'. It goes on to discuss the need for a privacy policy and also the potential need for a nominated officer in an organisation to manage privacy issues.

This leads naturally to a discussion of ISO//IEC 27018 [12]. This standard is focussed specifically on PII protection when it is processed in the cloud – more specifically when the processing is performed by a public cloud service provider. It provides a set of controls, supplementing ISO/IEC 27002, aimed at cloud service providers who act as PII processors on behalf of a PII controller. That is, the main focus of the standard is not those cloud service providers which act as PII controllers, although the controls in ISO/IEC 27018 will almost certainly apply to such entities (as well as many other controls besides, e.g. as given in the emerging standards ISO/IEC 27017 and ISO/IEC 29151 – see below).

The idea behind ISO/IEC 27018 is that a cloud service provider can have its ISMS audited using the ISO/IEC 27001 system, where the auditor will verify that the risk management process and subsequent ISMS implementation has properly taken into account the supplementary set of controls in ISO/IEC 27018. The certification resulting can then be used to both inform prospective users of the privacy-respecting properties of the cloud service and become part of the relevant contractual arrangements when the cloud service is used. It is hoped that this will greatly simplify the task of the PII controller when selecting a cloud service provider.

The set of controls in the standard was derived from a range of sources. Prior to producing the first draft of ISO/IEC 27018, an extensive analysis was performed of existing law relating to the third party processing of PII. The main result of this analysis was a set of 70 controls, which were documented in the original proposal to start work on the standard, published in November 2011 [13]. Only those not already covered in ISO/IEC 27002 were included in the subsequent working drafts of the standard. In July 2012, the European Union published an important review of cloud computing privacy issues [14]. This was carefully analysed, along with other published opinions, and used to derive a number of additional controls which were included in the second working draft of December 2012 [15]. In 2013 additional input was received from a number of parties and used to shape the final document published in 2014 [12].

The scope of ISO/IEC 27018 was kept deliberately tight for two main reasons. Firstly, those of us responsible for its development believed it was important to try to publish the standard quickly, and limiting the scope makes rapid progress much simpler. Secondly, the focus of the standard, namely, cloud service providers processing PII on behalf of the PII controller, was believed to be particularly important, and hence focussing on this subject made practical sense. Both these motivations appear to have been borne out by experience – the interval between the new work item proposal and publication of a completed standard was a little over 30 months, which is virtually as short a period as is possible within ISO/IEC SC 27, and the standard has rapidly become a 'best seller', at least in the context of ISO/IEC[1].

Of course ISO/IEC 27000, ISO/IEC 27001, ISO/IEC 27002 and ISO/IEC 27018 are only four of a major series of standards known collectively as the 27000 series. Some standards in the series seek to expand upon particular topics addressed within ISO/IEC 27001, including:

- ISO/IEC 27003: *Implementation guidance*, giving more details on the implementation of an ISMS
- ISO/IEC 27004: *Measurement*, covering security metrics
- ISO/IEC 27005: *Information security risk management*
- ISO/IEC 27006: *Requirements for bodies providing audit and certification of information security management systems*, setting out how certification of ISMSs against ISO/IEC 27001 should be carried out

Other 27000 series standards, like ISO/IEC 27018, act as a supplement to ISO/IEC 27002, providing an additional set of controls and accompanying guidance for a specific application domain, including:

- ISO/IEC 27011: *Information security management guidelines for telecommunications organizations based on ISO/IEC 27002*

Note that all these standards are available for purchase from ISO (www.iso.org), IEC (www.iec.ch) and also from national standards organisations such as BSI in the UK (www.bsigroup.com).

[1]For example, ISO/IEC 27018 was listed at number 7 in the April 2015 list of best-selling ISO standards, as published by the Singapore standards organisation – see http://www.singaporestandardseshop.sg/ISOStandards/BestSellingISOStandards.aspx (checked on 9th June 2015).

Whilst mentioning existing standards of relevance to privacy in the cloud, brief mention should also be given to ISO/IEC 29100 [1], the *Privacy Framework*. This standard was published back in 2011 and provides a set of 11 privacy principles (consent and choice; purpose legitimacy and specification; collection limitation; data minimisation; use, retention and disclosure limitation; accuracy and quality; openness, transparency and notice; individual participation and access; accountability; information security and privacy compliance). These principles were used to inform and motivate the supplementary control set given in ISO/IEC 27018. Indeed, the ISO/IEC 27018 supplementary controls are organised according to the 11 privacy principles.

1.3 Compliance: Emerging Standards

ISO/IEC 27018 was published in mid-2014. Two other standards directly relevant to cloud privacy, and with somewhat larger scopes, are currently under development. Both ISO/IEC 27017 and ISO/EC 29151, like ISO/IEC 27018, aim to provide a set of controls and associated implementation guidance aimed to supplement those given in ISO/IEC 27002 for a specific application domain. In some sense both of these emerging standards have the focus of ISO/IEC 27018 as a subset.

ISO/IEC 27017, which is nearing completion (as of mid-2015 it was at the Final Draft International Standard stage [16], the last stage before publication), aims to enhance the set of controls in ISO/IEC 27002 to cover all the security and privacy aspects of operating a cloud service. As stated in the introduction, it 'provides guidelines supporting the implementation of information security controls for cloud service customers and cloud service providers. Many of the guidelines guide the cloud service providers to assist the cloud service customers in implementing the controls, and guide the cloud service customers to implement such controls. Selection of appropriate information security controls, and the application of the implementation guidance provided, will depend on a risk assessment as well as any legal, contractual, regulatory or other cloud-sector specific information security requirements'.

The current draft of ISO/IEC 27017 [16] is, as one might expect, much larger than ISO/IEC 27018; indeed, it is something like half the length of ISO/IEC 27002 itself. It incorporates controls and guidance derived from a wide range of sources including standards and reports from Australia, Hong Kong, the USA (including NIST), Singapore, the Cloud Security Alliance, ENISA and ISACA. It looks set to be published in late 2015 or early 2016.

A somewhat complementary focus applies to the development of ISO/IEC 29151, which as of mid-2015 has just reached the committee draft stage [17]. ISO/IEC 29151 aims to document controls relevant to the protection of PII no matter where it is stored and which entity acts as the PII processor or controller. As it states in the introduction, 'The number of organisations processing PII is increasing, as is the amount of PII that these organisations deal with. At the same time, the societal expectation for the protection of PII and the security of data relating to the individuals is also increasing. A number of countries are augmenting their laws to address the increased number of high profile breaches. As the number of PII breaches increase, organisations controlling or processing PII, including smaller newcomers (e.g. small and medium enterprises (SMEs)) will increasingly need guidance on how they should protect PII in order to reduce the risk of privacy breaches occurring, and to reduce the impact of breaches on the organisation and on the individuals concerned. This document provides such guidance'.

The current draft is again an extensive document and builds on a wide variety of sources. At the current rate of development, publication is likely no earlier than 2017.

We conclude by providing in Table 1.1 a summary of the current and emerging standards of relevance to privacy compliance in the cloud.

Table 1.1 Summary of cloud privacy-relevant ISO/IEC standards

Standard	Title and scope
ISO/IEC 27000:2014	*Information security management systems – Overview and vocabulary*
	Sets the scene for the ISO/IEC 27000 series
ISO/IEC 27001:2013	*Information security management systems – Requirements*
	Defines general principles for an information security management system, including how an ISMS should be established and run – it is the foundation of the ISO/IEC 27000 series of standards
ISO/IEC 27002:2013	*Information security management systems – Code of practice for information security controls*
	Provides a catalogue of generally applicable security controls, to be used as part of an ISMS as defined in ISO/IEC 27001
ISO/IEC FDIS 27017 (2015)	*Code of practice for information security controls based on ISO/IEC 27002 for cloud services*
	Provides supplementary information for ISO/IEC 27002 controls and a set of new controls aimed specifically at the cloud (a superset of ISO/IEC 27018)
ISO/IEC 27018:2014	*Code of practice for protection of PII in public clouds acting as PII processors*
	Provides supplementary information for ISO/IEC 27002 controls and a set of new controls aimed specifically at cloud providers processing PII on behalf of a PII controller
ISO/IEC 29100	*Privacy framework*
	Lays down a general set of privacy principles for information storage and processing
ISO/IEC CD 29151 (2015)	*Code of practice for PII protection*
	Provides supplementary information for ISO/IEC 27002 controls and a set of new controls aimed at all processing and storage of PII (a superset of ISO/IEC 27018)

1.4 Compliance: Future Work

Even when ISO/IEC 27017 and ISO/IEC 29151 are completed and in use, the work on standards governing cloud privacy will not come to an end. Apart from anything else, all the standards we have discussed are subject to a continuing process of review and, where necessary, improvement. There are also further areas where standards guidance is needed.

One such area is that of data de-identification, i.e. the processing of PII so that it is no longer linked to a particular individual. Organisations processing PII, including cloud service providers, are required to comply with the applicable privacy-enforcing regulations and laws, which often prevents processing of personal data for purposes other than those for which the data was originally collected. Data de-identification techniques (e.g. pseudonymisation or anonymisation) are widely used as a way of enabling the reuse of large data sets to extract otherwise hidden information (so-called big data) without endangering user privacy. Such an approach is viable since in many cases the value of processing is maintained even if PII principals are no longer identifiable, directly or indirectly, either by the organisation alone as PII controller or in collaboration with any other party. Additionally, it may be permissible for an organisation to process data for purposes other than those for which the PII principals had given their consent, as long as the data has been rendered into a form in which identification of the PII principals is no longer reasonably feasible, taking into account the state of the art and the organisation's context. That is, de-identification techniques are tools that may enable the wide range of potential benefits arising from data processing to be maintained, whilst respecting privacy regulations and laws.

However, such data de-identification techniques need to be used with great care, not least because of the risk of data re-identification, in which, using contextual or other information, the data can be linked back to an individual. Organisations proposing to use de-identification must therefore carefully define the de-identification measures that are appropriate in their context in order to ensure results that are sufficiently robust given the risks of re-identification. As such it will be extremely helpful to end-user organisations, notably the many cloud service providers holding large data sets containing PII, to provide a detailed and practical description of these techniques, including their strengths and weaknesses.

This is an increasingly pressing issue since, in organisations of many types, the amount of data created and potentially being used continues to increase, as do the capabilities of data analytics. Furthermore, the state of the art shows (e.g. see [18]) that achieving robustness in de-identification processes is far from trivial. There is thus a need for a standard that will help organisations in defining and reviewing their processes according to the state of the art and their environment, including their regulatory context. Such a standard would also enable organisations to build trust with a variety of stakeholders (including PII principals, customers and data protection agencies) and to establish a common language for transparency regarding their processes.

At its May 2015 meeting in Kuching, WG 5 of ISO/IEC JTC 1/SC 27 (the standards committee responsible for ISO/IEC 27018 and ISO/IEC 29151) agreed to issue a new work item proposal [19] to create a standard covering data de-identification techniques to address this growing need. The proposed standard will provide information to organisations which aim to use de-identification techniques, with the goal of creating awareness of typical characteristics to consider and to help them avoid common pitfalls.

The new work item proposal [19] has an attached preliminary working draft, which draws extensively on a recent Article 29 Working Party report [20]. Apart from a comprehensive set of definitions of terminology, intended to enable unambiguous discussions of de-identification, the new standard is expected to contain clauses covering the usability of de-identified data, the risks of re-identification, techniques for pseudonymisation and techniques for achieving and metrics for measuring anonymisation. It will also draw on an existing health sector-specific ISO technical specification on pseudonymisation [21].

1.5 How Effective Is the Compliance Model?

As already discussed, the compliance model has been widely criticised, not least for encouraging a 'box-ticking mentality'. However, without doubt ISO/IEC 27002 (and its predecessors) has done much to inform organisations of the fundamental techniques of information security management. For better or worse, it would appear that the use of the 27000 series standards is considered as a fundamental part of security management for almost every large organisation, at least in the Western world.

One could reasonably ask critics of the compliance approach whether they would rather employ a cloud service provider which has verified that its security and privacy practices conform to the state of the art or one which has not. It seems hard to argue in favour of the latter. Indeed, the author is not aware of any research calling for routine security management measures to be abandoned; instead, what seems to be needed are better ways of managing the human side of security management. The compliance approach is still evolving, and there is clearly no cause for complacency. Ultimately there is no replacement for good management practices, both within IT and more broadly, and the 27000 series standards are just one part of the overall information security solution.

1.6 Concluding Remarks

We have attempted to review both recently published and emerging international standards of relevance to privacy, and in particular PII protection, in the cloud. ISO/IEC 27018 has made a significance in the short period since it was published and will be joined in the near future by ISO/IEC 27017 and, later on, by ISO/IEC

29151. In the longer-term future, it is hoped that we will see the development of detailed guidance on de-identification techniques, enabling greater confidence that data collected through the provision of cloud services is used for greater societal benefit in ways which respect end-user privacy.

1.7 Review Questions

1. What is PII and why is there an issue if PII is processed in the cloud?
2. Why are technical approaches to the protection of PII stored and processed in the cloud not widely used?
3. What is the compliance approach to security and privacy?
4. What is an ISMS and where is its operation defined in international standards?
5. What is the main scope and purpose of ISO/IEC 27018 and to who and what does it apply?
6. Why is data de-identification necessary and what is the main threat to such a procedure?

References

1. ISO/IEC 29100:2011, Information technology – security techniques – privacy framework
2. van Dijk M, Gentry C, Halevi S, Vaikuntanathan V (2010) Fully homomorphic encryption over the integers. In: Proc. Eurocrypt 2010, Springer LNCS 6110, pp 24–43
3. Duncan B, Whittington M (2014) Reflecting on whether checklists can tick the box for cloud security. In: Proc. of 2014 IEEE 6th international conference on cloud computing technology and science, IEEE, pp.805–810
4. Kwon J, Johnson ME (2014) Proactive versus reactive security investments in the healthcare sector. MIS Q 38:451–471
5. ISO/IEC 27000:2014, Information technology – security techniques – information security management systems – overview and vocabulary
6. ISO/IEC 27001:2013, Information technology – security techniques – information security management systems – Requirements
7. ISO/IEC 27002:2013, Information technology – security techniques – code of practice for information security controls
8. BS 7799:1995, Code of practice for information security management
9. BS 7799-1:1999, Information security management – Part 1: Code of practice for information security management
10. BS 7799-2:1999, Information security management – Part 2: Specification for information security management systems
11. BS 7799-2:2002, Information security management systems – specification with guidance for use
12. ISO/IEC 27018:2014, Information technology – security techniques – code of practice for protection of personally identifiable information (PII) in public clouds acting as PII processors
13. ISO/IEC JTC 1/SC 27 N10550, Proposal for a new work item on code of practice for data protection controls for public cloud computing services, November 2011
14. European Union, Article 29 Working Party, Opinion 05/2012 on cloud computing, adopted July 2012
15. ISO/IEC JTC 1/SC 27 N11742, 2nd WD 27018, Information technology – security techniques – code of practice for data protection controls for public cloud computing services, December 2012

16. ISO/IEC FDIS 27017 Information technology – security techniques – code of practice for information security controls based on ISO/IEC 27002 for cloud services, July 2015
17. ISO.IEC 1st CD 29151, Information technology – security techniques – code of practice for personally identifiable information protection, June 2015
18. Ji S, Li W, Gong NZ, Mittal P, Beyah R (2015) On your social network de-anonymizability: quantification and large scale evaluation with seed knowledge. In: Proc. NDSS'15, internet society
19. ISO/IEC JTC 1/SC 27 N15297, Proposal for a new work item on Privacy enhancing data de-identification techniques, June 2015
20. European Union, Article 29 Working Party, Opinion 05/2014 on Anonymisation Techniques, April 2014
21. ISO/TS 25237:2008, Health informatics – pseudonymization

Chris Mitchell has been Professor of Computer Science at Royal Holloway since 1990, previously working at HP Labs (1985–1990) and Racal Comsec (1979–1985). Soon after joining Royal Holloway he co-founded the Information Security Group and played a leading role in launching the Information Security MSc in 1992. His research interests cover information security and the applications of cryptography. He has edited around twenty international security standards and, in recognition of his contributions to international standards, in 2011 he received the prestigious IEC 1906 award. He has published around 250 research papers, is Co-Editor-in-Chief of Designs, Codes and Cryptography, a Senior Editor of IEEE Communications Letters, and Section Editor of The Computer Journal.

2 Cryptographic Tools for Cloud Environments

James Alderman, Jason Crampton, and Keith M. Martin

Abstract

Cryptography provides techniques that can be used to implement core security services such as confidentiality and data integrity. We review some fundamental cryptographic mechanisms and identify some of the limitations of traditional cryptography with respect to cloud computing environments. We then review a number of relatively new cryptographic tools that have the potential to provide the extended security functionality required by some cloud computing applications.

Keywords

Cryptography • Cloud security • Encryption • Functional encryption • Searchable encryption • Homomorphic encryption • Verifiable computation

2.1 Introduction

Cloud computing provides several advantages to end users in terms of economical outsourcing of data storage and processing. However, in many practical settings, client data may be sensitive in nature and should not be revealed to untrusted cloud service providers or transmitted in the clear over untrusted networks. Cryptography provides a mathematical toolkit of techniques for implementing core data security services. Traditionally, cryptography has focused on providing *confidentiality* and *integrity*: ensuring unauthorized entities cannot read data or modify data (without detection). However, modern cryptography can achieve significantly more functionality than this and has potential to provide effective solutions to specific security

J. Alderman • J. Crampton • K.M. Martin (✉)
Information Security Group, Royal Holloway, University of London, Egham TW20 0EX, UK
e-mail: Keith.Martin@rhul.ac.uk

S.Y. Zhu et al. (eds.), *Guide to Security Assurance for Cloud Computing*,
Computer Communications and Networks, DOI 10.1007/978-3-319-25988-8_2

issues arising in cloud environments such as the enabling of (limited) processing of encrypted data. In this chapter, we identify limitations of traditional cryptographic tools and then review a number of relatively recent cryptographic mechanisms that provide interesting functionality, all of which are potentially suitable for a wide range of cloud applications.

2.2 Fundamental Cryptographic Mechanisms

In this section, we review what can be considered as the fundamental tools of cryptography, including symmetric and public-key encryption, hash functions, message authentication codes, and digital signatures. We discuss the functionality of these tools, as well as their limitations.

2.2.1 Symmetric Encryption

Symmetric or *private key encryption* is perhaps the most fundamental cryptographic mechanism and relies on a pre-shared key between the sender and the recipient of a message (or writer and reader, respectively). *Plaintext* messages (data objects) to be encrypted are elements of a *message space*, M, while the symmetric key shared between (at least) two entities is usually drawn uniformly at random from a *key space*, K. The space M is often regarded as the set of all (finite length) binary strings, while the size of K depends on a *security parameter*, which varies the strength of the encryption (a security parameter of 128 usually means that keys are drawn uniformly from the set of all 128-bit binary strings).

A symmetric encryption scheme comprises three algorithms. A *key generation* algorithm takes the security parameter as input and randomly selects a symmetric key k from K. The *Encrypt* algorithm is a randomized algorithm taking the symmetric key k and a message m from M as input and outputting a ciphertext c. Finally, the *Decrypt* algorithm is deterministic and takes the symmetric key k and a ciphertext c and returns the message m.

There are many notions of security for symmetric encryption. Perhaps the most common is *indistinguishability against chosen plaintext attacks (IND-CPA)*. Intuitively, this states that an adversary with the ability to observe the encryption of arbitrary messages may not distinguish which of two messages of its choice has been encrypted – that is, a ciphertext should hide all information about the encrypted plaintext. *Indistinguishability against chosen ciphertext attacks (IND-CCA)* allows the adversary to also make decryption queries for ciphertexts of its choice. The choice of security notion depends on the context in which the scheme is used and what information an adversary is likely to observe in practice.

A symmetric encryption scheme that encrypts fixed size messages is often called a *block cipher* [1]. Longer messages may be split into fixed length blocks and chained together according to a *mode of operation* [2]. Particularly common modes of operation include *Cipher Block Chaining (CBC)* and *Counter Mode (CTR)*. The latter mode encrypts each block in parallel and is thus a good choice for encrypting particularly long plaintexts. The current standard for a block cipher is the *Advanced Encryption Standard (AES)* [3], which operates on blocks of 128 bits and supports key sizes of 128, 192, and 256 bits.

An alternative to a block cipher is a *stream cipher* [4], which generates a *key stream* of pseudorandom bits, which may be prepared ahead of time, and then combines (simply XORs) this stream with the message on a bit-by-bit basis. In this way, arbitrary length messages may be accommodated as long as a stream of the appropriate length can be generated. Block ciphers in certain modes of operation (such as CTR) can act as stream ciphers, albeit with a potential loss in efficiency compared to dedicated stream ciphers, which can be very fast. One of the most commonly used stream ciphers is RC4, but this is known to have severe security weaknesses.

It should be noted that all symmetric encryption mechanisms have a requirement to agree secret keys in advance; hence a major challenge in all applications is to find a secure and efficient means of key distribution.

2.2.2 Public-Key Encryption

Public-key encryption or *asymmetric* encryption [5] eases the problem of key distribution by removing the requirement for a pre-shared key. Instead, each entity A is associated with two keys: a *public key* used by an encryptor to send a message to A and a *private (secret) key* used by A to decrypt ciphertexts that were encrypted using A's public key. The public key may be transmitted in the clear (or published) so there is no requirement for a secure channel before transmitting a message (however, the public-key distribution channel should still be authenticated).

The public-key setting facilitates increased functionality as it is possible to encrypt objects *without* also having the ability to decrypt objects. It also allows a recipient to receive messages from multiple senders while keeping only a single private decryption key.

In general, public-key mechanisms are significantly slower than symmetric mechanisms. Thus, a *hybrid* model is often used whereby an object is (efficiently) encrypted using a symmetric encryption scheme, and the symmetric key itself is encrypted using a public-key scheme. Thus, the less efficient public-key scheme is only used to protect a reasonably short symmetric key, while the more efficient symmetric key scheme protects the larger data object.

Public-key encryption is formally defined in a similar way to symmetric encryption, with the key generation algorithm now outputting two keys. Security in the sense of IND-CPA and IND-CCA can also be defined for the public-key setting, where the adversary can form any ciphertext using just the public key.

2.2.3 Hash Functions

A *hash function* [6] is a compression function H that takes an arbitrary length string and outputs a shorter string. For cryptographic applications we must ensure that the mapping H does not produce predictable collisions and that the precise mapping is hard to determine. The most important security properties of a hash function are:

- *Collision resistance:* it should be computationally infeasible to find two distinct messages x and z such that $H(x) = H(z)$, that is, to find two messages that hash to the same value.
- *Pre-image resistance:* given the result $y = H(x)$ of H applied to a randomly chosen message x, it should be computationally infeasible to find a value z such that $H(z) = y$.
- *Second pre-image resistance:* given a message x, it should be computationally infeasible to find another message z such that $H(x) = H(z)$.

Hash functions find numerous uses in cryptography, from dedicated applications such as password protection through to acting as components in more complex cryptographic tools such as digital signature schemes.

2.2.4 Message Authentication Codes

A *message authentication code (MAC)* [7] detects any modification of a message. As with symmetric encryption, the sender and receiver of the message must pre-share a secret key k. The sender computes a *tag* t using the message and the secret key. The tag is transmitted alongside the message, and the receiver verifies the MAC using the message, tag, and secret key.

Formal MAC security is captured by *existential unforgeability under chosen message attack (EUF-CMA)*, which requires it to be computationally infeasible to generate a valid-looking tag for a new message, for which no tag has previously been seen, without access to the key k.

2.2.5 Digital Signature Schemes

Digital signature schemes [8] are public-key analogs of MACs, which preserve the integrity of messages without requiring a pre-shared secret. The key generation algorithm outputs both a private signing key, kept by the sender, and a verification key, which is published. The signing algorithm takes the secret signing key and the message and produces a signature. The verification algorithm takes the message, signature, and public verification key and accepts the signature if the message has not been altered. As with MACs, we define a notion of security known as *existential unforgeability under chosen message attack (EUF-CMA)*, whereby an adversary given the verification key and the ability to request signatures on arbitrary messages should not be able to generate a valid signature on a message that has not previously been signed.

As with encryption, the asymmetric setting eases key distribution, particularly when communicating with multiple parties (a single signature can be verified by multiple parties using the published verification key), but this comes at the expense of computational efficiency. Signatures are *publicly verifiable*, meaning that if one receiver verifies the signature correctly then it can be assumed that all other recipients may do the same; clearly this may not be true in the case of MACs where each recipient holds a different verification key and a MAC is created per key. Publishing the verification key also means that signatures are *transferable*; that is, given a message and a valid signature, a third party can verify the signature even if not the intended recipient. A final useful property of digital signatures is *non-repudiation,* which means that the signer of a message cannot deny having done so. MACs cannot provide such functionality since the key is shared between the signer and verifier only; it is not possible for a third party to verify that the signer held the particular signing key used. More advanced forms of signatures allow sets of users to jointly sign messages, signatures to be generated without the signer knowing the contents of the message, and for authorized users to modify designated portions of the message.

2.2.6 Authenticated Encryption

Authenticated encryption [9] combines the confidentiality properties of encryption with the integrity properties of MACs and digital signatures, thus assuring that a received message has not been read by unauthorized entities and has not been altered since its creation by the sender. Integrated methods to achieve this in the symmetric setting either combine a block cipher with a MAC or use a special authenticated mode of operation for a block cipher (such as GCM or CCM). Some modes allow for additional data to be authenticated but not encrypted. The public-key analog of an authenticated mode of operation is known as *signcryption* [10, 11], which integrates asymmetric encryption and digital signature schemes. Authenticated encryption schemes are typically more efficient than manual combinations of separate privacy and integrity mechanisms.

2.3 Limitations of Conventional Cryptography

Cloud environments provide several challenges that are not addressed by conventional cryptographic mechanisms. Three of the main limitations of conventional cryptography when applied to cloud settings are as follows:

Inability To Conduct Processing on Encrypted Data Conventional cryptographic mechanisms can be used to protect the confidentiality and integrity of stored and transmitted data. However, a natural requirement in the cloud is for a *cloud service provider* (CSP) who stores encrypted data to *process* data on behalf of a client. Without access to the data itself, it is hard for a CSP to perform meaningful processing, especially as conventional cryptography often requires it to be *hard* to meaningfully manipulate encrypted data. An inefficient solution would be to return the encrypted data to the client for local processing. However, some modern cryptographic tools (which we will discuss later) permit some computation directly over encrypted data.

Incorporation of Data Access Policies Conventional cryptography typically operates in a point-to-point setting where the sender knows the intended recipient, be that through a pre-shared key or through an associated public key. In cloud settings, however, it is likely that a dynamic set of clients may communicate with a CSP. It may be infeasible to compute a ciphertext for each potential user of a piece of encrypted data. Indeed, it may not even be possible to *define* (in terms of individual identities) the entities that should be given the capability to interact with particular encrypted resources. Moreover, in conventional systems, data is often stored in a single location within a trusted zone, with a trusted reference monitor enforcing access control to protected resources. In cloud environments, data may be outsourced to multiple locations over which the data owner exerts no control, making access to resources more problematic. As we will shortly discuss, some modern encryption schemes include built-in access control mechanisms that allow decryption policies to be enforced remotely on behalf of the data owner.

Reliability of the Encrypted Data Holder Most conventional cryptography, particularly symmetric cryptography, relies on a degree of trust between the communicating entities. However, in a cloud environment, a CSP typically lies outside of the trusted domain of the clients. In particular, a CSP could make unintentional errors, especially when asked to process encrypted data. In extremis, a malicious CSP could attempt to preserve resources by returning incomplete results or even deleting some outsourced data. We will discuss some new cryptographic mechanisms that reduce the necessary level of trust held by a client with respect to the holder of encrypted data.

One additional problem created by cloud environments is that operational requests made for the processing of encrypted data could be made over public channels and are certainly visible to the potentially untrusted CSP. A further problem is that optimization of storage costs is difficult when CSPs are not aware of raw data that is transmitted to them in encrypted form (in conventional cryptography, multiple ciphertexts encrypting the same data using different keys should appear completely unrelated). We will also discuss some tools for addressing both of these issues.

2.4 Cryptographic Mechanisms for the Cloud

We now discuss a range of relatively new cryptographic mechanisms that address some of the limitations of conventional cryptography and have potential for deployment in cloud environments.

2.4.1 Processing Encrypted Data

We first consider methods for performing specific computations on encrypted data, which could prove useful in cloud environments.

2.4.1.1 Searching Over Encrypted Data

One of the most basic processing tasks that might be required to be performed on encrypted data is to perform keyword search. However, once data has been encrypted, this operation becomes extremely difficult because conventional ciphertexts should not leak any information about the underlying plaintext. Additionally, queries themselves may need to be encrypted as they may reveal information about the data being searched for.

Searchable encryption (SE) schemes are encryption schemes designed to address this problem by encrypting data alongside special indices that permit a limited search capability. A range of SE schemes have been proposed, varying in the expressiveness of queries and the degree of privacy offered. Some SE schemes [12, 13] return all documents containing a *single* keyword, while other solutions [14] allow conjunctive searches for documents containing a set of keywords or allow for general Boolean formulas [15], range, and subset queries [16] or even SQL queries [17]. *Fuzzy* searches [18] seek words that are "close" to a given keyword. Security for SE schemes considers *data confidentiality* and *query confidentiality*, as well as *search pattern privacy* (so that an adversary that sees two queries with the same output cannot tell whether the queries were identical), and *access pattern privacy* (so that an adversary cannot learn the result of queries).

Early SE schemes allow a single data owner to issue queries. Subsequent work [19] enables many clients to write to a database by encrypting data segments with the public key of a single user who may form searches using the corresponding private key. Other solutions allow a single data owner to grant and revoke the ability to search their files [12] or combine both properties to allow multiple readers *and* multiple writers. In terms of efficiency, some schemes [12] include a search phase in which the workload of the server is not linear in the number of uploaded documents but rather in the number of documents that match the query.

2.4.1.2 Homomorphic Encryption

By default, traditional encryption schemes do not permit meaningful combinations of ciphertexts. However, some encryption schemes are *homomorphic* in nature and allow some computations to be performed on encrypted data. Certain operations can be applied to two ciphertexts such that the result, when decrypted, produces a plaintext as if the operation had been applied to the plaintexts themselves. For example, let C_1 be the encryption of a message m_1 and let C_2 encrypt m_2. Then, for example, in certain *homomorphic encryption schemes*, multiplying C_1 and C_2 together will produce a new ciphertext C_3 which will decrypt to reveal a plaintext equal to m_1 times m_2. It should be noted that, by design, homomorphic encryption schemes are *malleable* (ciphertexts can be altered and remain valid).

Schemes that exhibit homomorphic properties for a *specific* operation are known as *partially homomorphic encryption schemes*. On the other hand, if the set of permissible operations enables arbitrary computations to be performed, then the schemes are referred to as *fully homomorphic* [20]. Such schemes are very powerful since they allow arbitrary computation on encrypted data and thus potentially fit the cloud setting particularly well as the untrusted CSP never requires access to the plaintext data. Unfortunately, current schemes (referred to as *somewhat homomorphic*) that tend to be limited in the number of operations that may be applied before decryption will no longer succeed or are inefficient in terms of speed or the size of parameters and ciphertexts.

2.4.1.3 Computing Aggregates Over Encrypted Data

Since fully homomorphic encryption is not yet practical for general deployment, several cryptographic mechanisms have been designed for more specific uses. One such example is *privacy preserving data aggregation,* which allows specific types of computation to be performed (generally the sum) on encrypted data. The data is assumed to come from multiple independent sources, which are reluctant to share their sensitive information with either other sources or the aggregator. This has led to an active area of research where proposed solutions mainly rely on homomorphic encryption and secret sharing techniques. Some schemes achieve *aggregator obliviousness* using a trusted dealer that provides the aggregator with the sum of users' secret keys, which in turn allows the decryption of the sum of users' data. Other schemes handle dynamic user populations and arbitrary user failures. Recently, Leontiadis et al. [21] removed the need for trusted key dealers while supporting dynamic group management and user failures.

2.4.1.4 Order-Preserving Encryption

Order-preserving encryption [22–24] allows a CSP to perform *range queries* on encrypted data in order to return relevant results to a client query. This is a form of deterministic symmetric encryption where numerical comparison operators can be applied to encrypted numerical data. It has natural applications to querying encrypted databases. The scheme of Boldyreva *et al.* [23] claims to achieve such numerical range searches in logarithmic time (in the size of the database).

2.4.2 Functional Encryption

Functional encryption extends traditional public-key encryption to allow the holder of a private key to learn a specific function of an encrypted message, but nothing else. This function could return the message itself (as for traditional public-key encryption), return the message only if some additional criteria are met, or may produce the output of some computation specified by the message and private key. In the context of cloud, functional encryption can be deployed as a cryptographic enforcement mechanism for access control policies. Functional encryption allows the encryptor (client) to specify an access control policy in terms of identities or more general descriptive attributes; decryptors may access the data if and only if they satisfy this policy. Thus, data owners retain control of which entities may learn their data without requiring explicit prior knowledge of users.

There are several specific types of functional encryption scheme that could be of interest in cloud environments.

2.4.2.1 Identity-Based Encryption

Identity-based encryption (IBE) [25] allows encryptors to specify an arbitrary identity string (user name, email address, IP address, *etc.*) while preparing a ciphertext, rather than using a predefined public key. A decryptor can request (either beforehand or subsequently) a decryption key associated with an identity from a key generation authority (usually after proving authorization for the identity). The plaintext is successfully recovered if and only if the identity associated with the ciphertext matches that associated with the key. Since identity strings can be arbitrary, it is possible to append the current day, for example, in order to specify a lifetime for a decryption key. Similarly, one could append access rights or different separations of duty, *etc.*

2.4.2.2 Attribute-Based Encryption

Attribute-based encryption (ABE) is useful when the authorized set of decryptors cannot easily be stated explicitly in terms of identifier strings (*e.g.*, because the user population is too large or changes too frequently). Instead, authorized decryptors can be described in terms of *attributes*. ABE comes in several variants that vary based on the form of the key and ciphertexts. In *key-policy ABE (KP-ABE)* [26], the ciphertext contains a set of attributes that describe the classification and contents of the plaintext, while the decryption key is associated with an *access structure* (which describes the access policy). Decryption succeeds if and only if the set of attributes satisfies the access structure. Thus, a user can be issued a key for a formula specifying their access rights (*e.g.*, Manager (Clearance Level 2 and Accounts)), while ciphertexts can be associated with a set of attributes describing its contents or required level of protection (*e.g.*, {Yearly Report, Accounts, Clearance Level 2}). On the other hand, *ciphertext-policy ABE* (CP-ABE) [27] reverses the association of attribute sets and access structures. Ciphertexts are now formed with an associated formula over attributes (describing the users that should be able to read the contents), while decryption keys are issued for an attribute set.

2.4.2.3 Predicate Encryption

Predicate encryption (PE) [28] generalizes the previous notions of functional encryption, particularly KP-ABE. Decryption keys are associated with a *predicate* F over attributes and ciphertexts are associated with a set of attributes I. Decryption succeeds if and only if $F(I) = 1$. Thus, if $F(I) = 0$, then no information is learned about the encrypted message; this property is referred to as *payload hiding*. Furthermore, some schemes can achieve a stronger notion of *attribute hiding* whereby, as well as hiding the message, no information is learned about the attribute set I beyond what is naturally leaked by the decryption functionality – that is, the result of $F(I)$. Many PE schemes focus on the specific predicates of inner products, which have been shown to encompass useful functionality such as Boolean formulas in conjunctive normal form and disjunctive normal form, threshold policies, and polynomial evaluation.

2.4.3 Verifiable Computing

It is commonly suggested that CSPs should be "honest but curious," generally meaning that they are trusted to follow the rules of any process but cannot be fully trusted with respect to privacy of data that they happen to observe. However, it is not necessarily always the case that such a level of trust can be placed in a CSP. Several new cryptographic mechanisms provide services that may be appropriate in cloud environments with reduced levels of trust in CSPs.

2.4.3.1 Verifiable Outsourced Computation

One concern arises in environments where a CSP is not trusted to return the correct result of a processing computation. In *verifiable outsourced computation* (VC), a client delegates the execution of computationally demanding operations to the cloud and receives the results alongside a cryptographic proof of their integrity. These proofs allow the detection of any server misbehavior and, at the same time, do not let a client falsely accuse a server of misbehaving.

Features of verifiable computation schemes include *public verifiability*, which ensures that *anybody* can verify the correct execution of outsourced operations using only public information. Most VC schemes use *noninteractive proofs*, which restrict the necessary level of interaction between provers and verifiers. Many different techniques have been used to build VC schemes, including fully homomorphic encryption [29, 30] and KP-ABE [31]. Pinocchio [32] applies *succinct noninteractive arguments of knowledge* (SNARKs) to achieve public verifiable computation of arbitrary functions.

2.4.3.2 Verifiable Storage

Another concern arises when CSPs are not trusted to preserve the integrity of outsourced data in their charge. A simple solution is for the client to compute and store a checksum (such as a MAC) of the data. However, this kind of verification scales poorly in cloud environments where huge amounts of data are stored. *Verifiable storage* schemes aim to make verification more efficient than downloading the entire data set and allow clients to perform integrity checks as many times as needed. Solutions broadly fall into two categories: (i) *deterministic solutions* that offer an undeniable guarantee of integrity and (ii) *probabilistic solutions* in which the verifier is convinced of the integrity of the data with a certain probability only. Deterministic solutions incur considerable computation and communication complexity, generally linear in the size of the entire data. Most schemes propose probabilistic optimizations based on random sampling; instead of checking the entire file, these proposals check the integrity of a subset of segments included in the file. Probabilistic solutions can generally be classed as either *provable data possession* (PDP) (verifying that the data is held by the server) [33] or *proofs of retrievability* (POR) (verifying that data is recoverable from the server, even if small modifications have been made by a malicious server) [34]. Early proposals [33] deal with static data in the context of archival or backup storage, while others allow for efficient updates of the data (modification, deletion, or insertion of blocks) and for efficient integrity verification to ensure that the server stores the latest version of the outsourced data. Moreover, some solutions allow verification to be delegated to a third-party auditor [35] and to render this public verification privacy preserving [36].

2.4.4 Other Tools

In addition to the three classes of cryptographic mechanism just discussed, there are several other relatively recent cryptographic tools that have the potential for deployment in cloud environments.

2.4.4.1 Proxy Re-encryption

Proxy re-encryption [37] allows a semi-trusted intermediary (*proxy*) to convert a ciphertext intended to be read by one entity into one that can be read by another, without the proxy decrypting the ciphertext, or otherwise learning the message itself. One example application is to manage access to encrypted data stored on a cloud server, which acts as the proxy. The stored ciphertexts can be transformed such that they can be decrypted by authorized entities, yet the server itself remains unable to read the data.

2.4.4.2 Oblivious RAM

If a CSP is untrusted, a client may wish to access data and for the CSP to process stored encrypted data without revealing which data items are being used, how frequently they are accessed, and in what order. *Oblivious RAM (ORAM)* [38] aims to hide the memory locations accessed by RAM programs. Clients need only store a small amount of data, while servers store $O(n)$ data for n outsourced data items, and each access request can be replaced by $O(log^2 n)$ accesses [38]. Data must be stored in encrypted form and associated with an index. In order to hide the access patterns, further *dummy* accesses are made in other locations. If read and write requests should also look equivalent, then each read operation must include at least one dummy write operation to the same location and *vice versa*. The location that data is stored in must be independent of the index and two accesses to the same index should not necessarily access the same location. In general, ORAM schemes work by imposing some additional structure on the memory and then performing a read (or write) operation to a set of locations, using a combination of sorting and hashing algorithms. Since only the client knows which of these accesses was the desired one, no information is revealed to the CSP.

2.4.4.3 Format-Preserving Encryption

Format-preserving encryption (FPE) [39] enables formatted data to be symmetrically encrypted to ciphertexts that conform to the same formatting rules (*e.g.*, credit card numbers are encrypted to random, valid credit card numbers). The encryption induces a pseudorandom permutation over all validly formatted strings. This property can be useful for storing encrypted databases where data fields must follow specific formatting rules. In particular, it is useful when upgrading legacy outsourced database solutions to be secure; in general, it is not possible to simply encrypt the data using a non-format-preserving encryption scheme without changing the structure of the database itself. One way to achieve FPE is the *rank-then-encipher* approach where the set of all valid strings are numbered according to some ranking function. Then, using a simpler integer FPE scheme (which encrypts integers to integers), one can encrypt the rank of the message. The produced ciphertext will be an integer that indexes some random (correctly formatted) message from the message space, which forms the final ciphertext. Currently, such ranking functions exist for all formatted domains where the format can be expressed by a regular language.

2.4.4.4 Secure Deduplication

Secure deduplication [40] provides a space-efficient storage solution for outsourced data. If two users request to store the same data file, a cloud server may wish to save storage costs by only storing one copy of the file for both users. However, this is difficult if data is encrypted prior to being outsourced, as the security properties of a (randomized) encryption scheme will result in the ciphertexts for both files appearing entirely unrelated and, furthermore, storing just one ciphertext will prevent other users from recovering the data without holding the same decryption key. One solution to this problem is to use *message-locked encryption* (MLE) [40], which encrypts the message under a key derived deterministically from the message itself. For example, the key could be defined to be the result of a hash function applied to the message. A *tag* may also be generated that the server may use to detect duplicates. Privacy holds only when the message space has sufficient min-entropy. Another important security property is known as *tag consistency.* It is hard to enforce an honest client to recover a message different from that which is uploaded (*e.g.,* by forging a tag in such a way that the server believes the encryption of two different messages represent the same message and therefore deletes the second copy and returns the message).

2.5 Closing Remarks

In this chapter, we have briefly surveyed a number of relatively recent cryptographic mechanisms that have potential uses in security applications within cloud environments. While these tools show great promise in overcoming some limitations of conventional cryptography, it is important to apply some words of caution before recommending their immediate application.

While some of the discussed cryptographic tools are beginning to see deployment in cloud environments (such as searchable encryption and some functional encryption schemes), many others are still relatively young and the relevant theory is still under development. Several tools are only assured to be secure within the context of highly specific security models. As such, security levels may not yet be at acceptable levels.

Furthermore, cryptography is not (yet) able to *efficiently* provide all desirable functionality, especially when it comes to the processing of outsourced, encrypted data. For example, while fully homomorphic encryption remains promising to enable arbitrary computations on encrypted data, finding a truly practical, general-purpose scheme remains an open research area. In general, many of the tools discussed in this chapter are probably not yet efficient enough for practical deployment.

Cryptography is an area that has traditionally proved most effective when informed communities agree on the best available techniques. This is partly because of the difficulty of identifying effective mechanisms, but also because many applications benefit from compatibility. As yet, appropriate standardization activities are at relatively early stages for many of the mechanisms discussed in this chapter.

Nonetheless, the tools discussed in this chapter represent exciting developments in the theory of cryptography. We fully expect refinements and improvements to occur over the coming years that will result in these tools becoming effective practical mechanisms for securing data in cloud environments, and indeed elsewhere.

2.6 Review Questions

1. In general, what fundamental role does cryptography play in providing security for a computer system, whether in a cloud environment or otherwise?
2. What are the main limitations of traditional cryptography with respect to the security of typical cloud environments?
3. What types of processing operations is it possible to do on encrypted data using the tools described in this chapter?
4. How might a typical cloud environment benefit from the deployment of attribute-based encryption?
5. Searching over encrypted data is a potentially useful process to be able to conduct in a cloud environment, but what problems might arise from doing this over an insecure communication channel to an untrusted cloud server?
6. While the mechanisms described in this chapter appear to offer great promise, why should we be cautious about seeking to deploy them today?

Acknowledgements This chapter was adapted from a review conducted as part of the European Union project H2020-644024 "CLARUS." We would like to thank the following researchers who contributed to the initial deliverable: Monir Azraoui, Aida Calviño, Josep Domingo-Ferrer, Melek Önen, David Sánchez, Cédric Van Rompay, and Oriol Farràs Ventura.

References

1. ISO/IEC 18033-3:2010 Information technology – security techniques – encryption algorithms – Part 3: Block ciphers (2010)
2. Dworkin M (2001) Recommendation for block cipher modes of operation methods and techniques, National Institute of Standards and Technology special publication. National Institute of Standards and Technology, Gaithersburg
3. National Institute of Standards and Technology (2001) Advanced encryption standard (AES), Federal information processing standards publication, 197. National Institute of Standards and Technology, Gaithersburg, pp 311–441
4. ISO/IEC 18033-4:2011, Information technology – security techniques – encryption algorithms – Part 4: Stream ciphers, 2nd edn, (2011)
5. ISO/IEC 18033-2:2006 Information technology – security techniques – encryption algorithms – Part 2: Asymmetric ciphers (2006)
6. Dang Q (2008) Recommendation for applications using approved hash algorithms, National Institute of Standards and Technology special publication, 107. National Institute of Standards and Technology, Gaithersburg
7. ISO/IEC 9797-1:2011 Information technology – security techniques – message authentication codes (MACs) – Part 1: Mechanisms using a block cipher (2011)
8. National Institute of Standards and Technology (2009) Digital signature standard (DSS), Federal information processing standards publication, 186-2. National Institute of Standards and Technology, Gaithersburg, pp 1–119
9. ISO/IEC 19772:2009 Information technology – security techniques – authenticated encryption (2009)
10. Yung M, Dent AW, Zheng Y (2010) Practical signcryption. Springer Science & Business Media, Berlin
11. ISO/IEC 29150:2011 Information technology – security techniques – signcryption (2011)
12. Curtmola R, Garay J, Kamara S, Ostrovsky R (2011) Searchable symmetric encryption: improved definitions and efficient constructions. J Comput Secur 19:895–934
13. Bellare M, Boldyreva A, O'Neill A (2007) Deterministic and efficiently searchable encryption. In: Advances in cryptology – CRYPTO 2007. LNCS, vol 4622. Springer, Heidelberg, pp 535–552
14. Golle P, Staddon J, Waters B (2004) Secure conjunctive keyword search over encrypted data. In: Applied cryptography and network security, vol 3089, LNCS. Springer, Berlin/Heidelberg, pp 31–45
15. Cash D, Jarecki S, Jutla C, Krawczyk H, Rosu M-C, Steiner M (2013) Highly-scalable searchable symmetric encryption with support for boolean queries. In: Advances in cryptology – CRYPTO 2013, vol 8042, LNCS. Springer, Heidelberg, pp 353–373
16. Boneh D, Waters B (2007) Conjunctive, subset, and range queries on encrypted data. In: Theory of cryptography, vol 4392, LNCS. Springer, Berlin, pp 535–554
17. Popa R, Redfield C (2011) CryptDB: protecting confidentiality with encrypted query processing. In: Proceedings of the twenty-third ACM symposium on operating systems principles. SOSP'11, pp 85–100
18. Li JLJ, Wang QWQ, Wang CWC, Cao NCN, Ren KRK, Lou WLW (2010) Fuzzy keyword search over encrypted data in cloud computing. In: INFOCOM, 2010 proceedings IEEE, pp 1–5
19. Boneh D, Kushilevitz E, Ostrovsky R, Skeith WE III (2007) Public key encryption that allows PIR queries. In: Advances in cryptology – CRYPTO 2007, vol 4622, LNCS. Springer, Berlin, pp 50–67
20. Gentry C (2009) A fully homomorphic encryption scheme. PhD thesis, Stanford University. Available from: crypto.stanford.edu/craig
21. Leontiadis I, Elkhyaoui K, Molva R (2014) Private and dynamic time-series data aggregation with trust relaxation. In: Cryptology and Network Security, vol 8813, LNCS. Springer, Berlin, pp 305–320

22. Agrawal R, Kiernan J, Srikant R, Xu Y (2004) Order preserving encryption for numeric data. In: Proceedings of the 2004 ACM SIGMOD international conference on management of data. SIGMOD'04, pp 563–574
23. Boldyreva A, Chenette N, Lee Y, O'Neill A (2009) Order-preserving symmetric encryption. In: Advances in cryptology – EUROCRYPT 2009, vol 5479, LNCS. Springer, Berlin, pp 224–241
24. Wang C, Cao N, Li J, Ren K, Lou W (2010) Secure ranked keyword search over encrypted cloud data. In: Proceedings of Distributed Computing Systems (ICDCS), IEEE 30th International conference on, IEEE, pp 253–262
25. Boneh D, Franklin M (2001) Identity-based encryption from the Weil pairing. In: Advances in cryptology – CRYPTO 2001, vol 2139, LNCS. Springer, Berlin, pp 213–229
26. Goyal V, Pandey O, Sahai A, Waters B (2006) Attribute-based encryption for fine-grained access control of encrypted data. In: Juels A, Wright R. di Vimercati SDC (eds) ACM conference on computer and communications security. ACM, New York, pp 89–98
27. Waters B (2011) Ciphertext-policy attribute-based encryption: an expressive, efficient, and provably secure realization. In: Public key cryptography – PKC 2011, vol 6571, LNCS. Springer, Heidelberg, pp 53–70
28. Katz J, Sahai A, Waters B (2008) Predicate encryption supporting disjunctions, polynomial equations, and inner products. In: Advances in cryptology – EUROCRYPT 2008. Springer, Berlin, pp 146–162
29. Chung K-M, Kalai Y, Vadhan S (2010) Improved delegation of computation using fully homomorphic encryption. In: Advances in cryptology – CRYPTO 2010, vol 6223, LNCS. Springer, Berlin, pp 483–501
30. Barbosa M, Farshim P (2012) Delegatable homomorphic encryption with applications to secure outsourcing of computation. In: Topics in cryptology – CT-RSA 2012, vol 7178, LNCS. Springer, Berlin, pp 296–312
31. Parno B, Raykova M, Vaikuntanathan V (2012) How to delegate and verify in public: verifiable computation from attribute-based encryption. In: Theory of cryptography, vol 7194, LNCS. Springer, Berlin, pp 422–439
32. Parno B, Howell J, Gentry C, Raykova M (2013) Pinocchio: nearly practical verifiable computation. In: IEEE symposium on security and privacy. IEEE, pp 238–252
33. Ateniese G, Burns R, Curtmola R, Herring J, Kissner L, Peterson Z, Song D (2007) Provable data possession at untrusted stores. In: Proceedings of the 14th ACM conference on computer and communications security, pp 598–609
34. Juels A, Kaliski BS Jr (2007) PORs: proofs of retrievability for large files. In: Proceedings of the 14th ACM conference on computer and communications security. ACM, pp 584–597
35. Armknecht F, Bohli J-M, Karame GO, Liu Z, Reuter CA (2014) Outsourced proofs of retrievability. In: Proceedings of the 2014 ACM SIGSAC conference on computer and communications security. ACM, pp 831–843
36. Wang C, Wang Q, Ren K, Lou W (2010) Privacy-preserving public auditing for data storage security in cloud computing. In: Proceedings of INFOCOM. IEEE, pp 1–9
37. Ateniese G, Fu K, Green M, Hohenberger S (2006) Improved proxy re-encryption schemes with applications to secure distributed storage. ACM Trans Inf Syst Secur 9:1–30
38. Pinkas B, Reinman T (2010) Oblivious RAM revisited. In: Advances in cryptology – CRYPTO 2010, vol 6223, LNCS. Springer, Berlin, pp 502–519
39. Bellare M, Ristenpart T, Rogaway P, Stegers T (2009) Format-preserving encryption. In: Selected areas in cryptography, vol 5867, LNCS. Springer, Boston, pp 295–312
40. Bellare M, Keelveedhi S, Ristenpart T (2013) Message-locked encryption and secure deduplication. In: Advances in cryptology – EUROCRYPT 2013, vol 7881, LNCS. Springer, Berlin, pp 296–312

James Alderman is a postdoctoral research assistant in the Information Security Group at Royal Holloway, University of London. His research interests primarily revolve around verifiable outsourced computation and the cryptographic enforcement of access control policies. He is currently employed on the European Union's Horizon 2020 project CLARUS aiming to develop a secure framework for storing and processing data outsourced to the cloud.

Jason Crampton is a professor of information security at Royal Holloway, University of London. His research focuses on access control, including models for access control systems, languages for specifying access control policies, and the cryptographic enforcement of access control policies. He served on the editorial board of ACM Transactions on Information and System Security from 2007 to 2012 and regularly serves on program committees for a wide range of information and computer security conferences.

Keith M. Martin is a professor in the Information Security Group at Royal Holloway, University of London. After research positions at the University of Adelaide and Katholieke Universiteit Leuven, he rejoined Royal Holloway in January 2000 and became a professor of information security in 2007 and director of the Information Security Group between 2010 and 2015. Keith's current research interests include key management, cryptographic applications, and securing lightweight networks. He is the author of *Everyday Cryptography* by Oxford University Press. Aside from conventional teaching, Keith is a designer and module leader on Royal Holloway's distance learning MSc Information Security program and regularly presents to industrial audiences and schools.

Migrating to Public Clouds – From a Security Perspective

3

Thomas Holding, John Panneerselvam, and Lu Liu

Abstract

Given the growth of Cloud Computing in the recent years, the number of users adopting Cloud services is also increasing at a stupendous scale. Though the emergence of various service offering models and infrastructures in Cloud services widens the service options for the Cloud users, this also leaves the Cloud users in a state of chaos whilst choosing their appropriate Cloud services. To this end, defining policies for adopting Cloud services from the perspectives of both the individuals and organizations has become essential for choosing the right Cloud services. With this is mind, this chapter is aimed at uncovering the concerns incurred whilst migrating from private Cloud to public Cloud services. An important contribution of this chapter is the inferences, derived from a conducted survey amongst the Cloud users, which includes evaluating their satisfactory levels, requirements and desired improvements in their respective Cloud environments.

Keywords

Adoption • Chi-square • Migration • Performance • Provider • Satisfaction • Security

3.1 Introduction

Public Cloud Computing is growing in popularity for a number of reasons, one of which is the global economic crisis causing information technology (IT)-centric organizations to reduce the budgets spent towards their IT resources. As an impact of

---

T. Holding • J. Panneerselvam (✉) • L. Liu
Department of Engineering and Technology, University of Derby, Derby, UK
e-mail: t.holding101@gmail.com; j.panneerselvam@derby.ac.uk; l.liu@derby.ac.uk

S.Y. Zhu et al. (eds.), *Guide to Security Assurance for Cloud Computing*,
Computer Communications and Networks, DOI 10.1007/978-3-319-25988-8_3

this global crisis and also for preserving environmental sustainability, organizations relying heavily on IT are under immense pressure [24] to sustain their performance levels whilst reducing their usages of the IT resources. Cloud Computing is one amongst the first of choices for the organizations of all scales for effective IT provisions through the convergence of technologies that date back many years.

Nowadays, organizations of various purposes are becoming more IT centric and have started to deploy and maintain their own IT needs. For instance, higher education institutes (HEIs) are one of the major dependents of information technology and are deploying and maintaining their own IT requirements, rather than outsourcing their IT needs, since outsourcing is also becoming costlier when compared to that of own maintenance. Since public Cloud Computing [2] offers organizations with the access to computing resources at a reduced cost, a growing number of organizations are choosing to migrate to the public Cloud as a cost-effective solution to their IT infrastructure. Public Clouds are not only cost-effective with regard to the outlay and maintenance of IT infrastructure but also energy efficient in reducing the carbon footprints and associated bills.

Despite the cost-benefits [9] and sustainability, public Cloud Computing also causes concern amongst many, and some of them include data security and privacy, the lack of control of IT resources and the lack of interoperability between Cloud environments, etc. There is undoubtedly a question around the security of the data that resides within the public Cloud environment. Although vendors are working hard to fight this stigma through the use of security layers such as access control lists (ACLs) and security groups that can be implemented on, for example, Amazon Web Service's (AWS) Virtual Private Cloud (VPC), public Clouds are still certainly not exempt from security threats. Indeed, a total private Cloud can be implemented for improving the security; however, this solution does not accompany the cost-benefits that an IaaS offers the consumer. On-demand and future-proof IT infrastructure at an affordable cost can hardly be achieved through the implementation of a private Cloud.

Clearly, there has been a lack of discussion around the concerns of the organizations and the issues faced by the consumer, when moving from a private Cloud solution to a public Cloud solution. The distinctive growth of Cloud Computing into several forms of deployments such as Public, Private, Community and Hybrid Clouds has now brought up a situation to debate the benefits and drawbacks of the Cloud deployment types from various perspectives. With this in mind, this chapter is aimed at uncovering the issues faced by organizations or clients, in the process of migrating to the public Cloud services from private Clouds.

3.2 Clouds and Features

Public Cloud is a general-purpose environment, which is owned and managed by external service providers (such as Amazon's AWS or Microsoft's Azure), whom apply their own policies and costing and charging models [8]. A multi-tenancy model is applied in public Clouds; thus, consumers may be sharing the resources provided to them with other organizations [3]. Whereas, private Clouds are built solely for one organization and do not share the resources as in a multi-tenancy service type [6]. Private Clouds allow the organization to have greater control of their data and the architecture of their environment, in service of critical and dynamic decision-making and projects [8]. Private Cloud deployments are of two distinctive architectural patterns such as 'on-premise clouds' (OPC) and 'externally hosted clouds' (EHC) [25]. The OPC model is more appropriate for organizations requiring extremely secure environments [22], as this model maintains the resources within the organization applied with desired security levels [25]. Although a third party hosts the EHC, they are still dedicated to one organization and offer a less expensive Cloud solution. VMware [25] is a popular example of the EHC applications that are being widely used.

When different organizations have a common set of goals, interests or shared concerns, they can form a community Cloud [11]. Parallels can be drawn with the public Cloud, with the key difference being the management of the resources residing with the organizations collaborated to form the community Cloud [19]. The infrastructure, policies and values will all be shared amongst the participating parties, with the Cloud being either on- or off-premise [8]. As the name suggests, hybrid Clouds integrate attributes from more than one Cloud. The Clouds will be exclusive from one another, but have common attributes such as proprietary technologies [8]. This allows data and application portability as well as giving organizations the ability to manage their resources from a central hub [8].

In general, a more critical service that requires uncompromising security measures would be hosted on the private Cloud, whereas the less critical services on the public Cloud [25]. The hybrid Cloud can also be utilized when an organization has exhausted the resources on their private Cloud. Data (if not security critical) can be transferred to the hybrid Cloud, which is known as 'Cloud bursting', meaning the ability of acquiring extra resources when private Cloud resources are exhausted [6].

3.3 Migration Concerns

Whilst Cloud Computing is growing in popularity amongst the enterprises, the key attributes of their Cloud adoption policies are yet to be defined by the enterprises. Some of the common elements of public Clouds that enterprises taking Cloud initiatives need improvement, for the purpose of enhancing their business value, include security policies, cost, approval and access policies for the datacentre resources, disaster recovery policies, etc. A recent report of RightScale [18] defining the key elements of Cloud strategy for enterprises is presented in Fig. 3.1. It is evident from the Figure that only 36 % of the enterprises have actually defined policies based on their business requirements. This group falls into the minority of the total enterprises, insisting that companies adopting Cloud services should actually define their policies for various levels of Cloud adoption. In general, the

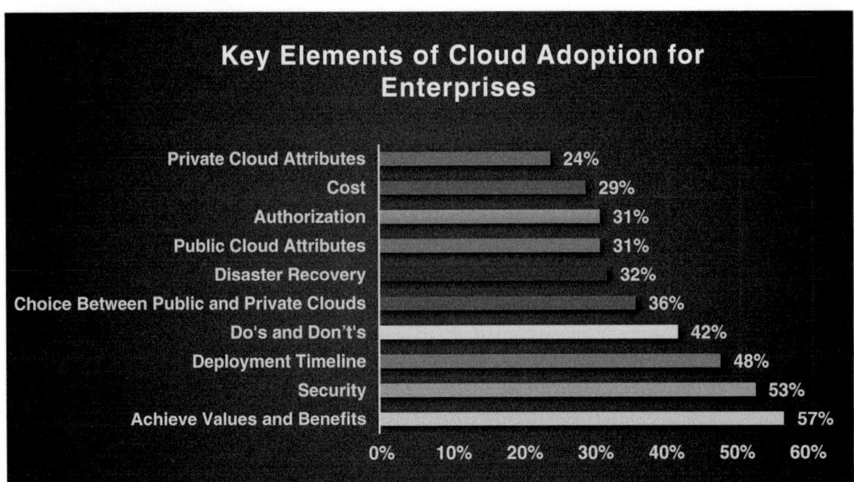

Fig. 3.1 Cloud attributes strategy for enterprises

statistics in Fig. 3.1 insists that enterprises are showing a keen interest in shifting towards public Cloud services, despite the demands for enhancing the service qualities of public Clouds.

One of the most prevailing issues in migrating to the public Cloud is the lack of control and total reliance of the clients on the public Cloud provider [5]. The total reliance on the service provider is precarious for the clients particularly for the stakeholders. Unforeseen circumstances in business-critical services (such as financial transactions) could affect the reputation of the provider, which highly concerns the stakeholders with their total reliance on the provider. Cloud Computing allows the client to trail and test the quality of the Cloud services before their actual adaptation or deployment of the Cloud applications [5]. Furthermore, the lack of control of the underlying infrastructure and the platform means that should the consumer of public Clouds wish to amend changes, the process could be long and arduous, which is not an acute issue in a private Cloud solution [12].

Indeed, there are advocates of moving from a private Cloud to a public Cloud solution [6]. Moore's law states that the number of integrated circuits and transistors doubles approximately every 2 years [21], which if holds true, the improvement in IaaS will be plain for all to see [6]. And this access to greater storage and more powerful IT infrastructures are delivered at a fraction of cost with the Cloud interventions [5]. This allows organization adopting private Clouds to deploy and implement such technological advancements within their own IT infrastructures, but incurred with excess IT spending when compared to that of a public Cloud solution [6]. Such an IT spending includes their hardware and software purchase requirements and also the employment of highly skilled staff and necessary training in order to ensure the smooth running of the architecture, and all of which, this process is time-consuming and tedious [12].

3.4 Security and Privacy in Public Clouds

The most concerning security issue faced by public Cloud users is the actual location of the data storage. For an instance, a single public Cloud provider may have several data servers located across Europe, Asia and other parts of the world, which in some cases causes issues with regard to privacy legislation that forbids certain data types (such as personal data) from being transmitted outside the EU [23]. In fear of breaking the UK's Data Protection Act (1998), UK-based organizations may seriously consider how secure the data is and also the location of the data servers prior to migrating to the public Clouds [23]. It is worth to add that many of the data privacy laws are predated to public Cloud Computing and so were created without the consideration of virtualization and other Cloud technologies, resulting in much uncertainty around the legalities of the data stored on a public Cloud [16]. It is important for the public Cloud consumers to have precise understanding of the potential legal implications involved within the provider, and also between the provider and other relevant organizations, since legal litigations of the providers always impact the security status of the consumer [3]. Such implications are extremely difficult to guard against, as they are out of the reach of the consumers [16]. There are several scenarios that could bring up such a situation for a client, and some of them are listed below [16]:

1. If the provider of the public Cloud service declares bankruptcy, all servers and the data within the servers could be seized.
2. A third-party organization taking legal action against the Cloud provider and acquiring a subpoena for access to all servers used by the public Cloud provider.
3. The data security could be compromised as the public Cloud provider may not have appropriate security measures.

Security measures suggested by Cloud experts for the consumers to consider for the purpose of safeguarding themselves from the above scenarios, whilst adopting public Cloud services, include encryption, backups and using a second Cloud provider, etc [16]. It is worth to add that some public Cloud providers are taking right measures in order to relieve concerns with regard to the relevant breaking government law [23]. Such measures include building datacentres within the EU and implementing state-of-the-art encryption techniques appropriately [23].

The inherent nature of the multi-tenancy model means that various resources and network addresses used by a single provider may be shared with other organizations, which introduces security challenges into the public Cloud service offering model [8, 7]. Also, hackers are using public Clouds in order to implement botnets, since such environments offer a relatively cheap and robust infrastructure, which is idyllic for launching attacks [17]. This is one of the major security concerns of the regular public Cloud users in two different perspectives. Firstly, if a network address is shared, malicious activity originating from that network address could be attributed to all the consumers using the same network address, without distinguishing the genuine users from the unscrupulous users. Secondly, pooled computing nature of the pubic Clouds incurs unexpected and unwanted side channels between regular resources and malicious resources [8].

Counteracting measures to such security challenges are also being confiscated by the public Cloud vendors in today's Cloud market. Amazon has acted by implementing VPC, which is the networking layer for Amazon EC2 [1]. VPC allows the consumer to launch the AWS resources into a predefined virtual network, which resembles a network that the consumer would have in their private Cloud, but with the added benefit of the scalable IT infrastructure of AWS [1]. Essentially, consumers are able to extend their existing security policies to their VPCs, with the aim of relieving some of the concerns with regard to control of the data security [23]. VPC ensures data security by isolating various virtual networks from one another and allows the consumers to configure their own routing tables, security settings and network gateways. Consumers can also create subnets and configure the IP address ranges in order to connect securely to their existing network infrastructure [1]. This is all achieved through the use of industry-standard encrypted Internet Protocol Security (IPSec) VPN connections [23].

In addition to the extra security control, there are several layers of security that can be implemented in a given subnet to ensure the security of the data, for example, security groups and network ACLs. Security groups act as a first line of defence firewall for the associated Amazon EC2 instances. They control the inbound and outbound traffic at the instance level [1]. ACLs act as the second layer of defence firewall for the associated subnets, controlling the inbound and outbound traffic at the subnet level [1]. In addition to this, identity and access management can be used in order to ensure that only the nominated people within the organization can manage the two layers of security [1]. Table 3.1 gives a brief overview of the differences between network ACLs and security groups.

Although these security measures tackle some issues, there is still concern from consumers and experts who admit Cloud service providers are yet to realize an all-encompassing security solution [20]. For instance, when a consumer amends the configuration for a security group, there is a period of transition time where the security group policies are not in place, during which, two or more machines can lose connectivity [14]. Furthermore, this also extends to the machines that are

Table 3.1 Comparison of security groups and ACLs [1]

Security group	Network Access Control Lists (ACLs)
First defence layer operating at the instance level	Second layer of defence operating at the subnet level
'Allow Rules' functionality	'Allow Rules' and 'Deny Rules' functionalities
Stateful: Allows return traffic automatically	Stateless: Explicitly allows return traffic
All the existing rules are evaluated when allowing traffic	Appropriate rules are processed in order when allowing traffic
Applies only to the specified instances	Applies to all the instances in the associated subnet automatically

not actually being deployed [14]. Also, the VPC implementation is addressed to be deviating from one of the primary purposes of public Cloud Computing – ease of use and reduced workload. Despite the added security, the added responsibility of managing the VPC network is not in the interests of the clients [14].

A research on uncovering public Cloud security frailties [4] revealed that out of 22 % of the virtual machines being created, the login credentials for the original creator of the machines are not being deleted [10]. And majority of the machines were found to be running with critical security weaknesses, and 98 % of the VMs contain undeleted data from the previous usage cycles [10]. This research on malware analysis insists the spreading of two popular infectors: firstly, Trojan-Spy that can perform key logging and monitoring of processes and secondly, a Trojan.Agent, which allows a user to modify Internet Explorer settings and download other malicious content [4].

In the recent years, the standards of Cloud Computing allow users to trail and test their applications before they actually deploy or migrate their applications to externally hosted Cloud datacentres. This feature of Cloud services allows users to assess the security levels that a particular Cloud provider can offer, and users can comparatively study the various security levels of the Cloud providers in the market. For instance, IBM Cloud maturity benchmark tool facilitates users to find out the way of stacking up their own Cloud. And HP Helion facilitates users with the visibility of governance control across its hybrid Cloud environment.

3.5 Migrating to Public Clouds – An Experimental Analysis

3.5.1 Research Design

The objective and purpose of this section is to establish a method of acquiring data in order to understand the benefits and drawbacks for an organization to move their IT infrastructure from a private Cloud to a public Cloud. This is achieved by conducting a survey through the use of questionnaires involving a set of seven questions each, amongst the Cloud users. The aim of this questionnaire is to draw conclusion on the end-user satisfaction amongst the users of the private Cloud and the public Cloud services. Two sets of survey have been conducted: one with the private Cloud users and the other with the public Cloud users, both of them belong to academia.

In general, workloads from educational institutions include a bag of tasks and are heterogeneous in nature, causing bottleneck effects on resources, such as the CPU. It is perceived that the survey amongst the Cloud users belonging to academia will have more diversity and contribute substantially in defining polices in public Cloud migrations. The final results of the two surveys have been compared and evaluated in order to draw inferences and conclusions with regard to public Cloud migrations. Analysis and interpretation of the obtained data help understanding the benefits and implications involved in migrating to a public Cloud from a private Cloud solution.

3.5.2 Statistical Analysis

Questionnaire-based strategy is adopted in this research study primarily for the purpose of evaluating the end-user satisfaction, something which can hardly be established by empirical research. Whilst it is important from a managerial perspective to have an overview of the performance differences between a private Cloud environment and a public Cloud environment, arguably the primary measure of the success of a given environment is the end-user satisfaction.

The questionnaire is created using an online platform based on eSurvey Creator and distributed to the Cloud users working with IT system in an educational organization, via the use of Internet forums and email. Due to the infancy of public Cloud systems within education, a concerted effort was also made to distribute the questionnaire to specific organizations that currently use public Cloud systems within their role.

A scientific statistical hypothesis test called chi-square (χ^2), which tests the null hypothesis, is applied on the results of the questionnaire data obtained. The null hypothesis is used for predicting differences between the expected and the observed results. Based on a relative standard value, this null hypothesis is either accepted or rejected for the purpose of driving further inferences [15]. The formula for χ^2 is shown in Eq. 3.1:

$$x_c^2 = \sum \frac{(\mathrm{O_i} - \mathrm{E_i})^2}{\mathrm{E_i}}. \tag{3.1}$$

where x_c^2 – chi-square
$\mathrm{O_i}$ – data collected
$\mathrm{E_i}$ – expected values

The process of testing the null hypothesis and calculating χ^2 is described as follows:

1. The *degree of freedom* for each question is established first. This is determined by calculating the number of possible answers in each question minus 1. For example, if there are five possible answers for a question, the degree of freedom is 4 [15].
2. Then, a relative standard is established as a basis for accepting or rejecting the null hypothesis value. The relative standard commonly used for the χ^2 test is $p > 0.05$. The value p is the probability for the returned results to deviate from the prediction, and it is the consequence of chance alone. Using the standard of 0.05, one would expect that any deviation to be due to chance alone a maximum of 5 % of the time [15].
3. Calculating χ^2 using Eq. 3.1 reduces the calculations to three significant digits, and it is rounded to two significant digits [15].

Table 3.2 Chi-square distribution table

Degrees of freedom (*df*)	Probability (*p*)										
	0.95	0.90	0.80	0.70	0.50	0.30	0.20	0.10	0.05	0.01	0.001
1	0.004	0.02	0.06	0.15	0.46	1.07	1.64	2.71	3.84	6.64	10.83
2	0.10	0.21	0.45	0.71	1.39	2.41	3.22	4.60	5.99	9.21	13.82
3	0.35	0.58	1.01	1.42	2.37	3.66	4.64	6.25	7.82	11.34	16.27
4	0.71	1.06	1.65	2.20	3.36	4.88	5.99	7.78	9.49	13.28	18.47
5	1.14	1.61	2.34	3.00	4.35	6.06	7.29	9.24	11.07	15.09	20.52
6	1.63	2.20	3.07	3.83	5.35	7.23	8.56	10.64	12.59	16.81	22.46
7	2.17	2.83	3.82	4.67	6.35	8.38	9.80	12.02	14.07	18.48	24.32
8	2.73	3.49	4.59	5.53	7.34	9.52	11.03	13.36	15.51	20.09	26.12
9	3.32	4.17	5.38	6.39	8.34	10.66	12.24	14.68	16.92	21.67	27.88
10	3.94	4.86	6.18	7.27	9.34	11.78	13.44	15.99	18.31	23.21	29.59
	Nonsignificant								Significant		

4. Conclusions drawn in terms of hypothesis:
   (a) If the value p for the calculated χ^2 is $p > 0.05$, the hypothesis will be accepted, meaning the deviation is small enough and is good enough to chance, and no other factors can impact the results [15].
   (b) If the value p for the calculated χ^2 is $p < 0.05$, the hypothesis will be rejected, meaning that the factors other than the chance are impacting the results of the survey [15].

Table 3.2 shows the χ^2 distribution table. Previously established *degree of freedom* is located in the *(df)* column. Working across the row, closest value to the calculated χ^2 is obtained, and the p value is obtained from the corresponding column of the closest value [15].

3.6 Results and Interpretation

In this section, the results of the questionnaire are interpreted using pie chart, and the values are depicted in a table with percentage values for the purposes of drawing inferences on the end-user satisfaction. For each questionnaire, χ^2 value calculations are presented. Unless otherwise stated, the following calculation (Eq. 3.2) will be used for each question in order to establish the expected values:

$$\frac{\text{Total participants for a given Cloud environment} \times \text{Total number of answers for a given question category}}{\text{Total number of overall participants}} \tag{3.2}$$

For a χ^2 test to be accurate and effective, every question category should include at least five responses. If not, the expected values would be too small for the approximation involved in the χ^2 test to be validated [13]. If such a scenario arises, then two question categories with less than five responses will be combined into one. For example, if a question has the categories of 'Needs Improvement', 'Quite Secure', 'Very Secure' and 'Totally Secure', but there are only three answers for 'Needs Improvement', the categories of 'Needs Improvement' and 'Quite Secure' will be combined in order to increase the expected values more than 5.

3.6.1 Question 1

How satisfied are the costings of the Cloud services? (Fig. 3.2)

Table 3.3 shows the *p value* for the χ^2 calculation as 0.70. Thus, $p > 0.05$. Therefore, the hypothesis of no significant difference is accepted, since the deviation is small enough and can be put down to chance. In other words, the users of the private Cloud and the public Cloud are equally satisfied with the cost of their Cloud environment.

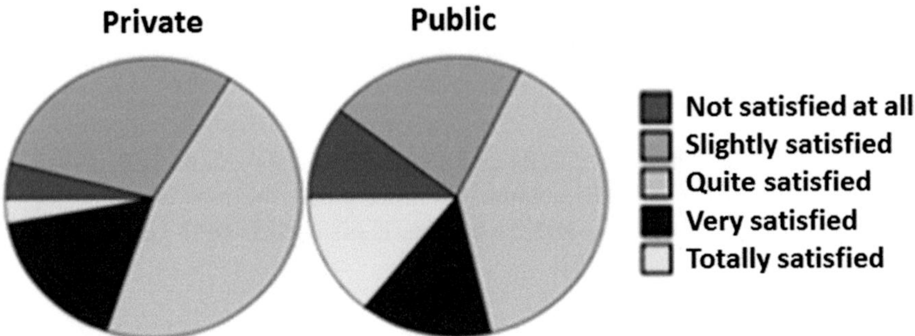

Fig. 3.2 Cost satisfaction pie chart

Table 3.3 Cost satisfaction figures and calculations

	Not satisfied at all	Slightly satisfied	Quite satisfied	Very satisfied	Totally satisfied	Total
Private Cloud	3	21	33	12	2	71
	4.23 %	29.58 %	46.48 %	16.90 %	2.82 %	
Public Cloud	3	6	11	4	4	28
	10.71 %	21.43 %	39.29 %	14.29 %	14.29 %	
Total	6	27	44	16	6	99
	6.06 %	27.27 %	44.44 %	16.16 %	6.06 %	
χ^2 Calculation = 0.96			*p value* = 0.70			

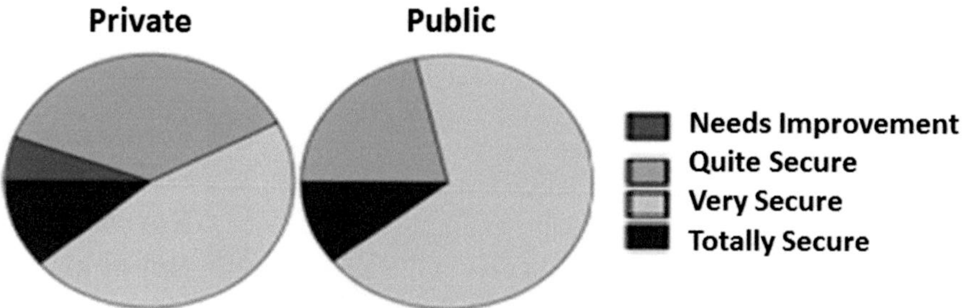

Fig. 3.3 Data security satisfaction pie chart

Table 3.4 Data security figures and calculations

	Needs improvement	Quite secure	Very secure	Totally secure	Total
Private Cloud	4	26	33	8	71
	5.63 %	36.62 %	46.48 %	11.27 %	
Public Cloud	0	6	19	3	28
	0.00 %	21.43 %	67.86 %	10.71 %	
Total	4	32	52	11	99
	4.04 %	32.32 %	52.53 %	11.11 %	
χ^2 Calculation = 3.76			*p value* = 0.05		

3.6.2 Question 2

Is your data secured in the Cloud? (Fig. 3.3)

Table 3.4 shows the *p value* for the χ^2 calculation as 0.05. Thus, $p = 0.05$, and therefore, the hypothesis of no significant difference is accepted, since the deviation is small enough and can be put down to chance. In other words, the users of the private Cloud and public Cloud are equally satisfied with the security of their Cloud environment.

3.6.3 Question 3

To what extent the performance issues in the Cloud affect your day-to-day jobs? (Fig. 3.4)

Table 3.5 shows the *p value* for χ^2 calculation as 0.001. Thus, $p < 0.05$, and therefore, the hypothesis of no significant difference is rejected, since the deviation is too large for it to be put down to chance. In other words, the users of the public Cloud and private Cloud have a different attitude towards the impact of the performance issues on their given environment.

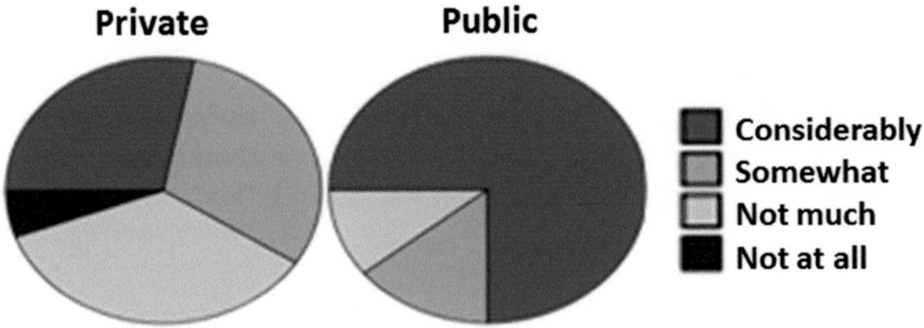

Fig. 3.4 Performance issues impact pie chart

Table 3.5 Performance issues impact table

	Considerably	Somewhat	Not much	Not at all	Total
Private Cloud	20	22	25	4	71
	28.17 %	30.99 %	35.21 %	5.63 %	
Public Cloud	21	4	3	0	28
	75.00 %	14.29 %	10.71 %	0.00 %	
Total	41	26	28	4	99
	41.41 %	26.26 %	28.28 %	4.04 %	
χ^2 calculation = 18.15			*p value* < 0.001		

From Table 3.5, as per the 21 public Cloud users, performance issues are 'considerably' impacting their day-to-day job processing. The expected value here is 12, and thus, there is a 32.14 % difference between expected and the observed results. The expected value for 'Considerably' for the private Cloud environment is 29, but the actual value is observed to be 20, which is a 10.49 % deviation, significantly smaller than that of the public Cloud environment. Seventy-five percent of the public Cloud users are finding reliability issues to 'considerably' impact their role which is 28.17 % in the private Clouds.

From these observations, it can be concluded that the users of the public Cloud environment are finding the performance issues to impact their environment, which affects their day-to-day job processing significantly more than in the private Clouds. This is because of the lack of internal control privileges to the clients in the public Clouds. Because of their total reliability in IaaS and PaaS Cloud service offering models, clients can hardly take measures in the event of job failures in the public Clouds. Also, the multi-tenancy model of the public Clouds exasperates this issue amongst the organizations sharing resources. Additionally, public Clouds also incorporate the lack of contingency processes, which could be the major reason for the performance concerns amongst the public Cloud users.

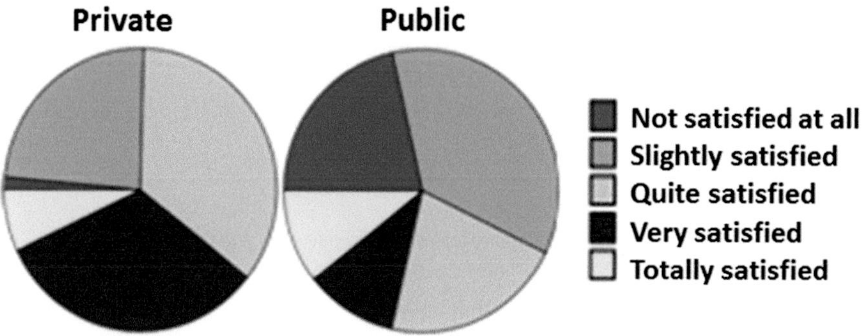

Fig. 3.5 Performance satisfaction pie chart

Table 3.6 Performance satisfaction table

	Not satisfied at all	Slightly satisfied	Quite satisfied	Very satisfied	Totally satisfied	Total
Private	1	17	25	23	5	71
	1.41 %	23.94 %	35.21 %	32.39 %	7.04 %	
Public	6	10	6	3	3	28
	21.43 %	35.71 %	21.43 %	10.71 %	10.71 %	
Total	7	27	31	26	8	99
	7.07 %	27.27 %	31.31 %	26.26 %	8.08 %	
χ^2 calculation = 9.02			*p value* = 0.01			

3.6.4 Question 4

How satisfied are you with the performance of the Cloud environment? (Fig. 3.5)

Table 3.6 shows the *p value* for χ^2 calculation as 0.01. Thus, $p < 0.05$, and therefore, the hypothesis of no significant difference is rejected, since the deviation is too large for it to be put down to chance. In other words, the users of both the public Cloud and the private Cloud experience different levels of satisfaction with regard to the performance of their given Cloud environment.

From Table 3.6, it is observed that 16 public Cloud users are either 'Not Satisfied At All' or 'Slightly Satisfied' with the performance of their Cloud environment. The expected value here is 10, and therefore, there is a difference of 21.43 % between the expected and the actual value. The expected value for 'Not Satisfied At All' and 'Slightly Satisfied' for the private Cloud environment is 24. And the actual value is 18, which is a difference of 8.45 %, significantly smaller difference to that of the public Cloud environment. So, 57.14 % of the public Cloud users are either 'Not Satisfied At All' or 'Slightly Satisfied' with the performance of their Cloud environment, compared to the 23.25 % in private Clouds. From these observations, it can be concluded that the public Cloud users are less satisfied with the performance of their Cloud environment. This could be because of the latency issues in the public

Clouds, and certainly, the distance of the data server location would have an impact on the latency, and this may well be exasperated in busier times, thus causing a greater dissatisfaction amongst the public Cloud users.

3.6.5 Question 5

To what extent the reliability issues affect your day-to-day jobs? (Fig. 3.6)

Table 3.7 shows the *p value* for χ^2 calculation as 0.01. Thus, $p < 0.05$, and therefore, the hypothesis of no significant difference is rejected, since the deviation is too large for it to be put down to chance. In other words, the users of the public Cloud and the private Cloud have different attitudes towards the impact of the reliability issues on their given environment.

From Table 3.7, it is clear that 22 public Cloud users feel that reliability issues 'considerably' impact their day-to-day job processing. Also, none of the public Cloud users opted for 'Not Much' and 'Not At All'. The expected value for 'Considerably' is 15, so there is a 25 % difference between the expected and the actual value. As there are no answers for 'Not Much' and 'Not At All', for

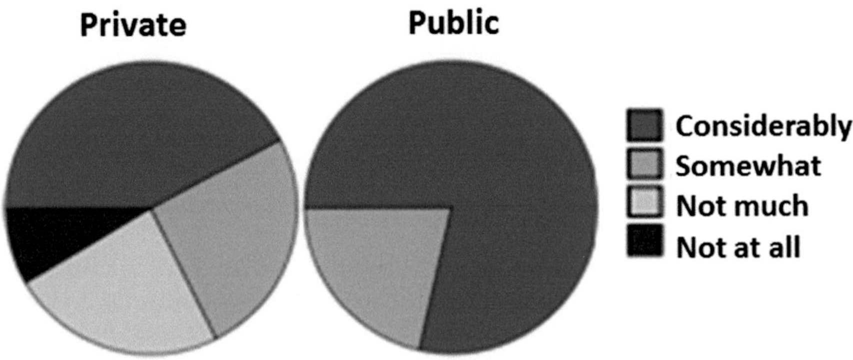

Fig. 3.6 Reliability issues impact pie chart

Table 3.7 Reliability issues impact table

	Considerably	Somewhat	Not much	Not at all	Total
Private	30	18	17	6	71
	42.25 %	25.35 %	23.94 %	8.45 %	
Public	22	6	0	0	28
	78.57 %	21.43 %	0.00 %	0.00 %	
Total	52	24	17	6	99
	52.53 %	24.24 %	17.17 %	6.06 %	
χ^2 Calculation = 10.62			*p value* = 0.01		

the purposes of the χ^2 calculation 'Somewhat', 'Not Much' and 'Not At All' are encompassed together in order to increase the response more than 5.

Now the expected value becomes 13, and still there is 24.99 % difference between the expected and the observed values. The expected value for 'Considerably' for the private Cloud environment is 37, and the actual value is 30, which is a difference of 9.86 %, which is significantly smaller to that of the public Cloud environment. Although the 78.57 % of the public Cloud users answered 'Considerably', a significant number of private Cloud users also answered 'Considerably'.

This shows that reliability issues have a major impact on whichever Cloud environment a client uses. What would be more eye-catching for the decision makers is the volume of answers for a public Cloud environment at one end of the scale. As discussed previously, one explanation for this is the lack of internal control an organization or a client has, when using a public Cloud environment.

3.6.6 Question 6

How satisfied are you with the reliability of your Cloud environment? (Fig. 3.7)

Table 3.8 shows the *p value* for χ^2 calculation as 0.01. Thus, $p < 0.05$, and therefore, the hypothesis of no significant difference is rejected, since the deviation is too large for it to be put down to chance. In other words, the users of the public Cloud and the private Cloud have different levels of satisfaction with regard to the reliability of their given Cloud environment. Table 3.8 shows a total of 16 public Cloud users answered either 'Not satisfied At All' or 'Slightly Satisfied'. For the purposes of the χ^2 calculation, 'Not Satisfied At All' and 'Slightly Satisfied' are encompassed together, as there are less than five responses for 'Not Satisfied At All'. Now, the expected value is 9, and there is a difference of 25 % between the expected and observed values. The private Cloud users opted 15 for the same categories and the expected value is 22.

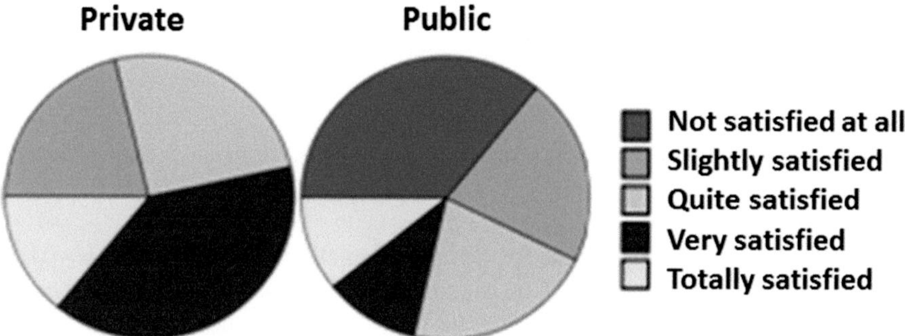

Fig. 3.7 Reliability satisfaction pie chart

Table 3.8 Reliability satisfaction table

	Not satisfied at all	Slightly satisfied	Quite satisfied	Very satisfied	Totally satisfied	Total
Private	0	15	18	28	10	71
Cloud	0.00 %	21.13 %	25.35 %	39.44 %	14.08 %	
Public	10	6	6	3	3	28
	35.71 %	21.43 %	21.43 %	10.71 %	10.71 %	
Total	10	21	24	31	13	99
	10.10 %	21.21 %	24.24 %	31.31 %	13.13 %	
χ^2 Calculation = 13.09			*p value* = 0.01			

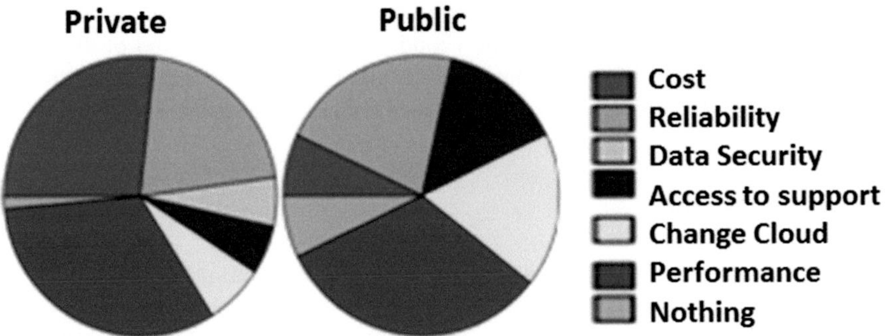

Fig. 3.8 Improvements to the cloud environment pie chart

This is a difference of 9.85 %, which is significantly lower than that of the public Cloud environment. Again, public Cloud users portray a more negative stance on their satisfaction of the reliability for their Cloud environment. A total of 57.14 % of public Cloud users show dissatisfaction compared to a total of 21.13 % in the private Cloud users. This could be because of the infancy of the public Cloud services being offered to the client organizations. Indeed, none of the private Cloud users opted for 'Not Satisfied At All' category, which again may be closely linked to the familiarity of the Cloud environment and the supported network within the organization.

3.6.7 Question 7

What is the most demanding feature of your Cloud services that needs improvement? (Fig. 3.8)

Table 3.9 shows the *p value* for the χ^2 calculation as 0.20. Thus, $p > 0.05$, and therefore, the hypothesis of no significant difference is accepted, since the deviation is small enough that it can be put down to chance. In other words, there is no significant difference between the answers from the users of the Cloud

Table 3.9 Improvements to the Cloud environment table

	Cost	Reliability	Data security	Access to support	Change Cloud	Performance	Nothing	Total
Private	19	15	4	4	5	23	1	71
	26.76 %	21.13 %	5.63 %	5.63 %	7.04 %	32.39 %	1.41 %	
Public	2	6	0	4	5	9	2	28
	7.14 %	21 %	0.00 %	14.29 %	17.86 %	32.14 %	7.14 %	
Total	21	21	4	8	10	32	3	99
	21.21 %	21.21 %	4.04 %	8.08 %	10.10 %	32.32 %	3.03 %	
χ^2 Calculation = 3.70					*p value* = 0.20			

environments. But, from the pie chart, it is evident that security is the most prevailing concern for the public Cloud users, and on the other hand, it is cost in the case of private Cloud users, requiring improvement.

3.7 Summary

From the seven questions asked, there are three criteria that showed no significant differences between the two Cloud environments. They are:

- Cost satisfaction
- Data security satisfaction
- What improvements the end user would most like to see from their Cloud environment

And four questions showed a significant difference between the Cloud environments. They are:

- Performance satisfaction
- Impacts of the performance issues on day-to-day job
- Reliability satisfaction
- Impacts of the reliability issues on day-to-day job

From the χ^2 test, it is established that the differences between the two Cloud environments are significant enough for factors other than chance to be playing a part in the responses. Indeed, the responses to the questionnaires indicated that the public Cloud environment users are less satisfied than the private Cloud environment users. But this difference in attitudes between the two Cloud environments is down to institutional culture and the nature of their job requests. Network latency is one of the major factors for the more negative responses from the public Cloud users. Users of the public Cloud environment are undeniably less satisfied with the performance and reliability of their Cloud services.

3.8 Conclusion

The primary aim of this chapter is to identify the key issues and challenges an organization faces when moving from a private Cloud and to a public Cloud, for the purpose of enhancing the quality of decision-making whilst incorporating the right and appropriate Cloud elements in migrating to the public Clouds. In order to assist and improve the quality of decision-making with regard to Cloud adoption, this chapter conducted a statistical analysis based on chi-square (χ^2), through the use of questionnaires amongst the Cloud users in order to reveal the end-user experiences in using public and private Clouds.

The questionnaire results depicted that the private Cloud users are satisfied with the performance and reliability of the Cloud environment by a significant margin than the public Cloud users. And there is no significant difference between public and private Cloud users regarding the cost, data security and potential changes in the Cloud environment. There is more negative attitude towards a public Cloud solution because of the institutional culture of the public Cloud users. Also, the lack of control of IT resources and limited access to the datacentre privileges might have implications on the reliability of the public Cloud environment.

This study reveals that there are both benefits and concerns in migrating to a public Cloud solution from a private Cloud solution. One of the major concerns in this migration is the uncertainty around data security. Vendor lock-in caused by the lack of interoperability is another prevailing issue in the public Clouds, and also, clients would have to pay more to switch their Cloud providers for a better service. Furthermore, the lack of control of IT services and troubleshooting are other limiting factors for the interests of the public Clouds. There are rising concerns with how problems can be resolved during reliability or performance issues. Despite the said concerns, public Cloud can offer huge cost-benefits for low-budget organizations. High-performance computing is another benefit, which is offered at an affordable price and allows organizations to stay ahead of the curve, when employing a public Cloud solution. In the end, it is down the trade-off between security and cost-benefits that one should consider based on the application requirements, whilst adopting their Cloud services. But it is worth to add that a balanced cost-security trade-off in the public Cloud services is not far away from now, with the technological advancements in today's Cloud arena.

3.9 Review Questions

1. What are the two distinctive architectural patterns of the private Cloud deployments?
   On-premise clouds (OPC) and externally hosted clouds (EHC)
2. What are the two popular infectors reported in the malware analysis report of Greenburg, and how do they affect the security status of the public Clouds?

This research on malware analysis insists the spreading of two popular infectors: firstly, Trojan-Spy that can perform key logging and monitoring of processes and secondly, a Trojan.Agent

3. What is the purpose of using the null hypothesis in the chi-square test?
   The null hypothesis is used for predicting differences between the expected and the observed results. Based on a relative standard value, this null hypothesis is either accepted or rejected for the purpose of driving further inferences.
4. What are the factors that lead to the more negative responses of the public Cloud users?
   Network latency, institutional culture, distance of the datacentre location, nature of their job requests and predated data privacy laws to public Cloud Computing
5. What is a multi-tenancy model?
   The inherent nature of the multi-tenancy model means that various resources and network addresses used by a single provider may be shared with other organizations.
6. What are the strategies that companies adopting Cloud services want to define?
   To benefit or value the needs of the company's goals and to strengthen the security policies of the Cloud

References

1. Amazon (2013) What is Amazon VPC? – Amazon Virtual Private Cloud. [online] Retrieved from: http://docs.aws.amazon.com/AmazonVPC/latest/UserGuide/VPC_Introduction.html. Accessed 25 Mar 2014
2. Antonopoulos N, Gillam L (2010) Cloud computing. Springer, London
3. Azeemi I, Lewis M, Tryfonas T (2013) Migrating to the cloud: lessons and limitations of 'traditional' IS success models. Procedia Comput Sci 16:737–746
4. Balduzzi M, Zaddach J, Balzarotti D, Kirda E, Loureiro S (2012) A security analysis of amazon's elastic compute cloud service. In: Proceedings of the 27th annual ACM symposium on applied computing, SAC'12, Italy, March 2012, pp 1427–1434. doi:10.1145/2245276.2232005
5. BCS (2012) Cloud computing: moving IT out of the office. British Computer Society, Swindon
6. Bento AM, Aggarwal A (2013) Cloud computing service and deployment models. Business Science Reference, Hershey
7. Chen Y, Paxson V, Katz R (2010) What's new about cloud computing security?. [report] University of Berkeley, Berkeley
8. Dillion T, Wu C, Chang E (2010) Cloud computing: issues and challenges. In: Proceedings of the 24th IEEE international conference on Advanced Information Networking and Applications (AINA), Perth, April 2010, pp 27–33
9. Gong C, Liu J, Zhang Q, Chen H, Gong Z (2010) The characteristics of cloud computing. In: Proceedings of the 39th International Conference on Parallel Processing Workshops (ICPPW), San Diego, September 2010, pp 275–279
10. Greenberg A (2011). Researchers find Amazon cloud servers teeming with backdoors and other people's data. [online] 11th August. Retrieved from: http://www.forbes.com/sites/andygreenberg/2011/11/08/researchers-find-amazon-Cloud-servers-teeming-with-backdoors-and-other-peoples-data/. Accessed 26 Mar 2014
11. Hill R, Hirsch L, Lake P, Moshiri S (2013) Guide to cloud computing. Springer, London
12. Leavitt N (2009) Is cloud computing really ready for prime time. Growth 27:5

13. Northwestern University (1997) PROPHET StatGuide: do your data violate goodness of fit (chi-square) test assumptions?. [online] Retrieved from: http://www.basic.northwestern.edu/statguidefiles/gf-dist_ass_viol.html. Accessed 1 Apr 2014
14. Pariseau B (2013) Networking, security issues still irk large AWS shops. [online] Retrieved from: http://searchCloudcomputing.techtarget.com/news/2240203992/Networking-security-issues-still-irk-large-AWS-shops. Accessed 26 Mar 2014
15. Pennsylvania State University (2013) CHI-SQUARE TEST. [online] Retrieved from: http://www2.lv.psu.edu/jxm57/irp/chisquar.html. Accessed 27 Mar 2014
16. Reese G (2009) Cloud application architectures. O'reilly, Sebastopol
17. Ren K, Wang C, Wang Q, Others (2012) Security challenges for the public Cloud. IEEE Internet Comput 16(1): 69–73
18. RightScale (2014) Retrieved from: http://www.rightscale.com/blog/Cloud-industry-insights/Cloud-computing-trends-2014-state-Cloud-survey
19. Rimal BP, Choi E, Lumb I (2009) A taxonomy and survey of cloud computing systems. pp 44–51
20. Rong C, Nguyen ST, Jaatun MG (2013) Beyond lightning: a survey on security challenges in cloud computing. Comput Electr Eng 39(1):47–54
21. Schaller RR (1997) Moore's law: past, present and future. Spectr IEEE 34(6):52–59
22. Seddon PB, Staples S, Patnayakuni R, Bowtell M (1999) Dimensions of information systems success. Communications Of The AIS, 2 (3es), p 5
23. Sultan N (2010) Cloud computing for education: a new dawn? Int J Inf Manag 30(2):109–116
24. Sultan N, Van De Bunt-Kokhuis S (2012) Organizational culture and cloud computing: coping with a disruptive innovation. Tech Anal Strat Manag 24(2):167–179
25. Wang L (2012) Cloud computing. CRC Press, Boca Raton

Thomas Holding is an MIS Support and Training Manager at ARK Schools in London, UK. He received the first-class honours bachelor degree on Computer Forensic Investigation from the University of Derby, UK.

John Panneerselvam is a Graduate Teaching Assistant and working towards the PhD degree under the supervision of Prof. Lu Liu and Prof. Nick Antonopoulos in the Department of Engineering and Technology at the University of Derby, United Kingdom. John received his M.Sc. in Advanced Computer Networks from the University of Derby (UK), and his primary research is in the area of green cloud computing. John has around 15 scientific publications in international conferences, journals and book chapters to his credit. His research interest includes cloud computing, big data, opportunistic networks, distributed systems and service-oriented computing.

Lu Liu is the Professor of Distributed Computing at the School of Computing and Mathematics in the University of Derby. Prof. Liu received his PhD degree from the University of Surrey (funded by DIF DTC) and M.S. in Data Communication Systems from Brunel University. He is the Fellow of British Computer Society and Member of IEEE. Prof. Liu's research interests are in areas of cloud computing, social computing, service-oriented computing and peer-to-peer computing.

Virtualization Security in Cloud Computing 4

Muhammad Kazim and Shao Ying Zhu

Abstract

Cloud computing is becoming popular among IT businesses due to its agile, flexible and cost effective services. Virtualization is a key aspect of cloud computing and a base of providing infrastructure layer services to tenants. In this chapter, we describe the different virtualization types and the security issues in cloud virtualization components such as hypervisor, virtual machines and guest disk images. The virtualization security analysis covers (i) attacks on virtualization components in cloud, (ii) security solutions for virtualization components provided in literature and (iii) security recommendations for virtualization environment that can be useful for the cloud administrators. Moreover, this chapter also discusses various industrial solutions developed for cloud virtualization security.

Keywords

Cloud computing • Virtualization • Security • Hypervisor • Virtual machines • Disk images

4.1 Introduction

Cloud computing has transformed the way the typical IT infrastructure was deployed by combining the technologies such as virtualization, web services, service-oriented architecture and grid computing. Unlike the traditional IT service model, businesses on cloud can grow rapidly without need of large capital invest-

M. Kazim (✉) • S.Y. Zhu
Department of Computing and Mathematics, College of Engineering and Technology, University of Derby, Derby, UK
e-mail: m.kazim@derby.ac.uk; s.y.zhu@derby.ac.uk

S.Y. Zhu et al. (eds.), *Guide to Security Assurance for Cloud Computing*,
Computer Communications and Networks, DOI 10.1007/978-3-319-25988-8_4

ments for purchasing new PC, servers and other dedicated hardware [1]. Therefore, the major advantages that cloud computing offers are reduced operational costs, scalability, increased efficiency and better utilization of hardware resources.

The deployment model of cloud can vary depending upon the requirements of provider and users. The major deployment models of cloud computing are public cloud, private cloud, hybrid cloud and community cloud. In public cloud model, the services are available to everyone on the Internet via web services. Vendors of private clouds manage infrastructure for one specific company to meet their requirements. Major benefits that private clouds offer are security and ease of management. Hybrid cloud model is the combination of two or more cloud models by using standardized technology that enables data and application sharing.

Cloud has three service models to define the type of services it provides to users. These models are Software as a Service (SaaS), Platform as a Service (PaaS) and Infrastructure as a Service (IaaS). IaaS is the base of all cloud services offering computing, network, storage and databases via the Internet. Virtualization is a primary feature of IaaS services in cloud. The cloud service models are shown in Fig. 4.1.

IaaS model enables customers to get the virtual machines on lease from the cloud providers instead of purchasing physical machines. Virtual machine (VM) is a software container that behaves like a physical machine with its own operating system and virtual resources including CPU, RAM and hard disk. VMs use disk images as their hard drives, which are virtual representation of a physical drive. Virtual disk image is a single file or directory representing the hard drive of a guest operating system.

Among all the security concerns related to cloud, Infrastructure as a Service (IaaS) layer security issues are the most critical. IaaS layer contains virtualization components such as virtual machines, hypervisor and virtual network. Virtual machines are vulnerable to many attacks, such as attacker accessing host disk files through his virtual machine, creating rogue virtual machines to occupy system resources and launch a DoS attack at cloud and using backdoor virtual machines to leak sensitive data. Providing security to virtual machines is the core of secure IaaS services in cloud.

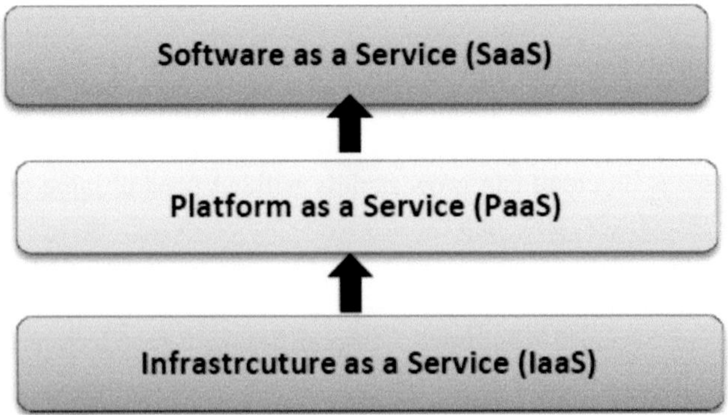

Fig. 4.1 Cloud service models

4.2 Virtualization

Virtualization is a primary feature of cloud computing that enables a single system to concurrently run multiple isolated virtual machines. It abstracts the underlying hardware to virtually provide interfaces similar to the hardware's physical platform [2]. It utilizes hardware in the best possible way by maximizing the jobs, which a single CPU can do. Organizations are using virtualization in private, public and hybrid clouds to gain efficiency in platform and application hosting.

Many virtualization approaches exist that can be applied to various system layers including hardware, desktop, operating system, software, memory, storage, data and network. Hardware virtualization is a form of virtualization that abstracts the underlying hardware [3]. It can be categorized into full virtualization, partial virtualization and para virtualization. Compared to the two other forms of virtualizations, full virtualization involves complete abstraction of underlying hardware to provide interfaces similar to the hardwares physical platform. Thus, it provides better operational efficiency by putting more workload on each physical system and hence more popularly used for servers virtualization. Full virtualization can be categorized into two forms: (i) bare-metal virtualization and (ii) hosted virtualization.

Hosted and bare-metal virtualizations are used in software-based partitioning approaches in latest UNIX/RISC and industry-standard x86 systems. In the hosted architecture, hypervisor lies on top of the standard operating system. However, running hypervisor on top of the host OS increases security risks and complexity of the system [4]. While in the bare-metal approach, hypervisor comes directly on top of the hardware which provides direct access to the hardware resources. Bare-metal approach is mostly used for server virtualization in large computing systems like cloud computing as it provides better performance, more robustness and agility.

Bare-metal approach is used for server virtualization in cloud. In the bare-metal virtualization architecture shown in Fig. 4.2 [5], hardware refers to the physical

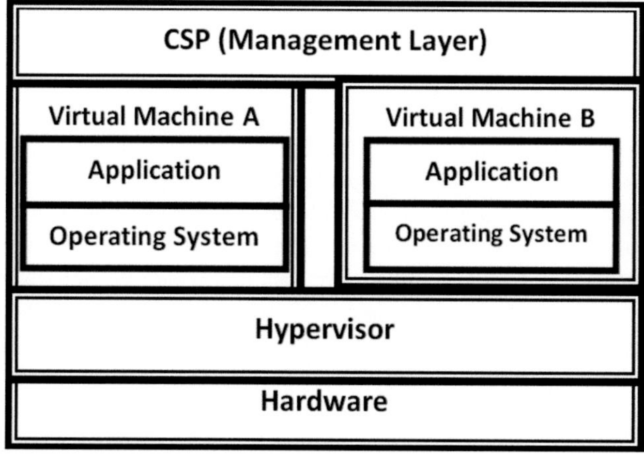

Fig. 4.2 Bare-metal virtualization architecture

resources such as CPU, RAM, storage disks, physical switches, I/O ports and BUS systems (PCI, LPC). Hypervisor is composed of resources necessary to run virtual machines including virtual machine manager (VMM), kernel layer and the driver layer. Hypervisor hides hardware resources of the system from the operating system running on it, manages the execution of the guest operating systems and partitions hardware platform into multiple logical units called virtual machines (VMs). Each virtual machine has its own operating system (called guest OS) and applications running on it.

4.3 Virtualization Security

Research has been done to explore major security issues related to virtualization in cloud. The standard bodies in computing security have issued guidelines on virtualization technologies. These guidelines cover different aspects of virtualization security. National Institute of Standard Technologies (NIST) guide [4] mentions security issues and recommendations for securing virtualization environment, whereas the Centre for Internet Security (CIS) guide [3] focuses on virtual machines security and their secure configuration. SANS guide sponsored by VMware [6] provides key configuration and security controls for VMware ESX and vSphere. Cloud Security Alliance (CSA) guide [7] and Payment Card Industry Data Security Standard (PCI DSS) [8] discuss security issues related to virtualization in cloud and provide recommendations for secure virtualization environments.

4.4 Virtualization Attacks

In this section, the attacks on various virtualization components including hypervisor, virtual machines and guest operating system images in cloud computing are detailed.

4.4.1 Hypervisor Attacks

A cloud customer can obtain a VM from service provider on lease that he can use to install a malicious guest OS. This guest OS can compromise the hypervisor by altering its source code and give attacker the access to guest VM data and code [9]. To control the complete virtualization environment, malicious hypervisors such as BLUEPILL rootkit, Vitriol and SubVir are installed which give attacker the admin privileges to control and alter VM data [10]. VM escape is another type of attack in which attacker can run an arbitrary script on the guest operating system to get access to the host operating system. This provides the attacker root access to the host machine.

Hardware devices such as hard disk, network and graphic cards have the ability to access main memory contents without going through the CPU. This feature is provided to facilitate the CPU so that peripherals can directly transfer data to and from memory without the involvement of the CPU. Without Direct Memory Access, CPU will remain fully occupied in any read/write operation. Allowing the device drivers to write at an arbitrary location in physical address space can result in many security threats. In virtualized environment, if any device driver is malicious, then it can write to hypervisor and any other address space in order to compromise the system.

4.4.2 Virtual Machine Attacks

Malicious programs in different virtual machines can achieve required access permissions to log keystrokes and screen updates across virtual terminals [11] that can be exploited by attackers to gain sensitive information. General attacks on OS of physical systems can also be targeted on guest OS of VMs to compromise them. Java applets can be installed through the Internet on virtual machines OS, which can install Trojans and malwares on VMs. Attackers can use Trojans and malwares for traffic monitoring, stealing critical data and tampering the functionality of VMs [12]. Other security attacks from OS are possible through buggy software, viruses and worms that attacker can exploit to take control of VMs.

Network DoS attacks can be launched on a cloud network, and one such attack is the TCP SYN attack. TCP performs a three-way handshake to establish a connection. The resources allocated for these three-way handshakes can be exploited to launch a TCP SYN flood attack. Attacker sends too many connection requests in the form of TCP SYN packers to the victim so that the victim cannot respond to the legal requests. After allocating resources for the incoming requests, victim replies to the attacker with a SYN-ACK packet. The attacker doesn't respond to the SYN-ACK, and the resources of the victim remain occupied [13]. Attacker can lease a VM in cloud, and through malicious software, he can consume extra resources from the system. This may lead to denial of service (DoS) attack as the system resources will be unavailable to legitimate users.

4.4.3 Disk Image Attacks

To create new VM image files, existing VM images can be easily copied which results in VM image sprawl problem, in which a large number of VMs created by customers may be left unnoticed. VM image sprawl results in large management issues of VMs including the security patches. Investigation of VM images on cloud (EC2, VCL) has shown that if patches are not applied, VM images are more vulnerable to attacks, and they may also not fulfil organization security policy. Secondly, some VM images are mostly online, and to patch these images, they will have to be started. This will add to the computation cost of cloud provider [14]. Attacker can access VM checkpoint present in the disk that contain VM physical memory contents and can expose sensitive information of VM state.

4.5 Security Solutions

This section provides the various security solutions that have been provided in literature for cloud virtualization. We analyze these security solutions and describe how these solutions can be used to mitigate attacks on hypervisor, virtual machines and guest operating systems.

4.5.1 Hypervisor Security

Hypersafe secures the hypervisor against the control hijacking attacks by protecting its code from unauthorized access [15]. Also, in a system there are dedicated portions of memory to which only hardware has access. These dedicated portions of memory (which hypervisor can't access) can be used to store information related to memory regions of VMs. So a compromised hypervisor cannot write at the memory locations of VMs.

Device drivers can be restricted from writing into memory resources by using input/output memory management units (IOMMU). It is used to connect a DMA-capable memory bus to I/O units. When the machine starts, hypervisor checks if IOMMU is enabled and correctly initialized. If not, then hypervisor must stop the boot process for checking. Hypervisor may utilize DMA remapping hardware to limit DMA from input/output device to physical memory of Dom0 [9].

VM escape attack can only be executed through a local physical environment. Therefore, the physical cloud environment must be prevented from insider attacks. The interaction between guest machines and host OS must also be properly configured [16].

4.5.2 Virtual Machine Security

TVDc [17] is developed by IBM to address strong isolation, integrity and security in virtualized system. All the security measures for OS in physical machines must also be applied on the OS of VMs (guest OS). To prevent OS from java applet attacks, java installation must be avoided until it is essentially required by any program. Furthermore, guest OS and applications running on it must be hardened by using best security practices [18]. These practices include installing security software such as antiviruses and anti-spyware to detect any suspicious activity and to notify the user or admin about such activity.

sHype system, a secure hypervisor architecture for XEN, offers isolation of VM systems with flexible security of mandatory access control (MAC) [19]. MAC systems are designed to control information flow and communication between VMs across multiple machines. To authorize the communication between VMs on the same machine, sHype adds hooks to XEN authorization mechanism and uses type enforcement (TE) model. Bell-La Padula policy restricts information flow at access class level, but implementing this model to have network per access class is impractical. To minimize cost, some risk must be taken by defence communities. Accepted risk may be expressed by using Chinese wall policy model. Chinese wall policy model allows selection of any policy in data access, but once the policy has been selected, future choice gets limited according to the selection [20].

To provide protection from networked DoS attacks, firewall proxies can be used so that attacker request is forwarded only after client side ACK is received. HOP count altering achieves 90 % detection of DoS attacks, by inspecting packet TTL field and dropping suspected spoofed packets. However, such solutions can result in excessive overhead on infrastructure as I/O devices such as network interfaces are being used. KVM is one of the standard hypervisor-based virtualization systems. KVM supports VirtIO drivers which are standard drivers in virtualization. KVM generates an interrupt when a message has to be sent from host to VM or from VM to host. VirtIO drivers can be modified to bundle together a series of packets so that when several packets are received, only a single interrupt is generated. A timer can be used to send all packets to VM received during a specific time [13].

Traditional security solutions for virtual machines have significant limitations and cannot deal with most threats. For example, Seongwook J. et al. [21] proposed real-time log monitoring to verify the integrity of virtual machines. Trent J. et al. used sHype [19] and added hooks to XEN authorization mechanism to prevent covert channel communication between virtual machines in the same network.

4.5.3 Disk Images Security

J. Wei et al. [22] proposed an image management system to manage the disk images in an efficient way in cloud and detect security violations. Nuwa [23] is a tool designed to apply patching to VM images in cloud. It uses the techniques to apply patches to VM images when they are offline. For the protection of images in storage, cryptographic techniques such as encryption can be applied. Similarly, encryption also helps to protect checkpoint files from attacks. SPARC is a mechanism which is specifically designed to protect the security of checkpoint files [24]. Table 4.1 shows the summary of various security aspects of virtualization which are discussed in this chapter.

4.6 Recommendations for Secure Usage of Virtual Machines

In order to secure the virtualization environment in cloud, administrators must implement certain security measures. This section presents the measures that must be adopted for a secure cloud implementation.

4.6.1 Secure Network

Network security must be provided to virtual machines to protect them from the network layer attacks. Virtual machines might have some open ports other than ports

Table 4.1 Summary of security aspects of virtualization described in chapter

Component	Attack	Solution
Hypervisor	VM Escape attack	Properly configure the interaction between guest machines and host VM
	Customers can lease a guest VM to install a malicious guest OS	VMs can be protected from compromised hypervisor by encrypting the VMsR
	HyperJacking, BLUEPILL, Vitriol, SubVirt and DKSM attacks	
	Increased code size has resulted design and implementation vulnerabilities	Hypersafe is a system that maintains the integrity of Hypervisor
Virtual Machines	Security attacks through worms etc. can be exploited to control the VMs	Use anti-viruses, anti-spyware programs in guest OS to detect any suspicious activity
	Saved state of guest virtual machine as a disk file appears as plaintext to Dom0. Attacker can compromise the integrity and confidentiality	Use encryption and hashing of VMs state before saving
Disk Images	VM checkpoint attacks	Checkpoint attacks can be prevented by encrypting the checkpoints or using SPARCR
	Unnecessary images can result in a security compromise	Organizations using virtualization must have a policy that manages issues of unnecessary images

that normally remain open, which may allow others to connect remotely to virtual machine and change its configuration. A firewall must be there to allow access to these open virtual machine layer service ports [3].

4.6.2 Disabling the Non-required Features

Using the features of screensavers, search tools and system update may create some issues if they are run in virtual machines. The processor intensive applications may consume the resources of system when these resources are needed by some other virtual machine. Similarly, the operating system of the virtual machines runs the low priority processes at the same time which can affect normal priority tasks. So the low priority tasks should be disabled, and if any task has to be run, its start time must be staggered [3].

4.6.3 Disconnect Unused Hardware Devices

Virtual machines can control physical devices out on host such as CD drives. If any virtual machine has access to physical drive, then all virtual machines requesting access to that particular drive will remain blocked. Host must be configured to access these devices only when required [25].

4.6.4 Backup of Virtual Machine Images

Backup of the virtual machine images must be maintained. However, the security of backup data stream and virtual machine backup image on disk is an issue. Cryptographic techniques such as encryption may be employed to protect the data stream. Similarly, data in transit may be protected by securing network through techniques such as VLANs [8]. If any VM is deleted, then its backup must also be removed from the system.

4.6.5 Hardening of Virtual Machines

Virtual machines must be deployed in cloud by following the industry standards. Some recommendations for hardening virtual machines are to put limit on virtual machine resource usage, ensure that OS of each virtual machine is hardened, harden the hypervisor and harden each of the VM virtual hardware [15].

Virtual machines must be deployed in cloud by following the industry standards. Some recommendations for hardening virtual machines are to put limit on virtual machine resource usage, ensure that OS of each virtual machine is hardened, harden the hypervisor and harden each of the VM virtual hardware [16].

4.6.6 Auditing

Administrators can find offline VM guests by using a logging server to monitor logs. VM power status, change of hardware configuration and changes to virtual machines on host should be audited [14]. Some other recommendations to secure VMs on cloud are that in VMs mixed mode deployment may occur; as a result, VMs that have different classes of data may lie on the same physical machine. Moreover, inter VM interactions must be monitored carefully to look for malicious behaviour of VMs in case of any attack.

4.7 Industrial Survey

In this section, we will discuss a few industrial solutions available for the security of virtualization in cloud computing. These solutions are mostly based on open source cloud platforms such as OpenStack [26] and provide additional features such as security and control.

4.7.1 Storage Made Easy

It is a commercial solution [27] that provides many different security features in cloud environment. It is designed to unify the information stored securely. Storage

Made Easy (SME) can be used with different cloud networks such as OpenStack, Amazon S3, Azure, RackSpace, HP Storage and other clouds. It is available to be used as a SaaS application as well as an IaaS application.

The major features of SME include secure image storage in cloud through strong encryption of AES-256, cloud data protection gateway, secure authorization and storage of company data, versioning of all files, file sharing and collaboration with other clouds.

Storage Made Easy APIs are also available for developers. These APIs are based on REST interface, and some libraries written in .NET. SME can be integrated with the security standards such as OpenID and Kerberos.

Other identity features that can be integrated with SME are LDAP/Active Directory. The user integration using SME with the OAuth server is provided in SME documentation.

4.7.2 Piston Cloud

Pistons Enterprise [28] Operating System offers secure cloud services to the enterprises. It is powered by OpenStack [26] and contains all its features with the added security components. It makes use of the private infrastructure while maintaining security and control over infrastructure. Its major benefits are the ease of use as complete private cloud can be built in less than an hour. For installation, a USB drive is used that contains installation software to fully configure servers with secure cloud stack. Pistons Enterprise Operating System is very efficient for handling big data as data is present closer to virtual machines. Scaling the cloud is easy as each new server is automatically detected in the Null Tier Architecture. To protect the sensitive data from single point of failures, data is usually replicated.

Pistons Enterprise Operating System runs on security hardened Linux Kernel. This Linux kernel is based on HLFS (Hardened Linux from Scratch). This distribution follows the basic security principle of having minimum packages required to run OpenStack. Updates are usually automatic to prevent cloud from zero day attacks. Along with security patches, updates also involve installation of new packages issued by OpenStack. To provide access security, Piston cloud offers Role-Based Access Control. Moreover, secure booting is also ensured to protect system from possible attacks. Additional features offered by Piston cloud include an availability framework to reduce downtime and virtual machines access through dashboard.

4.7.3 Metacloud

Metacloud [29] delivers public cloud services based on OpenStack with the security and privacy features. It provides a fully functional, highly available and easy to use cloud. It provides a complete support to monitor, troubleshoot, upgrade, fix bugs and provide other services. Users and admins access Metacloud through dashboard. Dashboard also provides information about cloud visibility. Metacloud OpenStack is fully compatible with OpenStack APIs and OpenStack CLI.

4.8 Conclusion

Cloud computing delivers software, platform and infrastructure services over the Internet. Virtualization is a technology that is the base of delivering infrastructure services over cloud. Therefore, the security of cloud cannot be maintained unless the virtualization environment is secured. This chapter analyzes general architecture of bare-metal virtualization and covers the security aspects of its different components. Cloud virtualization environment can be compromised by different attacks at hypervisor, virtual machines and guest disk images. We have identified attack scenarios at these components and different existing security schemes that provide security to virtualization environment. Various industrial solutions for virtualization security have also been discussed in this chapter.

4.9 Review Questions

1. Which virtualization approach is most suitable for cloud computing and what are its advantages?
2. What are the network attacks to which virtual machines are most vulnerable?
3. What are main the functionalities of hypervisor in virtualization environment?
4. What are the attacks to which disk images in cloud are most vulnerable?
5. Summarize the key steps that a cloud service provider must follow to secure the virtualization environment.

References

1. Armbrust M, Fox A, Griffith R, Joseph AD, Katz R, Konwinski A, Lee G, Patterson D, Rabkin A, Stoica I et al (2010) A view of cloud computing. Commun ACM 53(4):50–58
2. Bugnion E, Devine S, Govil K, Rosenblum M (1997) Disco: running commodity operating systems on scalable multiprocessors. ACM Trans Comput Syst (TOCS) 15(4):412–447
3. Kirch J (2007) Virtual machines security guidelines. Technical report, The Center for Internet Security
4. Hoffman P, Scarfone K, Souppaya M (2011) Guide to security for full virtualization technologies. National Institute of Standards and Technology (NIST), Gaithersburg, pp 800–125
5. Kazim M, Masood R, Shibli MA, Abbasi AG (2013) Security aspects of virtualization in cloud computing. In: Computer information systems and industrial management. Springer, Berlin/New York, pp 229–240
6. Shackleford D (2010) A guide to virtualization hardening guides. Technical report, SANS
7. Brunette G, Mogull R (2009) Security guidance for critical areas of focus in cloud computing v2.1, Cloud Security Alliance, pp 1–76

8. V. S. I. G. P. S. S. Council (2011) Pci dss virtualization guidelines, vol 2.0. pp 1–39
9. Szefer J, Lee R (2011) A case for hardware protection of guest vms from compromised hypervisors in cloud computing. In: 31st international conference on distributed computing systems workshops (ICDCSW), Minneapolis. IEEE, pp 248–252
10. Ibrahim A, Hamlyn-harris J, Grundy J (2010) Emerging security challenges of cloud virtual infrastructure. In: Proceedings of the APSEC 2010 cloud workshop, Sydney
11. Reuben J (2007) A survey on virtual machine security. Helsinki University of Technology
12. Kazim M, Zhu SY (2015) A survey on top security threats in cloud computing. Int J Adv Comput Sci Appl 6(3):109–113
13. Shea R, Liu J (2012) Understanding the impact of denial of service attacks on virtual machines. In: Proceedings of the 2012 IEEE 20th international workshop on quality of service, Coimbra. IEEE, p 27
14. Zhou W, Ning P, Zhang X, Ammons G, Wang R, Bala V (2010) Always up-to-date: scalable offline patching of vm images in a compute cloud. In: Proceedings of the 26th annual computer security applications conference, Austin. ACM, pp 377–386
15. Wang Z, Jiang X (2010) Hypersafe: a lightweight approach to provide lifetime hypervisor control-flow integrity. In: 2010 IEEE symposium on security and privacy (SP), Oakland. IEEE, pp 380–395
16. Szefer J, Keller E, Lee R, Rexford J (2011) Eliminating the hypervisor attack surface for a more secure cloud. In: Proceedings of the 18th ACM conference on computer and communications security, Chicago. ACM, pp 401–412
17. Berger S, Cáceres R, Pendarakis D, Sailer R, Valdez E, Perez R, Schildhauer W, Srinivasan D (2008) Tvdc: managing security in the trusted virtual datacenter. ACM SIGOPS Oper Syst Rev 42(1):40–47
18. Rueda S, Sreenivasan Y, Jaeger T (2008) Flexible security configuration for virtual machines. In: Proceedings of the 2nd ACM workshop on computer security architectures, New York. ACM, pp 35–44
19. Sailer R, Valdez E, Jaeger T, Perez R, Doorn L, Griffin JL, Berger S (2005) Shype: secure hypervisor approach to trusted virtualized systems. Technical report RC23511
20. Jaeger T, Sailer R, Sreenivasan Y (2007) Managing the risk of covert information flows in virtual machine systems. In: Proceedings of the 12th ACM symposium on access control models and technologies, Sophia Antipolis. ACM, pp 81–90
21. Jin S, Huh J (2011) Secure mmu: architectural support for memory isolation among virtual machines. In: 2011 IEEE/IFIP 41st international conference on dependable systems and networks workshops (DSN-W), Hong Kong. IEEE, pp 217–222
22. Wei J, Zhang X, Ammons G, Bala V, Ning P (2009) Managing security of virtual machine images in a cloud environment. In: Proceedings of the 2009 ACM workshop on cloud computing security, Chicago. ACM, pp 91–96
23. Jin S, Ahn J, Cha S, Huh J (2011) Architectural support for secure virtualization under a vulnerable hypervisor. In: Proceedings of the 44th annual IEEE/ACM international symposium on microarchitecture, Porto Alegre. ACM pp 272–283
24. Gofman M, Luo R, Yang P, Gopalan K (2011) Sparc: a security and privacy aware virtual machinecheckpointing mechanism. In: Proceedings of the 10th annual ACM workshop on privacy in the electronic society, Chicago. ACM, pp 115–124
25. Shackleford D (2012) Virtualization security: protecting virtualized environments. Wiley, New York
26. Openstack (2015) http://www.openstack.org. Accessed 28 July 2015
27. "Storage made easy." https://storagemadeeasy.com/files/07bbead85c6467c40f69f20156d23524.pdf. Last accessed 6 Feb 2015
28. Piston cloud computing (2015) http://www.pistoncloud.com. Accessed 21 Feb 2015
29. Metacloud Inc. (2015) www.metacloud.com. Accessed 21 Feb 2015

Muhammad Kazim is a PhD student at the University of Derby, UK. His research area in PhD is cloud computing security. Before starting his PhD, he completed his master's degree in Computer and Communication Security from the National University of Sciences and Technology, Islamabad, Pakistan in 2014. Earlier, he completed his bachelor's degree in Information and Communication Systems Engineering also from the National University of Sciences and Technology in 2011. Other research areas of his interest are computer networks, computer security and communication systems.

Shao Ying Zhu is a Senior Lecturer in Computing at the University of Derby, UK. She mainly teaches computer networks and security. She has published a number of conference and journal papers on image processing, e-learning, computer networks and cloud security. She has served as programme committee member for many conferences and reviewer for several international journals.

Security of Cloud-Based Storage

5

Shweta Saharan and Gaurav Somani

Abstract

Cloud computing is an emerging paradigm which allows to enhance the capabilities of users dynamically. It requires no investment in setting up new infrastructure and saves the cost of human resources, i.e., capabilities are increased with the available man power. Despite the presence of all the facilities, enterprise customer hesitates in transferring their business over the cloud. One major reason behind this reluctance is security. In cloud computing, data privacy and protection are always seen as the major concerns. The users of the cloud services need to be careful in understanding the risks of data breaches in cloud environment.

Clouds have variant models for different types of services that are made available to the user. In Infrastructure as a Service (IaaS), cloud storage is offered as a service. Cloud storage is an online storage that can be accessed through network, i.e., both storing and accessing operations are performed with the help of network usage. The data is stored in virtualized pool of storage. This chapter gives the detailed overview of the cloud storage architecture and its detailed security architecture. It covers various possible security risks for cloud storage techniques and methods developed so far for making cloud storage secure. We have provided a detailed overview of the storage deduplication techniques, which are deployed for making cloud storage more efficient and free from various security risks caused due to deduplication. It provides comparison between

S. Saharan (✉)
Computer Engineering Department, Indian Institute of Information Technology, Kota, India
e-mail: shweta.17oct@gmail.com

G. Somani
Department of Computer Science and Engineering, Central University of Rajasthan, Ajmer, Rajasthan, India
e-mail: gaurav@curaj.ac.in

S.Y. Zhu et al. (eds.), *Guide to Security Assurance for Cloud Computing*,
Computer Communications and Networks, DOI 10.1007/978-3-319-25988-8_5

different techniques used for security of cloud storage. Additionally, an effort has been made to include various case studies considering security aspects. This chapter provides detailed guidelines to secure various parts of cloud storage.

Keywords
Cloud computing • Cloud storage • Deduplication • Encryption • Storage security

5.1 Introduction to Cloud Storage

Cloud computing has seen enormous growth in the last few years, which will continue for years to come. Cloud computing relies on sharing a pool of physical/virtual resources, rather than deploying local or personal hardware or software. Out of all cloud computing models, Infrastructure as a Service (IaaS) is the most widely used and popular model as it offers storage space and compute power to the user as a service. As estimated by IDC [2], data is growing at an alarming rate of 40 % per year in enterprise storage banks. Cloud offers many storage models, viz., private, public, community, and hybrid cloud models. "Cloud storage" is basically defined as data storage that is made available to the customers as a service via a network. Major examples of industry products include Amazon S3 [1], Microsoft azure [49], Rackspace [38], and Dropbox [13]. Among all models of cloud, IaaS is the most widely used service among the multiple layers of service offered. IaaS largely altered the way applications are deployed. Instead of spending amount on maintaining the infrastructure and hiring staff, the enterprise can concentrate on its core work without worrying about secondary issues. IaaS offers its customer only basic security like firewall, load balancing, etc., but along with it, the applications which are being transferred to cloud need higher level of security.

While storing data at a remote location, the major question is about the security of data. Security remains a major challenge for cloud providers. The security of the cloud should be engineered in such a way that the critical data is safe from leakage in both storage and transit. In the last few years, many cases related to security breach of cloud storage have come up. The major challenges for cloud computing are not only limited to vulnerabilities related to accessibility, virtualization, or web application only, but identity management, data loss and theft, integrity, confidentiality, authentication, etc. have also become prevalent.

5.2 Organization

The rest of the paper proceeds as follows: Sect. 5.3 provides overview of cloud storage architecture. Section 5.4 lays emphasis on various component of cloud storage security architecture. Section 5.5 describes deduplication, and Sect. 5.6 consists of various security techniques for storage. Comparison between various available techniques is provided in Sect. 5.7. Section 5.8 consists of various case studies related to cloud storage security. Various security guidelines are covered in Sect. 5.9. Section 5.10 summarizes the chapter, and Sect. 5.11 enlists the review questions based upon chapter.

5.3 Cloud Storage Architecture

Though cloud storage architecture consists of many distributed components, but still it acts as one uniform resource. Cloud storage typically refers to a hosted object storage service. Object storage services like Amazon S3 and Microsoft Azure Storage are all examples of storage that can be hosted and deployed with cloud storage characteristics.

Figure 5.1 depicts various components of cloud storage architecture. Clouds at remote locations consist their own storage servers and compute servers. All requests made by customer are either for compute server or storage server. Linking of remote cloud storage location is done via a logical storage pool. Through this logical pool, sharing and transferring of data among remotely located clouds takes

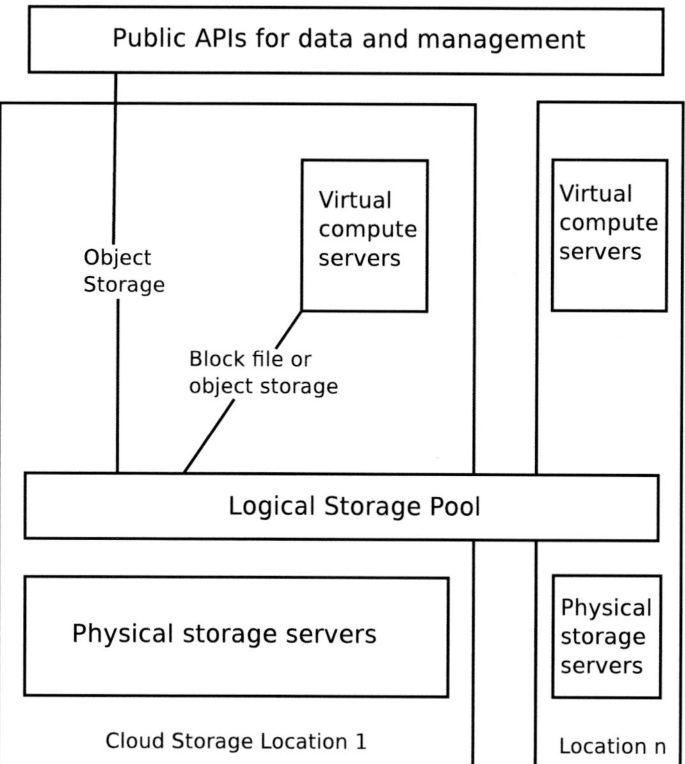

Fig. 5.1 Cloud storage architecture

place. In this chapter, main focus is on storage server and its vulnerabilities keeping aside the compute server vulnerabilities. Each location has its own virtual compute servers.

5.4 Cloud Storage Security Architecture

Cloud computing security [11, 26, 30, 48], also known as cloud security, is a sub domain of computer and network security itself. Broadly, it covers information security. It comprises of all the set of protocols, rules, policies, control, and technologies which are essentially required to ensure protection of data and application over the cloud. For each model, i.e., PaaS, IaaS, and SaaS, there are variable set of rules that are deployed for data protection [4, 45]. As per Gartner [20], a customer needs to consider seven parameters at the time of cloud vendor selection. The parameters are data segregation, recovery, regulatory compliance, privileged user access, data location, long-term liability, and investigate support. There are security issues in all aspects of infrastructure model.

One of the most useful features, cloud comes up with, is data sharing. Along with this advantage, many security concerns arise related to data security and privacy. The data owner provides access to the data to one party. That party in turn made that data available to another party which causes threat to the data security and integrity. Therefore, rules and policies should be set in order to limit the usage of data by third party. The data stored over the cloud can be categorized into two categories. One is the IaaS data where the user request for "Storage as a Service" from the cloud. Only the data owner can access the stored data. The second category is of SaaS and PaaS. All the data generated by the application which are used by the user as a service falls under this category. The security aspects considered over the cloud are the same as for traditional data storage, i.e., integrity, confidentiality, and availability. Figure 5.2 depicts the Infrastructure Security Architecture consisting of both the virtual environment security and shared storage security [6]. In this chapter, our main focus is on storage security of cloud so all the aspects of shared storage security are discussed in detail in the next section.

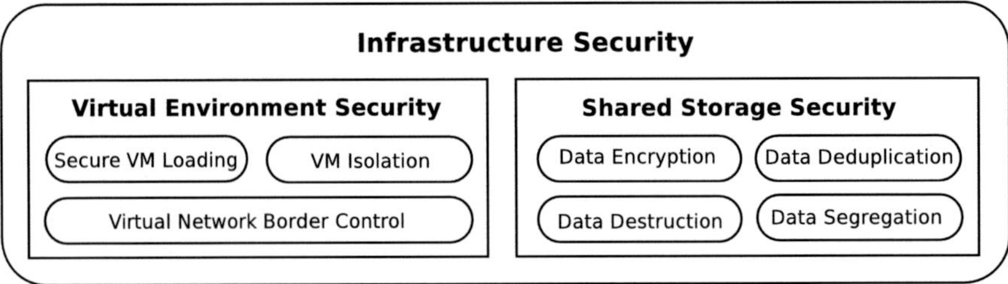

Fig. 5.2 Infrastructure security architecture

1. **Data Segregation**
   Data is categorized based on the similarity of the data in order to make searching more efficient and easier. Data can be user data, application-generated data, cloud's own application data, etc. Along with providing the ease of searching, segregation makes the data more susceptible to attack as the domain in which user has to search the sensitive data is greatly minimized. For example, in order to get the bidding information related to particular user, the attacker just have to search in the user's data section and to extract password application data over the cloud to be checked.
2. **Data Encryption**
   The best and widely used solution for obtaining data confidentiality is via encryption [18, 22, 47]. The confidentiality level provided by the encryption depends upon the encryption algorithm used and the key length. As over cloud, large amount of data is being stored and retrieved, and using heavier encryption over it makes this process slower and costly. Here, considering the time efficiency, symmetric key algorithm is preferable over asymmetric because the overhead to maintain extra keys is minimized. Using asymmetric algorithm, another issue of key management arises. The customers again have to use the cloud service for key management. In this, the risk that cloud vendor can even check the encrypted data still persists as all keys are managed by the cloud service provider itself.

   Along with confidentiality, data integrity is equally important as users upload several gigabytes of data over the cloud for both storage and processing. So checking integrity of such large data pool is a cumbersome task. The users are not even aware about the location of the data since it keeps on migrating, and for all this process, the customers are charged by the service provider. Therefore, downloading the data, checking its integrity, and again uploading and paying for all this process are not an advisable solution. Due to dynamic nature and elasticity of cloud, the traditional techniques are not useful to check the integrity [19, 21].
3. **Data Destruction**
   When the data is no longer needed by the customer, the data over the cloud is destroyed. The same as in traditional storage, the data is not completely erased. Data remains are left over the cloud, and since the data travels or stored at remote locations on different clouds, so it is difficult to destroy all the data completely and it can be restored. Through this, any sensitive user's information can be disclosed.
4. **Data Deduplication**
   Since several TBs of data is stored over the cloud, so it need to be stored efficiently. Data deduplication is a widely used technique for efficient storage of data. Almost all cloud vendors make use of deduplication to save space over their cloud. The detail and risks related to cloud will be discussed in detail in the next section.

The reliability of the data stored over the cloud also depends upon the hardware used by the service provider. In the era of increasing virtualization in information security, the owner of the data is losing their ultimate control over the data. This makes the data prone to more security attacks. Both the cloud service provider and the customer are responsible for the security of data. Many cloud service provider even provide "Security as a Service." This comprises security to hypervisor, environmental security, and virtualization security.

5.5 Deduplication for Efficient Storage

Cloud holds enormous amount of data, and for utilizing the available space more efficiently, deduplication is used. Deduplication [10,27,33,40,51] refers to removing duplicacy. Instead of storing the same block twice, it is stored only once saving space. Deduplication is widely being used by almost all cloud service providers. Along with efficiency, deduplication also leads to many security concerns for cloud storage. There are many advantages of using deduplication in virtual machines over the cloud such as higher storage utilization and multi-tenancy support, which improve disk cache efficiency and reduce VM sprawl.

Figure 5.3 depicts the simple block storage before and after deduplication. As per a report in 2011 [24], complaint was filed against Dropbox since it uses deduplication which causes threat to the data since it leads to timing attacks.

One of the major security concerns related to deduplication is that plain text can be deduplicated easily. Once encryption is used in order to make the data, the efficiency of deduplication falls [32, 34, 44]. Encryption is used to make the data seems random, so that the third person is not able to identify the data. But in deduplication, we check for similarity in order to save the storage space. The issue which comes up is that whenever the same block is encrypted with different encryption key, it leads to different ciphertext. Most of the attacks in case of deduplication occur when the client is able to detect which data is deduplicated over the server. There is always a time difference between deduplicated and non-deduplicated data while uploading and downloading it to storage. This time difference allows the attacker to know whether the data is duplicated or not. By knowing this, the attacker can upload its own randomly generated file, and if he is able to know that it is deduplicated, that means he knows the content of other

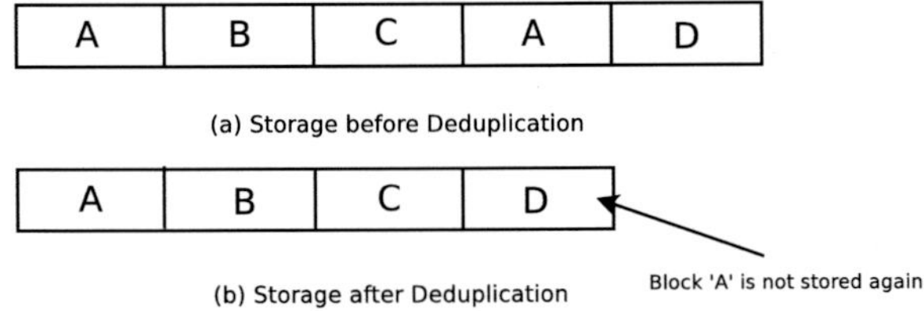

Fig. 5.3 Cloud storage architecture

user's file over the cloud which breaches the confidentiality of a cloud service user. Other issues with deduplication are how to identify the owner of the data since one deduplicated data can be used and shared by more than one user. As duplication is checked based upon hash of the data, so just passing the hash of data and getting its ownership leads to data integrity breach. All these issues require new set of policies to provide integrity and confidentiality to data.

5.6 Techniques Used for Maintaining Security in Cloud Storage

Cloud storage being a sub-offering of cloud computing also has privacy concerns. In cloud storage technology, user's data is stored not only on dedicated provider as in traditional networked storage but on many third-party providers [7, 8, 28]. The data storage services are provided through network to the user.

Cryptography is a key solution for providing security and privacy in traditional storage systems. Cryptography plays a significant role in providing confidentiality to user's data. It plays a vital role in protecting user's data on different storage servers. The security risk to user's data is high in cloud storage as compared to traditional storage because in cloud storage the users don't have direct control over the data. Users are able to access their data only through the cloud service provider. Attackers have high chances to access the data either from the cloud directly after claiming to be its owner or in between the real user accessing its own data from the cloud [16, 37]. Among all the security issues, data confidentiality is most significant. Data should be confidential both from the attacker and from the cloud service provider where the data is stored. For data integrity, the data should not be modified, and if modified, then the user should be able to detect the changes performed on the data. Data availability in case of cloud storage is different from traditional storage since in cloud storage, the data is stored at third party and accessed through network, so availability also depends on the network resources and the load on cloud service provider [43, 46].

5.7 Comparison Between Various Available Secure Cloud Storage Techniques

Peng et al. [35] provided a clear categorization of secure cloud storage techniques and comparison between them. According to them, all available cloud storage techniques can be classified into two categories: Category A and Category B. Category A consists of all those techniques which uses cryptographic techniques for their design purpose but are not in cryptographic theory framework. Category B refers to those cloud storage techniques which are designed using cryptographic techniques and also fall under cryptographic framework.

5.7.1 Cloud Storage Techniques of Category A

5.7.1.1 ESPAC Scheme

Barua et al. [5] designed a secure cloud storage scheme for privacy of personal health information (PHI). It consists of patient self-controlled access privilege known as ESPAC (Efficient and Secure Patient-Centric Access Control). This scheme is based on ciphertext policy, attribute, and identity-based encryption. In this scheme, the user can access the data based on the role which is assigned to them, and accordingly, different attribute set is assigned to them. This scheme comprises of two major phases. In former phase to make sure that data communication is secure, identity-based encryption is used. In later phase for realizing the data requester's access control, attribute-based encryption is employed.

5.7.1.2 Kamara et al.'s Scheme

Kamara et al.'s [29] work was the first and most vital contribution in cloud storage security using cryptography. They make use of nonstandard cryptographic technique like searchable encryption, attributed encryption, etc. for designing secure cloud storage architecture. The architecture was designed from perspective of both cloud service provider and service user. The main component in any cloud storage implementing cryptographic security is how to make use of cryptographic technique for achieving security and privacy goals. The detailed work of Kamara et al. gives complete discussion about how nonstandard cryptographic techniques are implemented in cloud storage for security and how it affects the security of the storage.

5.7.1.3 Key to Cloud (K2C) Scheme

Zarandioon et al. [50] used attribute-based encryption and signature. Their work proposes a user centric scheme which is privacy preserving and is a cryptographic access control protocol and named it Key to Cloud (K2C). This scheme provides the customer a protocol through which they can share, store, and manage their data securely. Figure 5.4 depicts the major participants in the K2C scheme. In case of a metadata directory, all the participates in the hierarchy have both the read access revision and write access revision. This scheme makes use of attribute-based cryptography for access control.

5.7.1.4 Cryptonite Scheme

For achieving security for data storage, Kumbhare et al. [31] have designed Cryptonite, which offers security over public cloud infrastructure. For assuring integrity of data, digital signature was deployed. Digital signature was also useful in auditing purpose. For the distribution of the keys, broadcast encryption is used by them. In order to search within a file without decrypting it, searchable encryption was implemented in it. Both these encryptions are deployed in the client library of Cryptonite which enables these encryptions on client side and faster.

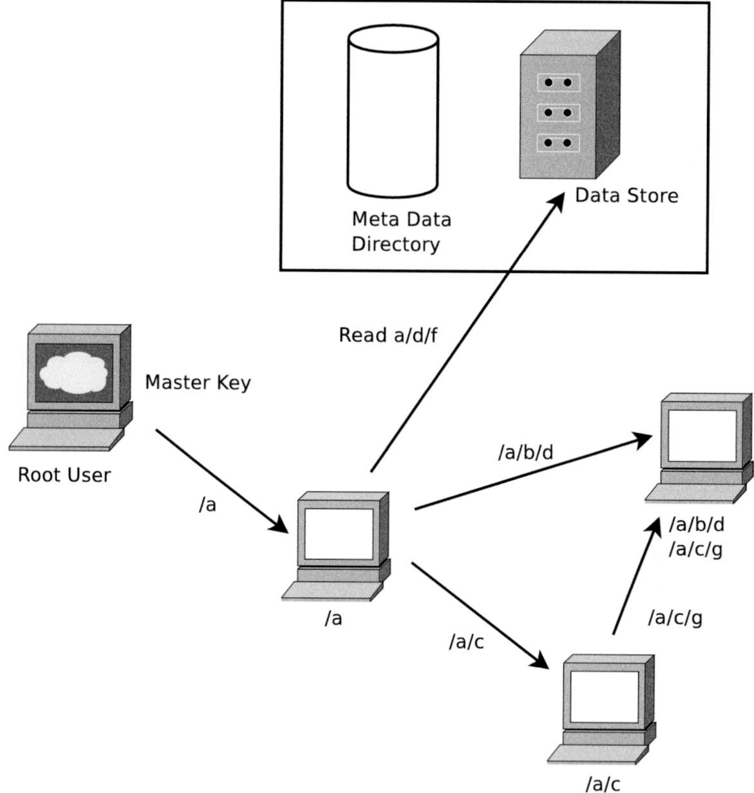

Fig. 5.4 Participants in K2C

5.7.1.5 Sec^2 Scheme

Sec^2 was proposed by Somorovsky et al. [42] using extensive markup language (XML) encryption as a secure solution in the cloud storage. The architecture of Sec^2 is illustrated by Fig. 5.5. The XML payload and the data are encrypted using XML encryption which is used in XML encryption engine.

5.7.2 Cloud Storage Techniques of Category B

5.7.2.1 Chow et al.'s Scheme

Chow et al. [9] provided a secure cloud storage scheme which supports addition of dynamic users and provides data provenance. This scheme not only proposed the cryptographic model but also provided a security model based on cryptography. Security model consists of anonymity, traceability, and confidentiality. They make

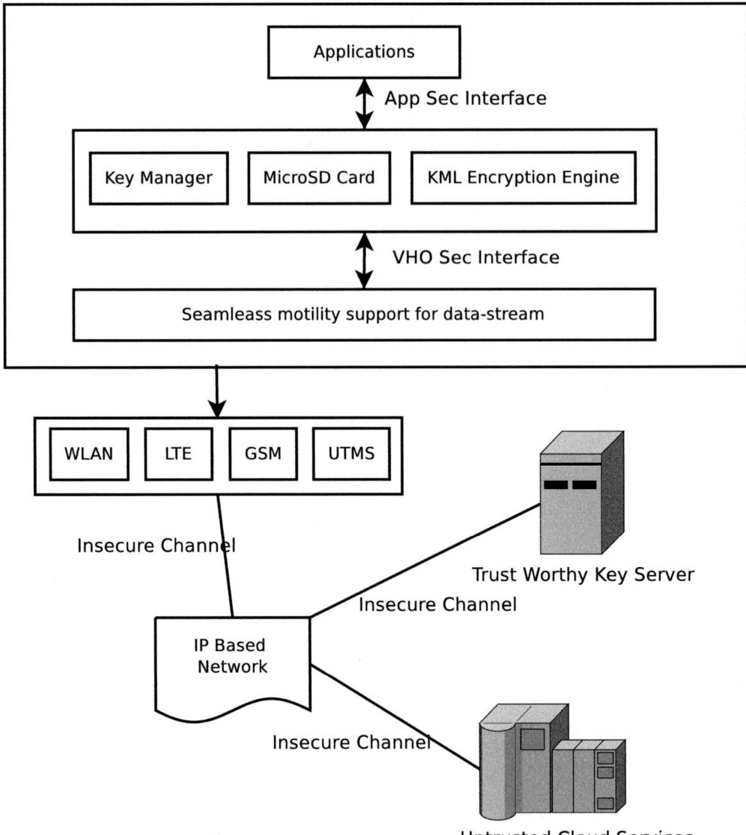

Fig. 5.5 Architecture of Sec^2

use of pairing-based cryptographic for data storage. Verifier Local Revocation (VLR) and a variant of identity-based broadcast encryption was used for designing purpose.

5.7.2.2 Cloud Storage System (CS2)

CS2 (Cloud Storage System) was proposed by Kamara et al. [29] for providing integrity, verifiability, and confidentiality. CS2 ensures all security features without compromising with the speed of the system. They make use of Symmetric Searchable Encryption (SSE) for data encryption by the client. Later on, search tokens are generated for storage providers. Cloud provider uses search authenticator for assuring that desired files are returned to the client. CS2 makes use of proofs of storage (PoS) for ensuring integrity.

Table 5.1 Comparison between various approaches for secure cloud storage

Cloud storage scheme	Cryptographic technique used	Functionality provided
ESPAC	Identity-based encryption, attribute-based encryption	Confidentiality, access control
Kamara et al.	Attribute-based encryption, searchable encryption	Confidentiality
Key to Cloud	Attributed-based encryption and signature	Access control
Cryptonite	Searchable encryption distribution of keys, broadcast encryption	Confidentiality
Sec^2	XML encryption	Confidentiality
Chow et al.'s	Identity-based broadcast encryption, group signature	Access control
Cloud Storage System	Search authenticator, searchable encryption	Confidentiality, integrity
Popa et al.'s scheme [36]	Unique signature, broadcast encryption	Attestation, access control
Feng et al.'s scheme [15]	Group encryption	Confidentiality
Ruj et al.'s scheme [39]	Sttribute-based encryption	Access control

Peng et al. [35] provided a comparison among the functionality provided by various schemes and the cryptographic techniques used by them. The comparison is provided in Table 5.1 given above.

5.8 Security-Related Case Studies in Cloud Storage

Outsourcing storage is always considered as risky business. The risk can be both from the insider, i.e., the cloud service provider or the outsider or attacker who can access the data illegally. There are various security concerns which arises like data loss, data breaches, traffic hijacking, DoS, abuse of cloud services, malicious insider, etc. [17,45,48].

From time to time, there are several cases related to security breach in the cloud storage. In this section, we have presented some case studies to achieve a comprehensive state-of-the-art analysis of cloud storage architecture in the area.

5.8.1 Dropbox

In 2014, it was discovered that the sensitive user information was leaked on Dropbox [25]. The reason for the leakage was the way in which the files are being handled using "Shared Links." When a Dropbox user shares a file with any other user, Dropbox creates a shareable link for anyone, even for the users who don't have a Dropbox account. Another recent case of Dropbox showed a great risk to unencrypted data. A Dropbox employee stored a document containing email addresses of Dropbox user in unencrypted form. An attacker gets access to that copy of the document and used all those email addresses to flood spams to all those users in order to get sensitive information of their accounts. Another alarming issue came up when a tool "DropSmack" [14] was able to deliver malware over Dropbox data and steal files from Dropbox. DropSmack was designed to monitor and synchronize folder over the Dropbox cloud which proves as a great threat to the data security over Dropbox.

5.8.2 Microsoft Azure

Capgemini's latest report [23] this year talks about Microsoft Azure-related security breaches and compliance issues. Most of the issues are related to data rules and Azure Disaster Recovery and Backup.

5.8.3 Amazon EC2

As per a report last year, a hacker had gained access into an Amazon Web Service (AWS) customer's account. The attack as accompanied by an extortion attempt resulted in the loss of the data the company had been storing for customers. Though there was redundancy, but still the data loss was unrecoverable. Balduzzi et al. [4] has performed security analysis on Amazon EC2 using virtual server images. Their results illustrate that both the cloud service provider and the cloud service user are prone to many security risks. These risks can be malware infection, loss of important and sensitive information, or any unauthorized access. They informed Amazon service provider about their findings, and accordingly, AWS service team took action to overcome those vulnerabilities. In 2014, Robert Westervelt [3] come up with security issues related to Amazon cloud. He determined that a simple configuration error enables a determined attacker pathway to control virtual instances and access critical resources store at AWS.

5.9 Security Guidelines for Cloud Storage

Various guidelines are being provided by many organizations to make cloud storage secure [12, 41]. For designing a cloud storage system, these guidelines should be followed so that the designed cloud storage is secured from various perspectives. Various cloud storage security guidelines are listed below:

5.9.1 Login Credential Safety

For accessing cloud storage, customer needs to set up their own account. At the registration time, both the customer and the cloud service provider agree upon credentials, which can be used later. If the attacker eavesdrops the connection and gets the credentials, then he can access the account as well as store data. The attacker might also change the data. So to avoid this, the communication between the customer and service provider should be confidential. The user should keep strong passwords to avoid password guessing attacks. There should be proper authentication mechanism, where the service provider proves its identity to the customer by providing certificate. This make sure that user is communicating to the legitimate service provider. Multifactor authentication can also be used to ensure higher level of security as used by Google.

5.9.2 Encryption of the Stored Data

Keeping data at remote location always remains a threat to confidentiality and integrity of data. The threat may be from external attacker or from cloud service provider itself. The data should be encrypted using cryptographically secure encryption algorithm. Some cloud service provider uses their own key to encrypt the data. This prevents external attacker from breaching the confidentiality and integrity of the data; the risk from internal attackers still persists. Therefore, the data should be encrypted at the client side by user with their own keys. Keys should be generated in such a way that two cryptograms of the same clear text are different.

5.9.3 Security Along with Deduplication

Deduplication, as explained earlier, is used to reduce the storage space requirements. Many security concerns also arise along with it. Deduplication applied either at client side or server side is prone to attack. The attacker may learn which file is stored on server or guess its contents. Many timing attacks are also possible which may reveal the user's data. The user should only be allowed to access the file of other user, i.e., authentication should be a must. Deduplication can be made secure by eliminating the time difference in accessing and uploading a deduplicated and non-deduplicated file.

5.9.4 Transport Security

For using cloud services, the users make use of client software provided by the cloud service provider. This arise the need for service provider's authentication as the client software can also access the local data stored at the user's system. Proper cryptographic algorithms with appropriate key length should be used. Hash function should be kept up to date. A well-accepted cryptographic protocol should be used instead of developing a new one. Standard TLS protocol solves the transport security issues.

5.9.5 Multiple Devices Accessibility

Nowadays, users access their storage accounts via various devices like mobile phone, laptop, PC, etc. All these devices need to be associated with the account. This limits the devices through which the user can access the account, but prevent the unauthorized access to the account. Whenever account is accessed from any unknown device, it causes a security alert. Whenever users want to add new device to the account, it need to provide the credentials. Credentials need to be saved securely in order to prevent security breach.

5.9.6 Update Functionality of System

Making use of old and outdated software always poses risk to system security. Timely updation of the system along with all software should be done. The latest version is made free from vulnerabilities reported in the previous versions. The updations should be made from legitimate site; otherwise the risk of malware attached with updated is also high. The system can be updated automatically with human interaction. This may comprise risk since it is without human interaction and an attacker can make an update which performs some unwanted action.

5.10 Summary

This chapter focuses on emerging storage facilities in cloud computing architecture and various security concerns emerging in the area. It also provides a comprehensive overview of cloud storage and how it is different from traditional architecture. The major focus is cloud storage security, specifically integrity and confidentiality of data. It also highlights the case studies where many security breaches took place over major cloud service providers. A detailed comparison has been made between traditional and cloud-based storage security. Additionally, various requirements of a good solution are discussed with cryptographic techniques at various levels of cloud storage.

5.11 Review Questions

1. What are the major aspects of Infrastructure as a Service (IaaS) security?
2. Why does VM security play an important role in cloud?
3. How does data deduplication lead to security threat to cloud data?
4. Why data encryption may not provide complete confidentiality to cloud data?
5. From security perspective, what are the major differences among available cloud storage techniques?

References

1. Amazon Web Services at http://aws.amazon.com/
2. Available at https://www.idc.com/prodserv/4Pillars/cloud
3. Available at http://www.pcworld.com/article/242598/researchers_demo_cloud_security_issue_\with_amazon_aws_attack.html
4. Balduzzi M, Zaddach J, Balzarotti D, Loureiro S (2012) A security analysis of Amazon's elastic compute cloud service. In: Proceedings of the 27th Annual ACM Symposium on Applied Computing (SAC'12), pp 1427–1434
5. Barua M, Liang X, Lu X et al (2011) ESPAC: enabling security and patient-centric access control for eHealth in cloud computing. Int J Secur Netw 6(2):67–76
6. Burt C (2014) Large volume DDoS attacks see exceptional growth in first half of 2014: arbor networks. http://www.thewhir.com/web-hosting-news/large-volume-ddos-attacks-see-exceptional-growth-first-half-2014-arbor-networks. Available online on 18 July 2014
7. Chor B, Goldreich O, Kushilevitz E, Sudan M (1995) Private information retrieval. In: Proceedings of the 36th annual symposium on foundations of computer science. IEEE, Washington, DC, pp 41–51
8. Chor B, Gilboa N, Naor M (1998) Private information retrieval by keywords Report 98-03. Theory of cryptography library
9. Chow SSM, Chu C, Huang X et al (2011) Dynamic secure cloud storage with provenance. In: Cryptography and security: from theory to applications. LNCS, vol 6805. Springer, Berlin, pp 442–464
10. Chun-ho Ng, Mingcao Ma, Wong T-y, Lee PPC, Lui JCS (2011) Live deduplication storage of virtual machine images in an open-source cloud, pp 80–99
11. Cloud Computing Architecture. Available at https://en.m.wikipedia.org/wiki/Cloud_computing_architecture
12. Cloud Security Standards What to Expect & What to Negotiate (2013) http://www.cloud-council.org/
13. Dropbox at https://www.dropbox.com/en/
14. DropSmack Available at http://www.techrepublic.com/blog/it-security/dropsmack-using-dropbox-to-steal-files-and-deliver-malware/
15. Feng J, Chen Y, Summerville DH (2011) A fair multi-party non-repudiation scheme for storage clouds. In: International conference on collaboration technologies and systems (CTS 2011), Philadelphia, pp 457–465
16. Feng J, Chen Y, Summerville D et al (2011) Enhancing cloud storage security against roll-back attacks with a new fair multi-party non-repudiation protocol. In: IEEE conference on consumer communications and networking (CCNC), Las Vegas, pp 521–522
17. Fernandes DAB, Soares LFB, Gomes JV, Freire MM, Inácio PRM (2014) Security issues in cloud environments: a survey. Int J Inf Secur 13:113–170. Springer
18. Fiat A, Naor M (1994) Broadcast encryption. In: CRYPTO93. LNCS, vol 773. Springer, Heidelberg, p 480–491
19. Freire MM, Inácio PRM (2014) Security issues in cloud environments: a survey. Int J Inf Secur 13:113–170
20. Hoffman S (2013) Ddos: a brief history. https://blog.fortinet.com/post/ddos-a-brief-history. Available online on 25 March 2013
21. Gupta U (2015) Survey on security issues in file management in cloud computing environment. 5
22. Herley C, van Oorschot P, Patrick A (2009) Financial Cryptography and Data Security. In: 13th international conference, Accra Beach, vol 5628. Washington, DC
23. https://www.in.capgemini.com/resource-file-access/resource/pdf
24. http://www.wired.com/2011/05/dropbox-ftc/
25. http://www.tripwire.com/state-of-security/security-data-protection/dropbox-security/

26. Jensen M, Gruschka N, Iacono LL, Horst G (2009) On technical security issues in cloud computing. In: Cloud Computing (CLOUD '09)
27. Jin K, Miller EL (2009) The effectiveness of deduplication on virtual machine disk images. In: Proceedings of SYSTOR 2009: the Israeli experimental systems conference, Haifa. ACM, p 7
28. Juels A, Burton J, Kaliski S (2007) PORs: proofs of retrievability for large files. In: Proceedings of CCS 07, Alexandria, pp 584–597
29. Kamara S, Papamanthou C, Roeder T (2011) CS2: a semantic cryptographic cloud storage system. Microsoft research, Technical report MSR-TR-2011-58
30. Kandukuri BR (2009) Cloud security issues. In: 2009 IEEE international conference on services computing, Bangalore, pp 517–520
31. Kumbhare A, Simmhan Y, Prasanna V (2012) Cryptonite: a secure and performant data repository on public clouds. In: Proceedings – 2012 IEEE 5th international conference on cloud computing, CLOUD 2012, Honolulu, pp 510–517
32. Li J, Chen X, Li M, Li J, Lee PPC, Lou W (2014) Secure deduplication with efficient and reliable convergent key management. IEEE Trans Parallel Distrib Syst 25(6):1615–1625
33. Meyer DT, Bolosky WJ (2012) A study of practical deduplication. ACM Trans Storage 7(4):1–20
34. Ng WK, Wen Y, Zhu H (2012) Private data deduplication protocols in cloud storage. In: ACM symposium on applied computing, Trento, p 441
35. Peng Y, Zhao W, Xie F, Dai ZH, Gao Y, Chen DQ (2012) Secure cloud storage based on cryptographic techniques. J China Universities Posts Telecommun 19(Suppl 2):182–189
36. Popa RA, Lorch JR, Molnar D et al (2010) Enabling security in cloud storage SLAs with CloudProof. Microsoft TechReport MSR-TR-2010, 46
37. Prasad P, Ojha B, Shahi RR, Lal R (2011) 3-dimensional security in cloud computing. Comput Res Dev (ICCRD) 3:198–208
38. Rackspace Open Cloud at http://www.rackspace.com/cloud
39. Ruj S, Nayak A, Stojmernovic I (2011) DACC: distributed access control in clouds. In: International joint conference of IEEE TrustCom-11/IEEE ICESS-11/FCST-11. IEEE Computer Society, Los Alamitos, 91–98
40. Schwarzkopf R, Schmidt M, Rüdiger M, Freisleben B (2012) Efficient storage of virtual machine images. In: Proceedings of the 3rd workshop on scientific cloud computing date – ScienceCloud '12, New York, p 51
41. SIT (2012) Technical reports On the security of cloud storage services
42. Somorovsky J, Meyer C, Tran T et al (2012) SEC2: secure moblie solution for distributed public cloud storages. In: 2nd international conference on cloud computing and services science (CLOSER), Porto, pp 555–561
43. Sood SK (2012) A combined approach to ensure data security in cloud computing. J Netw Comput Appl 35(6):1831–1838
44. Storer MW, Greenan K, Long DDE, Miller EL (2008) Secure data deduplication. In: Proceedings of the 4th ACM international workshop on storage security and survivability StorageSS 08, New York, p 1
45. Subashini S, Kavitha V (2011) A survey on security issues in service delivery models of cloud computing. J Netw Comput Appl 34(1):1–11. Elsevier Conference
46. Wang C, Wang Q, Ren K, Lou W (2009) Ensuring data storage security in cloud computing. In: IEEE 17th international workshop on quality of service, IWQoS 2009, Charleston, p 19
47. Wang C, Cao N, Li J, Ren K, Lou W (2010) Secure ranked keyword search over encrypted cloud data. J ACM 43(3):431–473
48. Wei L, Zhu H, Cao Z, Dong X, Jia W, Chen Y, Vasilakos A (2014) Security and privacy for storage and computation in cloud computing. Inf Sci 258:371–386. Elsevier conference
49. Windows Azure at http://azure.microsoft.com/en-us/
50. Zarandioon S, Yao D, Ganapathy V (2012) K2C: cryptographic cloud storage with lazy revocation and anonymous access. In: Security and privacy in communication networks. Lecture notes of the institute for computer sciences, social-informatics and telecommunications engineering LNICST, vol 96. Springer, Berlin/Heidelberg, pp 59–76
51. Zhao X, Zhang Y, Wu Y, Chen K, Jiang J, Li K (2014) Liquid: a scalable deduplication file system for virtual machine images. IEEE Trans Parallel Distrib Syst 25(5):1257–1266

Shweta Saharan has completed her Bachelor of Technology (B.Tech) from Rajasthan Technical University and received her master's degree in Computer Science and Engineering (Information Security) from Central University of Rajasthan, India, in 2015. Currently, she is a lecturer in Computer Engineering Department, Indian Institute of Information and Technology (IIIT), Kota. Her research interests include cloud computing, information and network security, and networking.

Gaurav Somani is an Assistant Professor at Department of Computer Science and Engineering, Central University of Rajasthan, India. He has completed his Bachelor of Engineering (BE) in Information Technology from University of Rajasthan with honors and Master of Technology (MTech) in Information and Communication Technology from DAIICT, Gandhinagar, India, with distinction. He is pursuing his PhD from Malviya National Institute of Technology, Jaipur, India. His research interests include Distributed Systems and Security Engineering. He has authored a book/monograph on Scheduling and Isolation in Virtualization. He has published a number of papers in various conferences and journals of international repute like ACM SINCONF, ACM CGC, IEEE CLOUD, and Elsevier FGCS. He has served as TPC member in multiple international conferences and reviewer of top journals like IEEE transactions on cloud computing. He is a member of IEEE and ACM.

Cloud Computing Governance, Risk, and Compliance – The Quintessential Globalization Challenge

6

Rhonda L. Farrell

Abstract

As cloud computing innovations move at warp speed, technology at light speed, and associated legislation at a snail's pace, the penultimate globalization challenge appears to be the reduction of the governance, risk, and compliance bottlenecks that continue to plague industry, especially within the security assurance arena world-wide.

Keywords

Cloud computing • Governance • Risk • Standards • Innovation

6.1 Industry Buy-in, Consensus, and Reciprocity

As cloud computing innovations move at warp speed, technology at light speed, and associated legislation at a snail's pace, the penultimate globalization challenge appears to be the reduction of the governance, risk, and compliance bottlenecks that continue to plague industry, especially within the security assurance arena world-wide.

What is the most likely culprit of potential root causes associated with these bottlenecks? In a nutshell, it is lack of industry buy-in, consensus, and reciprocity at the most vital levels, including definitions, governance focus areas, primary organizations, standards, policies, methodologies, reference architectures, control frameworks, innovation, and legislation. While choice is certainly valued in the industry from a product technology perspective, eventually convergence must occur within these other vital areas in order to keep technologists sane, the industry

R.L. Farrell (✉)
Booz Allen Hamilton, Annapolis Junction, MD, USA
e-mail: rhondalfarrell@aol.com

S.Y. Zhu et al. (eds.), *Guide to Security Assurance for Cloud Computing*, Computer Communications and Networks, DOI 10.1007/978-3-319-25988-8_6

moving forwards efficiently, and venture capitalists and law firms prospering. For cloud computing technologies, the ability to collect, categorize, understand, apply, and eventually assess for prospective use is made even harder given the wide variety of innovations falling into this category and the ever widening security boundary associated with the Internet of Things.

While the governance situation is currently problematic for the practitioner, there are growing signs of convergence, synergy building, re-use, and reciprocity, all of which bode well for industry advances, supporting the next 25 years of progress.

6.2 Definitions

Definitions exist in order to build a common lexicon which aids in the creation of relevant industry artifacts, which in turn enable broader technological and security assurance understanding by cloud providers, consumers, and practitioners alike [27]. Given that cloud computing innovations encompass many practice areas, including cyber, engineering, operations, compliance, audit, among others, it should be no surprise that there are multiple seminal definitions for the term security assurance as applied within this complex operating arena. The following four definitions for "security assurance" are taken from NIST IR 7298 and depict the integrated nature of the practice area as applied to "the cloud" [25].

- Grounds for confidence that the other four security goals (integrity, availability, confidentiality, and accountability) have been adequately met by a specific implementation. "Adequately met" includes (1) functionality that performs correctly, (2) sufficient protection against unintentional errors (by users or software), and (3) sufficient resistance to intentional penetration or by-pass (SOURCE: SP 800-27).
- The grounds for confidence that the set of intended security controls in an information system are effective in their application (SOURCE: SP 800-37; SP 800-53A).
- Measure of confidence that the security features, practices, procedures, and architecture of an information system accurately mediates and enforces the security policy (SOURCE: CNSSI-4009; SP 800-39).
- In the context of OMB M-04-04 and this document, assurance is defined as (1) the degree of confidence in the vetting process used to establish the identity of an individual to whom the credential was issued, and (2) the degree of confidence that the individual who uses the credential is the individual to whom the credential was issued (SOURCE: SP 800-63).

These definitions focus on the complex and integrated nature of security assurance and offer a unique perspective that suggests utilization of a robust, holistic approach, which includes seminal elements of governance, risk, and compliance, which should better allow security assurance practices to be successful in this complex and continuously evolving technology area.

6.3 Governance Focus Areas

Governance has traditionally been used as an overarching organizational term which includes heightened responsibilities, practices, and scrutiny placed on ensuring strategic business alignment, risk minimization, and best utilization of enterprise resources as applied to the cybersecurity operational arena [5, 24]. Risk management, on the other hand, includes taking a "risk-based approach to security control selection and specification [which] considers effectiveness, efficiency, and constraints due to applicable laws, directives, Executive Orders, policies, standards, or regulations" [30]. Compliance includes evaluation and assessment activities in support of verification, validation, and accreditation activities of technologies, as specified within relevant security requirements and control frameworks [28, 29].

All three of these vital operational activities must be understood, integrated, and incorporated into day-to-day continuously evolving practices in order for security assessment outcomes to be successful from a practitioner's perspective. Figure 6.1 puts these concepts into perspective from a Cloud Computingperspective [12].

6.4 Organizations and Standards

Even in the currently non-converged compliance state, the practitioner has access to seminal organizations that provide cloud computing guidance within the security assurance space, thus enabling a quicker ramp up time and shorter path for those whom are operating within this rather nascent technology space. These include Cloud Security Alliance (CSA), European Network and Information Security Association (ENISA), Institute of Electrical and Electronics Engineers (IEEE), International Organization for Standardization (ISO), and a plethora of additional cloud standards organizations including the Cloud Standards Customer Council (CSCC), Distributed Management Task Force, European Telecommunications Standard Institute, Global Inter-Cloud Technology Forum (GICTF), ISO/IEC JTC 1, International Telecommunications Union (ITU), National Institute of Standards and Technology (NIST), Open Grid Forum (OGF), Object Management Group (OMG), Open Cloud Consortium (OCC), Organization for the Advancement of Structured

<table>
<tr><td colspan="4">Testing-as-a-Service</td></tr>
<tr><td colspan="4">Management/Governance-as-a-Service</td></tr>
<tr><td rowspan="5">Security-as-a-Service</td><td rowspan="4">Integration-as-a-Service</td><td colspan="2">Application-as-a-Service</td></tr>
<tr><td>Process-as-a-Service</td><td rowspan="5">Platform-as-a-Service</td></tr>
<tr><td>Information-as-a-Service</td></tr>
<tr><td>Database-as-a-Service</td></tr>
<tr><td colspan="2">Storage-as-a-Service</td></tr>
<tr><td colspan="3">Infrastructure-as-a-Service</td></tr>
</table>

Fig. 6.1 Categorization of cloud computing provider services–granular level

Information Standards (OASIS), Storage Networking Industry Association (SNIA), The Open Group, Association for Retail Technology Standards (ARTS), TM Forum, and Open Cloud Connect [9].

6.4.1 Industry Community Groups

From a broader security assurance perspective, community groups such as the Department of Homeland Security (DHS) affiliated Build Security In, and Software Assurance groups, as well as Mitre's Making Security Measurable offer practices, tools, guidelines, rules, principles, languages, standardized processes, and other resources that software developers, architects, and security practitioners can use to build security into and assure software and systems across every phase of the life-cycle.

Offering high levels of both relevancy and timeliness, a quick review and inventory of the content associated with each organization's offerings will be well worth the security assurance practitioner's time, enabling them to gain valuable industry expertise far beyond that of the majority of their peers. For those whom the knowledge areas resonate, a plethora of community workshops and associated working groups enable on-going professional development and high visibility industry involvement, thus offering value-add at many professional levels.

6.4.2 FEDRAMP

The Federal Risk and Authorization Management Program (FEDRAMP) arena offers great value within the Federal Government space, including offering a "government-wide program that provides a standardized approach to security assessment, authorization, and continuous monitoring for cloud products and services" ([10], 'About Us'). Additionally, their documented goals align well with the intent of closing the divergence gap and include the following:

- Accelerate the adoption of secure cloud solutions through reuse of assessments and authorizations
- Increase confidence in security of cloud solutions achieve consistent security authorizations using a baseline set of agreed upon standards to be used for cloud product approval in or outside of FedRAMP
- Ensure consistent application of existing security practice and increase confidence in security assessments
- Increase automation and near real-time data for continuous monitoring

Additionally, their documented benefits align well with the aforementioned governance model which is focused on achieving ever greater efficiencies, including the following:

- Increase re-use of existing security assessments across agencies
- Save significant cost, time, and resources – "do once, use many times"
- Improve real-time security visibility
- Provide a uniform approach to risk-based management
- Enhance transparency between government and Cloud Service Providers (CSPs)
- Improve the trustworthiness, reliability, consistency, and quality of the Federal security authorization process

This is true industry collaboration, with cybersecurity and cloud expert representatives from the General Services Administration (GSA), National Institute of Standards and Technology (NIST), DHS, Department of Defense (DOD), National Security Agency (NSA), Office of Management and Budget (OMB), the Federal Chief Information Officer (CIO) Council and associated working groups, as well as private industry. Private organizations have a somewhat similar place to utilize centralized security assessment and related tools, called the Software Assurance Marketplace (SWAMP) [35].

6.4.3 ISO

Other signals of convergence include the ISO standard set, where a plethora of standards are converging around risk, assurance, and process standardization, including the 9001:2015, 12207, 15504, 20000, 26262, and 27000 families. While none of these are cloud specific standards, all of them are technology, process, and security oriented, thus allowing for broad application and use across the wider Internet of Things supported by the cloud, including automobile safety and reliability issues [1, 2, 4, 6–8, 13–17, 26, 33, 34].

6.4.3.1 ISO 9001:2015

ISO 9001:2015 offers the following value-adds to adopting organizations and applies readily to the governance area of most cybersecurity programs world-wide [3].

- Reducing costs
- Increasing profits
- Increasing leadership involvement
- Ensuring customer satisfaction
- Ensuring employee competency and involvement
- Heightened resource management
- Improving system planning
- Developing of mutually beneficial supplier relationships
- Accomplishing objectives that support the organization's mission

Additionally, the recently approved changes for this standard family will be the catalyst to drive other industry sector standards forward from an integration standpoint [32]. Additionally, it provides fodder for undertaking a larger business management review, including an organization wide effort which is inclusive of personnel at all levels within the recommended controls and monitoring methods [31].

6.4.3.2 ISO 12207:2008

ISO 12207:2008 is an international systems and software engineering standard focused on examining the software life cycle processes and defining all the tasks required for developing and maintaining software. It establishes a process lifecycle for software and includes processes and activities applied during the acquisition and configuration of the services of the system. There are 43 system and software processes, and over 95 activities, 325 tasks, and 224 process outcomes. It supplies a common structure for all practitioners involved with the software development use a common lexicon. The standard is modular in support of use and quick adoption and can be adapted to the special needs of any software project. Major focus areas include those associated with acquisition/supply, development, operation, maintenance, and destruction [18].

6.4.3.3 ISO 15504:2012

ISO/IEC 15504: 2012 was initially derived from process lifecycle standard ISO/IEC 12207 and from maturity models like Bootstrap, Trillium, and the CMM and is the reference model for the maturity models. It is labeled ISO/IEC 15504 Information technology – Process assessment, also known as SPICE (Software Process Improvement and Capability dEtermination) and is a set of technical standards documents for the computer software development process and related business management functions. It enables assessors to offer an overall determination of the organization's capabilities for delivering products (software, systems, and IT services). The reference model defines a process dimension and a capability dimension. The process dimension defines processes divided into five categories: customer/supplier, engineering, supporting, management, and organization. Aligning to each process is a capability level, which utilizes the following scale (Table 6.1):

The capability of processes is measured using process attributes. The international standard defines nine process oriented attributes, including process performance, performance management, work product management, process definition, process deployment, process measurement, process control, process innovation, and process optimization. Each process attribute is assessed on a four-point (N-P-L-F)

Table 6.1 ISO 15504:2012 capability levels

Level	Name
5	Optimizing process
4	Predictable process
3	Established process
2	Managed process
1	Performed process
0	Incomplete process

rating scale: not achieved (0–15%); partially achieved (>15–50 %); largely achieved (>50–85 %); and fully achieved (>85–100 %). This standard is recommended to be used in two contexts, primarily process improvement and capability determination which is the evaluation of a supplier's process capability, and can readily be applied to technological undertakings. Process improvement is paramount. Additionally, the standard can be used to inform supplier selection decisions, either in-house or through independent assessors. The capability assessment area also includes practical process profiles – which use risk as the determining factor in setting target process profile, in order to practice active risk reduction, and hence reducing the likelihood of problems occurring [21].

6.4.3.4 ISO 20000-1:2011

ISO 20000-1:2011 is a service management system (SMS) standard. It specifies requirements for the service provider to plan, establish, implement, operate, monitor, review, maintain and improve an SMS. The requirements include the design, transition, delivery and improvement of services to fulfil agreed service requirements" [19]. ISO/IEC TR 20000-5:2013 is an example of implementation plan and provides guidance to service providers on how to implement a service management system which adheres to ISO/IEC 20000-1 or for service providers who are planning service improvements as a business initiative. It also advises service providers on how to best achieve the requirements outlines within 20000-1 [22].

6.4.3.5 ISO 26262:2011

ISO 26262:2011 addresses functional safety features across the lifecycle within each automotive product development phase, ranging from specifications, to design, implementation, integration, verification, validation, and production release. It applies to all automotive equipment which fall into the electronic and electrical safety-related systems area, with the aim of addressing possible hazards caused by the malfunctioning behavior of electronic and electrical systems.

It is a risk-based safety standard, where the risk of hazardous operational situations are qualitatively assessed and safety measures are defined to avoid or control systematic failures and to detect or control random hardware failures, or mitigate their effects. It provides an automotive safety lifecycle (management, development, production, operation, service, decommissioning) and supports tailoring the necessary activities during these lifecycle phases.

Additionally, it covers functional safety aspects of the entire development process including such activities as requirements specification, design, implementation, integration, verification, validation, and configuration. This standard provides an automotive-specific risk-based approach for determining risk classes (Automotive Safety Integrity Levels, ASILs) and uses those for specifying the item's necessary safety requirements for achieving an acceptable residual risk. Additionally, the standard provides requirements for validation and confirmation measures to ensure a sufficient and acceptable level of safety is being achieved [20].

Table 6.2 Severity classifications

S0	No injuries
S1	Light to moderate injuries
S2	Severe to life-threatening (survival probable) injuries
S3	Life-threatening (survival uncertain) to fatal injuries

Table 6.3 Exposure classifications

E0	Incredibly unlikely
E1	Very low probability (injury could happen only in rare operating conditions)
E2	Low probability
E3	Medium probability
E4	High probability (injury could happen under most operating conditions)

Much like the RMF Framework, hazardous events are classified according to the severity (S) of expected injuries, per Table 6.2.

Also like the RMF, it includes exposure classifications (EC), per Table 6.3, where exposure (E) is the relative expected frequency of the operational conditions in which the injury can possibly happen, and control (C) is the relative likelihood that the driver can act to prevent the injury.

6.4.3.6 ISO 27000 Series

The ISO 27000 family includes eight primary standards which can greatly enhance the security practitioner's ability to assess technological solutions, such as cloud, among others. 27001:2013 provides requirements for establishing, implementing, maintaining, and continuously improving an Information Security Management System (ISMS). 27002:2013 offers a comprehensive set of controls and tailoring advice. 27004:2009 offers measures and metrics aligned to 27002, while 27005 covers ISMS risk management [23].

In addition to the merits of each of the separate standards, the family of standards allows for heightened continuous improvement processes like Six Sigma's Define, Measure, Analyze, Improve, and Control (DMAIC) method to be implemented. Additionally, it seeks to align more strongly with ISO 9000 and ISO/IEC 20000. Lastly, the standards introduce information security risk analysis to drive the selection and implementation of information security controls across multiple categories. The authors strive to keep the standards relevant despite the evolving nature of information security threats, vulnerabilities and impacts, and trends in the use of certain information security controls.

6.5 Way Forward

Making order out of the chaos, i.e., the plethora of partially conflicting and divergent information currently existing within this practice area, appears to be a journey not for the faint-of-heart, but with patient research, industry aggregation sites reward the hearty researcher by providing a plethora of vitally connected information areas, allowing the practitioner to see the 'forest in spite of the trees' or rather the 'stars in spite of the clouds'.

This researcher suggests converging the cloud computing assurance knowledge areas within a breakout similar to the often-times referenced industry IA Policy Chart, which logically aligns authorities, policies, regulations, standards, and guidance and color codes them per their relevant Office of Primary Responsibility (OPR) area [11]. Creating a like map for the broader cloud assurance practice area would go a long way towards achieving convergence, enabling end-to-end traceability, as well taming the heightened complexity surrounding cloud computing technologies, which continues to be daunting to new entrants and senior practitioners alike.

6.6 Review Questions

1. Name and explain the purpose of three ISO standards relating to services.
2. Name and explain the purpose of three Cloud Technology-related standards bodies.
3. Identify three cloud provider services.
4. Explain the FEDRAMP initiative conceptually.

References

1. Ab Rahman NH, Choo KKR (2015) A survey of information security incident handling in the cloud. Comput Secur 49:45–69
2. Ali M, Khan SU, Vasilakos AV (2015) Security in cloud computing: opportunities and challenges. Inform Sci 305:357–383
3. Aston B (2015) Expert answers: ISO 9001 internal audit. Qual Prog ASQ (8):8
4. Bertolino A, Blake MB, Mehra P, Mei H, Xie T (2015) Software engineering for internet computing: Internetware and beyond [Guest editors' introduction]. IEEE Software 32(1):35–37
5. Bodeau DJ, Graubart RD, Fabius-Greene J (2010) Cyber security governance, MTR100308, PR 10-3710. The MITRE Corporation, Bedford
6. Borgohain T, Kumar U, Sanyal S (2015) Survey of security and privacy issues of Internet of Things. arXiv preprint arXiv:1501.02211. Retrieved from http://arxiv.org/ftp/arxiv/papers/1501/1501.02211.pdf
7. Breslin P (2014) Security updates: the upcoming revision of ISO/IEC 27001. DNV Business Assurance. Retrieved 27 Jan 2015
8. Buckholtz B, Ragai I, Wang L (2015) Cloud manufacturing: current trends and future implementations. ASME J Manuf Sci Eng. doi:10(1.4030009)
9. Cloud Standards Org (2015) Cloud standards Wiki. Retrieved from http://cloud-standards.org/wiki/index.php?title=Main_Page
10. Council IA (2012) Federal risk and authorization management program (FedRAMP)
11. DoD Deputy CIO for Cybersecurity (2015) Cybersecurity-related issuances and policies. Retrieved from: http://iac.dtic.mil/csiac/download/ia_policychart.pdf
12. Farrell R (2010) Securing the cloud – governance, risk, and compliance issues reign supreme. Inf Secur J – A Global Perspect 19(6):310–319

13. Garitano I, Fayyad S, Noll J (2015) Multi-metrics approach for security, privacy and dependability in embedded systems. Wireless Pers Commun 81(4):1359–1376
14. Glas B, Gebauer C, Hänger J, Heyl A, Klarmann J, Kriso S, Vembar P, Wörz P (2015) Automotive safety and security integration challenges. In: Proceedings of the automotive safety & security
15. Gope P, Hwang T (2015) Untraceable sensor movement in distributed IoT infrastructure. Retrieved from http://ieeexplore.ieee.org/xpl/login.jsp?tp=&arnumber=7120086&url=http%3A%2F%2Fieeexplore.ieee.org%2Fxpls%2Fabs_all.jsp%3Farnumber%3D7120086
16. Granjal J, Monteiro E, Silva JS (2015) Security in the integration of low-power Wireless Sensor Networks with the Internet: a survey. Ad Hoc Netw 24:264–287
17. Hogan M (2014) Understanding automotive reliability and ISO 26262 for safety-critical systems. Retrieved from Mentor Graphics Website: http://s3.mentor.com/public_documents/whitepaper/resources/mentorpaper_86209.pdf
18. ISO (2008) ISO/IEC 12207:2008. Systems and software engineering – software life cycle processes. Retrieved from ISO Website: http://www.iso.org/iso/catalogue_detail?csnumber=43447
19. ISO (2011a) ISO/IEC 20000-1:2011. Information technology – service management – Part 1: Service management system requirements. Retrieved from ISO Website: http://www.iso.org/iso/catalogue_detail?csnumber=51986
20. ISO (2011b) ISO 26262-1:2011. Road vehicles – Functional safety – Part 1: Vocabulary. Retrieved from ISO Website: http://www.iso.org/iso/catalogue_detail?csnumber=43464
21. Gupta U (2015) Survey on security issues in file management in cloud computing environment. *arXiv preprint arXiv*:1505.00729
22. ISO (2013) ISO/IEC TR 20000-5:2013. Information technology – Service management – Part 5: Exemplar implementation plan for ISO/IEC 20000-1. Retrieved from ISO Website: http://www.iso.org/iso/home/store/catalogue_ics/catalogue_detail_ics.htm?csnumber=60329
23. ISO 27000 Directory (2013) Retrieved from http://www.27000.org/
24. IT Law Wiki. Cybersecurity governance. Retrieved from http://itlaw.wikia.com/wiki/Cybersecurity_governance
25. Kissel R (2013) Glossary of key information security terms. NIST Interagency Reports NIST IR, 7298, 3. Retrieved from the NIST Website: http://nvlpubs.nist.gov/nistpubs/ir/2013/NIST.IR.7298r2.pdf
26. Li S, Da Xu L, Zhao S (2014) The Internet of Things: a survey. Inf Syst Frontiers 17(2):243–259
27. Liu F, Tong J, Mao J, Bohn R, Messina J, Badger L, Leaf D (2012) NIST cloud computing reference architecture: recommendations of the National Institute of Standards and Technology (Special Publication 500–292)
28. Mellado D, Blanco C, Sánchez LE, Fernández-Medina E (2010) A systematic review of security requirements engineering. Comp Stand Inter 32(4):153–165
29. NICCS (2015) Cyber glossary. Retrieved from http://niccs.us-cert.gov/glossary
30. NIST, SP. 800-30 (2012) Risk management guide for information technology systems
31. Palmes P (2015) ISO 9001:2015 transition starts with top management. New 2015 requirements make leadership involvement critical first step in transition. Retrieved from ASQ Website: https://secure.asq.org/perl/msg.pl?prvurl=http://asq.org/2015/05/standards/iso-9001-2015-transition-starts-with-top-management.pdf
32. Reid D (2015) Open to change: how expected revisions to ISO 9001: 2015 may affect sector-specific standards. Qual Prog ASQ 7
33. Sicari S, Rizzardi A, Grieco LA, Coen-Porisini A (2015) Security, privacy and trust in Internet of Things: the road ahead. Comput Netw 76:146–164
34. Singh J, Pasquier T, Bacon J, Ko H, Eyers D (2015) 20 cloud security considerations for supporting the internet of things. Retrieved from http://ieeexplore.ieee.org/xpl/login.jsp?tp=&arnumber=7165580&url=http%3A%2F%2Fieeexplore.ieee.org%2Fxpls%2Fabs_all.jsp%3Farnumber%3D7165580
35. Software Assurance Marketplace (SWAMP) (2015) Retrieved from https://continuousassurance.org/

Rhonda L. Farrell is an Associate at Booz Allen Hamilton. She began her career in computer operations with the US Marine Corps in 1982 at Quantico, VA, progressing on to private enterprise beginning in 1984 when she joined Amdahl Corporation. Since that time period, she has worked in Silicon Valley, CA, within the operations, engineering, quality, and security portions of Fortune 500 firms, such as Cisco Systems, Inc. and VISA, among others. She graduated in 2009 from Concord Law School with her JD focusing in Technology, and in 2010 relocated to the East Coast to continue her cybersecurity career in the DC Metro area. She has earned her CISSP, CSSLP, CSQE, CMQ/OE, and CMAP certifications. She recently successfully completed her Doctoral defense as a student at the University of Fairfax. In her "spare time", she supports three professional non-profit organizations in multiple leadership capacities, including: American Society for Quality (ASQ), IEEE, and ISSA.

Cloud Computing and Security in the Future 7

Nigel McKelvey, Kevin Curran, Benny Gordon, Edward Devlin, and Kenneth Johnston

Abstract

We are starting to depend more and more on 'cloud' technology, in business and in our own personal lives. With so much personal data being stored in our personal clouds, questions are being asked about where the responsibility lies for the protection of data. For instance, is it with the consumer or with the provider? People have a right to know where their files are being stored and what is protecting them. The same goes for the consumer. They are obligated to ensure that their passwords are of a good strength and that they are safe while browsing the web, especially on public networks. The personal cloud industry is on the rise, and if the experts are correct in their predictions, the business world will be a better place for it, better in terms of portability and flexibility. The power to set your office up wherever you happen to be sitting, anywhere in the world, will be what personal cloud providers are offering. This is the future for cloud computing. Security and privacy are now more relevant than ever. This chapter examines the issues around cloud data protection and security and also

N. McKelvey
School of Computing, Letterkenny Institute of Technology, Letterkenny, Co. Donegal, Ireland
e-mail: nigel.mckelvey@lyit.ie

K. Curran (✉)
Faculty of Computing and Engineering, School of Computing and Intelligent Systems, Ulster University, Londonderry BT48, 7JL, UK
e-mail: kj.curran@ulster.ac.uk

B. Gordon • K. Johnston
Letterkenny Institute of Technology, Co. Donegal, Ireland

E. Devlin
Logistics Department of General Motors, Limerick, Ireland

S.Y. Zhu et al. (eds.), *Guide to Security Assurance for Cloud Computing*,
Computer Communications and Networks, DOI 10.1007/978-3-319-25988-8_7

investigates if the current Data Protection Act defines sufficient guidelines for data controllers on how they should collect and store user information in relation to thin-based clients using online or cloud-based service or if a lack of clarity in the Data Protection Act could cause these services to misuse the user's data.

Keywords
Cloud computing • Security • Privacy • Encryption • Public clouds

7.1 Introduction

Since the inception of the internet in the early 1990s, the variety and volume of services on offer have increased exponentially. In recent times, a new computing paradigm has emerged to further expand the online universe: cloud computing. Despite what may largely appear to be a general zeitgeist of mass approval and an unstoppable drift towards universal implementation, the adoption rate amongst many business sectors has been slower than expected. The generally offered justification for this caution is perceived to be an underlying fear that the technology does not offer the same level of security that can be achieved by the traditional, on-site, model of computing. Big business especially seems hesitant to embrace the model. Cloud computing is now an almost ubiquitous concept in modern information technology. First conceived in the early 1960s by John McCarthy, a researcher at MIT, who suggested that one day computing service provision would essentially become a utility, delivered and metered much like the telephone or electricity services. Today, cloud computing, in its various forms, is the dominant force in the IT industry, with market research giant Gartner suggesting that cloud computing-based activities will form the bulk of IT spending by 2016 [29].

'Security concerns the confidentiality, availability and integrity of data or information. Security may also include authentication and non-repudiation.' [27]. With the vast majority of people now using multiple devices during their daily lives, personal cloud computing has become a major factor in storing our data from multiple devices to the same location. With so many devices which are connected to the internet, it is more important than ever to be able to access your files from every one of those devices: from your phone to your laptop, your iPad to your smart TV. An easily accessible, user-friendly personal cloud storage system that does not compromise on security is what many users are looking for [32]. Clients using either personal or public cloud services may suffer anxiety due to a lack of control over such things as availability, portability, isolation, integrity, transparency and the confidentiality of their data [26].

Privacy is a major concern when referring to the cloud. Every cloud service provider must adhere to the law. This law is dependent on where the service provider is located. In Europe, the service must comply with European Data Protection Regulations [27]. Clients need to be made aware of the terms of such a service, and users need to be aware of where liability lies if their accounts are breached. For this to work, there needs to be a certain amount of trust between the client and provider: trust the client will not abuse what rights they have and trust that the provider will behave in the way that is expected. According to the National Institute of Standards and Technology (NIST), 'Cloud providers should protect the assured, proper, and consistent collection, processing, communication, use, and disposition of personal information (PI) and personally identifiable information (PII) in the cloud system' [24]. It goes on to state that, even though the cloud is available to provide a platform for shared software, resources and information, the services also pose privacy and security problems to the consumer [24].

The term cloud computing could be considered to have multiple meanings in information technology; from a technical perspective, cloud computing may be considered as a means of allowing an application to be deployed to an environment that is easily accessible and one that can be scaled to meet user demand [33]. Alternatively, it could be used as a marketing or business tool to describe a service that allows a user to access data or software from any location in the world [1]. In both senses, cloud computing may be interpreted as online services accessible via the internet. However, it should be realised that although cloud computing supports a remote logical processing environment accessible via the internet, in reality, the cloud is manifested in physical servers which may be storing and/or processing user data remotely, and like any form of data processing and storage, it needs to adhere to the Data Protection Act.

An increase in the number of mobile device has seen more people using cloud-based service and application [6]. It could be suggested that with an increase in demand, there may be an increase in the number of cloud services offered to user. These services may be storing and processing user data; therefore, it could be suggested that cloud-based services need to adhere to legal requirements defined in the Data Protection Act. However, if these cloud services are focused on marketing and profit, the user's data protection may take a back seat [4].

7.2 The Cloud Model

Grance and Mell [14] outline a generally accepted definition of what comprises the cloud. Cloud computing is a blanket term used to describe a computing model where data, resources and/or infrastructure are stored remotely, shared amongst multiple consumers and accessed via the internet rather than on a local computer or network. The cloud model is considered to consist of five essential characteristics and three service models. The five characteristics outline the minimum properties a computing service must possess before it can be considered to be part of the cloud (Fig. 7.1).

1. *On-demand self-service*. The services offered by a vendor must be always available and should be easily configurable by the consumer without intervention from the service provider.

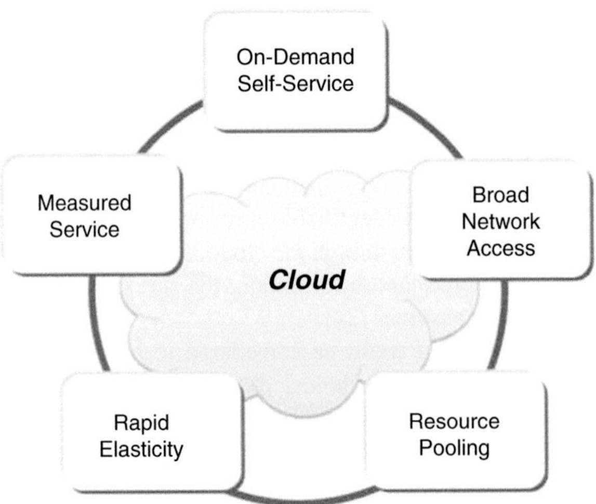

Fig. 7.1 The five essential characteristics of the cloud computing model (The Open group, 2013)

2. *Broad network access*. Services should be available over the internet and should be inclusive in terms of access platforms and client models.
3. *Resource pooling*. Resources provided by the vendor are pooled and shared amongst multiple consumers and should be sufficiently dynamic to quickly react and adapt to changing consumer requirements.
4. *Rapid elasticity*. Service provision should be able to scale quickly, and with little effort, to provide the correct level of service the consumer requires, when it's required.
5. *Measured service*. Vendors should adopt a system which allows service provision to be measured and monitored using a metric that is appropriate to the services being provided. This ensures transparency between consumer and vendor.

The cloud can be conceptually considered to be comprised of a three-layered model for service provision. The first layer, *software as a service,* is a software deployment model where the required functionality is offered as a remote, often bespoke, facility which is adaptable the customer's demands providing a service which is flexible, scalable and cost-effective. The second layer, *platform as a service,* offers a development environment and associated solution stack as a remote service package. This provides the consumer with the facilities required to conduct a development project using software and services based on the internet, without the need to be concerned with the underlying hardware or infrastructure. The final layer, *infrastructure as a service,* offers fundamental computing infrastructure delivered as a service. Storage, processing and network capabilities are accessible as a remote, often virtualized, scalable product. This service can be considered analogous to computing as a utility with a similar pricing model [19].

Supplementary to these characteristics and service models are a further four classifications: the deployment models. In reference to cloud computing, a deployment model is the term used to attempt to classify and group the different configuration possibilities that exist under the cloud computing model. It outlines four different deployment categories, loosely based on access rights.

Public Cloud The service vendor provides resources, typically applications or storage, to the public via the internet often using traditional web browsers. This service may be offered free but is more commonly charged using a 'pay as you use' model. Leading to the belief that cloud computing may evolve to become the fifth utility. These clouds are usually hosted at the location of the provider.

Private Cloud The service is provided for the use of a single organisation. This reduces concerns over security and maintenance as all resources are managed in-house by the organisation and access is restricted to approved persons. The service may be provided by the organisation itself, purchased from a third party or a combination of both.

Hybrid Cloud This category describes a deployment model that combines aspects of both public and private (even community) models. All the components of a hybrid cloud remain discrete entities but are connected in some way via standards or technology, to offer increased business value. A hybrid cloud can have the security of a private cloud but can also employ the resources of the public cloud when required.

Community Cloud Similar to a private cloud, this model allows the infrastructure and services of the provider to be shared amongst different organisations that share a common purpose or concern or have complimentary requirements and policies.

Cloud computing offers many advantages over traditional computing models. The most obvious is financial savings. Research from Microsoft suggests that in pre-2010, up to 89% of a company's IT budget was spent on maintenance and infrastructure [21]. The availability of computing infrastructure, software and processing power to be purchased as a service changes IT overheads from being capital expenses into operational costs, eliminating significant upfront outlay and increasing fiscal efficiency. The cloud model also offers greater flexibility than traditional models. In the past, if a company wanted to expand its capabilities, it would be required to invest in equipment, software licences and premises to locate them. Now, infrastructure and processing can be purchased when required and can expand and contract as demand dictates. This scalability offers greater control and cost-efficiency. The cloud model also provides greater convenience and availability. As services and infrastructure are offered remotely, they can be accessed from any geographical location, cultivating collaboration and improving the work/life balance of users. Backup and recovery issues are also improved by the adoption of cloud technology. At its most basic, the cloud can be used as a location to store backups of data held on physical machines. In most cases, cloud vendors will offer flexible solutions to backup issues. These benefits can be derived logically from the architectural and deployment structures outlined by Grance and Mell and are increasingly being corroborated both anecdotally and statistically. It is important however to realise that it is only one-half of the narrative. The adoption of new technology has never been an entirely positive event, and many people believe cloud technology to be no different. Larry Ellison, chairman of IT giant Oracle, suggests a cautious approach: '*The interesting thing about cloud computing is that we've redefined cloud computing to include everything that we already do. I can't think of anything that isn't cloud computing with all of these announcements. The computer industry is the only industry that is more fashion-driven than women's fashion. Maybe I'm an idiot, but I have no idea what anyone is talking about. What is it? It's complete gibberish. It's insane. When is this idiocy going to stop?*'[23]

The argument exists that there is no such thing as a 'personal cloud' system, that the cloud is there to benefit big entities and there is nothing personal about it [28]. The 'cloud' is an extremely technical term. The 'cloud', thanks in part to its name, is extremely marketable; therefore, it was only a matter of time before a cloud existed for everyone to utilise [5]. The cloud in this sense is personal: a personal cloud, for anyone to use. In general, there are two main types of personal cloud technologies out there: public and private. Public cloud systems such as Box, Dropbox, Google Drive, iCloud, etc. are public because it is free and widely available to use. All anyone would need is an internet-accessible device and a connection. Public also means that my data is beside your data [5]. A private personal cloud however is different when we have companies such as Younity that will create a personal and private cloud service for anyone that is willing to pay. This cloud, built using the users' own software and hardware, is the users' and the users' alone [5]. This dramatically reduces the risk involved in using a personal cloud. This service is without doubt the most secure way of moving to the cloud. This is the future, and the only reason people seem to be slow to move towards the cloud is that they have so much data which is spread across so many devices. According to Gartner in 2013, the average household contained 1 terabyte of data, and Gartner also suggests that this figure will rise to 3.3 terabytes by 2016 [5].

7.3 Privacy and Security

Rajat Bhargava, co-founder of JumpCloud has stated that, "There's no more debate. When you don't own the network, it's open to the rest of the world, and you don't control the layers of the stack, the cloud – by definition – is more insecure than storing data on premises" [25]. By 2017, it is estimated that the amount of cloud IP traffic will be up to 443 exabytes per month; this figure will have risen from 98 exabytes a month 5 years previous [20]. Cloud security is growing and is now an industry on its own, there to protect what privacy we have left. In the past year, we have seen a large amount of hacks on various high-profile individual's cloud accounts. This makes cloud security and more locally personal cloud security more poignant and important than ever. What is the best way for users to protect their data, to stop pictures leaking to the web? There are a few steps that a user can take to secure their cloud accounts as best as possible: data encryption, securing their machines and securing their network is just a few [20]. There are many methods to secure your network. Vigilance is key when browsing the web. If you feel that a website is unsafe, then the best approach to take would be to stay well away from it. Never access a banking or high-risk site from a public network where a hacker could retrieve some very important details. With some of these practices, the user can reduce their chance of account violation. New security concerns seem to appear every week, if not more often. We need to question why we would want to keep all our data online, in the same place, where anyone with the means and motive could try to harvest some of our most personal details. Take iCloud, for example, and the recent security breaches.

Security practices are ever evolving and now after the most recent batch iCloud hacks there is no doubt that Apple will be concentrating a great deal of their resources on ensuring that no more iCloud accounts are hacked in the future [11]. The one benefit about these extremely high-profile hacks is that cloud companies will not want this to happen to them and hoping not to be at the forefront of another international scandal. What can the public learn from what Apple claims are 'very targeted attack on user names, passwords and security questions, a practice that has become all too common on the Internet [13]. None of the cases we have investigated has resulted from any breach in any of Apple's systems including iCloud or Find my iPhone.' [13]. This has happened before and will no doubt happen in the future. The reputation of iCloud and other mobile cloud services has been blemished before, and they are no stranger to attacks like this. It was first thought that this attack was what was known as a brute-force attack, where a hacker or a group has forcefully gained access to these peoples' accounts through repeatedly attacking the Find My iPhone app to try and get the password using two separate 'dictionary' files to crack the passwords of the users' accounts. This was an error in the application as it would not lock the user out for failing to provide the right answer a number of times [13]. Apple denied this, and it is now thought that the hacker(s) used 'phishing' emails to gain entry or by using personal information to guess the password on the account [13]. There is very little that could have been done to prevent this although the affected users' account passwords may have been quite weak and a strong password always leads to stronger security [13].

A public cloud service stores all the data they are given, yours, mine, ours, in the same location. This puts an enormous target on the back of these service providers, a gold mine of information that is just a security breach away. There are methods that can be taken to try prevent any breaches on these sites. Although total security is a thing of the past, or future, these methods can help reduce the risk of your files being breached. Client-side encryption, for example, is something that all consumers should think about although very few do [5].

7.4 The Data Protection Act and Cloud Computing

In the past, a user may have used software installed locally on their computing devices. If the client machine processed the data, and stored the data locally on their machine, then this data may not have been retained remotely. However, a paradigm shift in computing has seen data processing and storage moved online to the cloud, with only a thin client application installed on the user's device [17]. The growth in usage of mobile device has seen an increased usage of application installing thin client application on the user's device and the user's data being stored and processed remotely on the cloud [16]. These thin client applications may be collecting and processing user information. However, it may not be clear to the user how their information is being used and how much of their data is being collected and stored by the data controller. There are a number of key aspects in the Data Protection Act. For the purpose of this chapter, the focus will be on those of the data controller and also the data processor.

A data controller is considered the individual or company who controls and is responsible for the storing and controlling of user's personal information. The data controller is legally responsible; therefore, it needs to be clear if the party storing or using the data is the data controller as the responsibilities for data protection will fall with that individual or company [8]. A data controller stores personal information about a person, controls which data is stored, controls how the data is stored and controls how the data is used. All data controllers must comply with certain rules about how they collect and use personal information.

Ultimately, the data controller should ensure that data is obtained and processed lawfully and fairly; data is only stored for a specific purpose; data is only processed as initially defined; data is stored safely and securely; data is accurate and up to date; that it is adequate, relevant and not excessive; and data is not retained longer than is necessary and a copy of the users' data can be provided to them on request.

If an individual or company holds or processes user data on behalf of another party, then the other party is the data controller, and individually or company holding or processing the data is a data processor [8]. A data processor may maintain or process user's personal data, but does not exercise responsibility or control over the personal data. In contrast to data controllers, data processors have a limited set of responsibilities under the Data Protection Act. A data processor should only process data under the instructions of the data controller. The data processor should ensure the data is stored securely and must ensure that it complies with the contract defined by the data controller and does not process and/or share the data in any way that is not defined by the data controller [9].

Twenty-six privacy enforcement authorities participated in the second Global Privacy Enforcement Network Privacy Sweep. The Sweep had identified mobile apps as a key area of focus in light of the privacy implications for consumers [10]. In total, 1,211 apps across a number of platforms and categories were examined. Approximately one-third of the apps (31%) were considered to be requested access to data that was not related to the purpose of their functionality; this was according to the sweepers' understanding of the app and the associated privacy policy. Three-quarters of all apps examined requested access to potential sensitive data with little transparency to what purpose the data was collected and how the apps would use the data [10]. The results of the mobile application sweep offer some insight into the types of information companies are seeking and the extent to which organisations are informing consumers about their privacy practices. The sweep suggested that more information may have to be collected that is required.

It could be suggested that the mobile application was collecting information to improve the user's experience that may not have been apparent during the investigator carrying out the sweep. However, as per the Data Protection Act, the data controller should only collect information that is required. It could be suggested that the Data Protection Act provides a set of rules that may help protect and ensure the user data is managed correctly by the data controller. However, if the data controller does not adhere to these rules or provide transparency, then it is difficult to determine if the user's data is being stored safely and not being misused. In the case where an investigation was carried out on a number of mobile applications, it was suggested that a number of them were collecting information that was not related to their main purpose or there was no clarification to why and how the data was being used. As defined in the Data Protection Act, a data controller most only collects pertinent data and indicates their intention for collecting it. As a result, it could be suggested that any application not adhering to this is not protecting the user's data correctly. In summation, the Data Protection Act may define rules for handling user data, but due to the changes in how users are disclosing their information to online and cloud services, then a new set of rules may be required to manage these type of data controllers, otherwise, it may be difficult to ensure user data is protected.

7.5 The Future

At the keynote at the NetEvents EMEA Press & Service Provider Summit in Portugal, Tom Homer, Telstra's Head of EMEA and the Americas, Global Enterprise & Services, stated that in the future, employees will be able to bring their own 'cloud' to their respective jobs with them. This is a major development for the technology. This would lead one to believe that before long, cloud computing's influence would lead to the workplace of the future no longer being a physical location; that wherever the employee is, that is their office. This in effect will significantly reduce the daily operating costs for any company. If this really is the future, which many think it, then many personal cloud service providers will be overjoyed. This will mean a great surge in business for companies like Box which Homer says Telstra has invested in with his predictions in mind. According to Homer, 'We are responding to the evolution of cloud technologies right now and recognise that computer power is required in many different forms.' [15]

There is a new wave coming called *anything as a service* (XaaS). This poses new risks that will need to be addressed. XaaS companies provide the consumer with integrated features of cloud-based data, infrastructure, software and platforms [2]. Using the cloud so extensively is putting so much faith in a company which you physically cannot see. Trust is most important in these business partnerships. Trust that a business will not regret putting so much faith in one service provider. Although, it has to be said, using a XaaS provider also minimises the risk involved with cloud computing as all of the security needs are going to be dealt with by one product provider whereas with multiple providers it may be difficult to customise the security to the company's needs [2]. The emergence of these XaaS providers will shape cloud computing in the near future.

7.6 Conclusion

Aside from the security considerations that are inherent in all internet-based activities, the cloud model of computing has its own specific concerns. The multilayered architecture, combined with different modes of deployment, produces numerous specific security issues that continue to affect both the reputation and pervasiveness of the model [3]. The security and integrity of the underlying infrastructure that permits the cloud model of computing have been the subject of much research and are still very much an open topic for both consumers and providers. From the work of Behl and Behl [3] and Keshavarzi et al. [21], it is possible to identify and address three major concerns related to the infrastructure of the cloud. The nature of the cloud model means that not only are the data and applications of users stored and accessed remotely, the responsibility for controlling access and keeping these assets secure has also been devolved. To ensure trust in this system, a water-tight understanding between consumers and service providers must exist that addresses the authorisation, authentication and auditing of individuals interacting with the system [22]. The shared computing paradigm that underpins cloud computing evidently involves multiple users accessing the same infrastructure, both virtualised and physical. This, coupled with the characteristic of rapid elasticity, implies that it is possible, even likely, that resources acquired for the use of one tenant were recently under the control of another. For this situation to be considered safe, there must exist some mechanism that ensures that data remains isolated and cannot be recovered either by direct methods or inference.

A significant portion of the technology that supports and enables the cloud model of computing was not initially intended for that purpose. Many of the physical components (CPUs, GPUs, etc.) were not designed for a multi-tenant architecture and as such may lack the isolation properties required for the model to be secure [34]. The relative infancy of the cloud model can also lead to software-based vulnerabilities. Poorly designed APIs and user interfaces can lead to possible exposures that not only affect the user involved but may impact other organisations using the same cloud provider [21], massively increasing the potential attack surface for anyone with malicious intent. The cloud security alliance identifies cloud abuse as one of the nine critical threats for cloud security. This report also outlined the daunting scenario of the cloud being used to essentially attack itself, through distributed encryption key cracking or massive DDos attacks. [34]. Considerable research has been conducted into ways of mitigating these concerns [3, 22]. The author believes that the combined approach of a bespoke, systematic risk assessment such as described by Djemame et al. [12] coupled with detailed service level agreements negotiated between provider and consumer can at least ensure that security expectations from both parties are consistent and achievable. This can, and should, be enhanced by adopting a structured testing framework similar to the process developed by Iyler and Easwar [18] to ensure that assurances are met and undertakings are being adhered to. While it is ultimately unlikely that the threat of infrastructure intrusion will never disappear, collaboration from everyone involved can significantly reduce the potential and increase stakeholder confidence in the integrity of the cloud model.

The structure and characteristics of the cloud computing model intrinsically suggest many potential data protection issues. The distributed nature of the model increases data mobility and raises concerns over where data is stored. It can often be difficult for consumers to find out where exactly their data is being housed and if suitable measures are in place to protect that data. Storage locality may also have serious legal implications as data protection and compliance regulations often vary between countries and jurisdictions [30]. The research of Chen and Hong [7] outlined how the cloud model requires specific security considerations at every stage in the data life cycle. Data is not only being shared, stored and archived in the cloud but also increasingly generated and destroyed. The privacy and integrity of this data, and any associated metadata, must be assured if confidence in the cloud model is to grow. Assuring the integrity of data is a major open question within the cloud community. Traditional methods of integrity verification are not suitable for data stored remotely as it would require significant data transfer and associated costs. The ACID framework conventionally used to aid data integrity is becoming increasingly irrelevant in the modern world of Big Data and NoSQL. The work of Sugumaran et al. [31] and Behl and Behl offers practical solutions to many of these issues, but significant further research and discussion are required if a unilateral approach is ever to be agreed.

The advocates of cloud computing are consistently the darlings of the media offering an ever-growing array of sound bites and evangelical predictions on where this journey will take us all. Many of these claims may transpire to be correct, but the initial impulse to migrate one's business interests to the cloud should be tempered by a thorough audit of expectations and a realistic assessment of what the technology has to offer. Cloud computing, like every innovation, has its benefits and its limitations. The commercial and economic factors outlined above make it likely that an increasing number of small-to-medium businesses will indeed be tempted to deploy their IT concerns onto the cloud. If the security and data protection concerns described previously are to be eradicated, further research is needed to identify the security requirements of stakeholders at every level.

7.7 Review Questions

1. Why is privacy such a major concern when referring to the cloud?
2. What are the five essential characteristics and three service models of the cloud?
3. What comprises the three-layered model for service provision in the cloud?
4. What are the key differences between public, private, hybrid and community clouds?
5. How important is the Data Protection Act when it comes to cloud computing?

References

1. Amazon Web Services (2013) Amazon Elastic Compute Cloud (Amazon EC2). http://aws.amazon.com/ec2/
2. Balaciart D (2014) What The Future Of Cloud Computing Will Bring | clouderPC. clouderPC, Trivandrum, India. Available at: http://www.clouderpc.com/the-future-of-cloud-computing-includes-combining-all-services-together/#.VD67AGewIiY
3. Behl A, Behl K (2012, Oct. 30 2012–Nov. 2 2012) An analysis of cloud computing security issues. Paper presented at the Information and Communication Technologies (WICT), 2012 World Congress on
4. Borrill S (2014) Telstra Keynote Urges CIOs to Master the Art of Shaping Cloud ServicesT-elecomsTalk. Telecomstalk.com. Available at: http://www.telecomstalk.com/?p=3823
5. Caso, E. (2014). *The Rise of the Personal Cloud | WIRED*. [online] WIRED. Available at: http://www.wired.com/2014/01/rise-personal-cloud/
6. Cisco (2014) Cisco visual networking index: global mobile data traffic forecast update, 2013–2018. Available: http://www.cisco.com/c/en/us/solutions/collateral/service-provider/visual-networking-index-vni/white_paper_c11-520862.pdf
7. Chen D, Hong Z (2012, 23–25 March 2012) Data security and privacy protection issues in cloud computing. Paper presented at the Computer Science and Electronics Engineering (ICCSEE), 2012 International Conference on, Hangzhou, China
8. Data Protection Commissioner (2005) Are you a data controller? Available: http://www.dataprotection.ie/docs/Are-you-a-Data-Controller-/43.htm
9. Data Protection Commissioner (2010) Data security guidance. http://www.dataprotection.ie/viewdoc.asp?DocID=1091
10. Data Protection Commissioner (2014) Global privacy sweep raises concerns about mobile apps. Available: http://www.dataprotection.ie/viewdoc.asp?Docid=1456&Catid=66&StartDate=01+January+2014&m=
11. Dinadayalan P, Jegadeeswari S, Gnanambigai D (2014, Feb. 27 2014–March 1 2014) Data security issues in cloud environment and solutions. Paper presented at the Computing and Communication Technologies (WCCCT), 2014 World Congress on, Tiruchirappalli, India
12. Djemame K, Armstrong D, Guitart J, Macias M (2014) A risk assessment framework for cloud computing. Cloud Computing, IEEE Transactions on, PP(99), 1–1
13. Gallagher S (2014) Update: what Jennifer Lawrence can teach you about cloud security. Ars Technica, Boston. http://arstechnica.com/security/2014/09/what-jennifer-lawrence-can-teach-you-about-cloud-security/
14. Grance T, Mell P (2011) The NIST definition of cloud computing. National Institute for Standards and Technology, Gaithersburg, Tamil Nadu, India
15. Homer T (2014) 2020 vision for cloud services to the enterprise what service should the enterprise expect and demand by 2020?, 1st edn. [ebook] EMEA, Quinta do Lago

16. ICS (2015) ICS predicts data protection will be a hot topic in 2015. http://www.ics.ie/news/view/1341
17. Intel (2015) Intel's vision of the ongoing shift to cloud computing. Available: http://www.intel.ie/content/dam/www/public/us/en/documents/white-papers/cloud-computing-intel-cloud-2015-vision.pdf
18. Iyler K, Easwar D (2013) Cloud computing and modelling of cash flows. In: International conference on business analytics, Lisbon, Portugal, 18–21 January 2013, pp 34–42
19. Jadeja Y, Modi K (2012, 21–22 March 2012) Cloud computing – concepts, architecture and challenges. Paper presented at the Computing, Electronics and Electrical Technologies (ICCEET), 2012 International Conference on
20. Kelyman B (2014) How I secure my personal cloud. Dark Reading. Available at: http://www.darkreading.com/cloud-security/how-i-secure-my-personal-cloud/d/d-id/1113941
21. Keshavarzi A, Haghighat AT, Bohlouli M (2013, 12–14 Sept. 2013) Research challenges and prospective business impacts of cloud computing: a survey. Paper presented at the Intelligent Data Acquisition and Advanced Computing Systems (IDAACS), 2013 IEEE 7th International Conference on, Berlin, Germany
22. Kulkarni G, Chavan N, Chandorkar R, Waghmare R, Palwe R (2012) Cloud security challenges. Paper presented at the Telecommunication Systems, Services, and Applications (TSSA), 2012 7th international conference on, New York, 30–31 Oct 2012
23. McKendrick J (2013) 10 quotes on cloud computing that really say it all. http://www.forbes.com/sites/joemckendrick/2013/03/24/10-quotes-on-cloud-computing-that-really-say-it-all/, 29th September 2013, Chicago
24. NIST Cloud Computing Standards Roadmap (2011) 1st ed. [ebook] The US Department of Commerce. Available at: http://www.nist.gov/itl/cloud/upload/NIST_SP-500-291_Version-2_2013_June18_FINAL.pdf
25. Perlroth N (2014) Security needs evolve as computing leaves the office. [online] Bits Blog. Available at: http://bits.blogs.nytimes.com/2014/06/11/security-needs-evolve-as-computing-leaves-the-office/
26. Rai A, Sharma S (2013) Privacy issues regarding personal data in cloud computing, 1st edn. International Journal of Advanced Research in Computer Science, New York, USA
27. Robinson N (2011) The cloud, 1st edn. Rand, Santa Monica
28. Searls D (2013) Bringing "Personal cloud" to market. Harvard Blog. https://blogs.law.harvard.edu/doc/2013/05/04/how-marketable-will-personal-cloud-be/
29. Shetty S (2013) Gartner says cloud computing will become the bulk of new IT spend by 2016. Analysts examine cloud strategies and adoption at gartner symposium
30. Subashini S, Kavitha V (2011) A survey on security issues in service delivery models of cloud computing. J Netw Comput Appl 34(1):1–11
31. Sugumaran M, Murugan BB, Kamalraj D (2014) An architecture for data security in cloud computing, computing and communication technologies (WCCCT), 2014 World Congress on, Delhi, India, 27 February 2014–1 March 2014, pp 252–255. doi:10.1109/WCCCT.2014.53
32. Tomonari K, Yukio E (2010) Achieving a "Personal Cloud" environment, 1st edn. NEC Technical Journal
33. Varia J, Mathew S (2013) Overview of amazon web services. Available: http://media.amazonwebservices.com/AWS_Overview.pdf
34. Walker K (2013) The Notorious Nine: cloud computing top threats in 2013. www.cloudsecurityalliance.org/topthreats. Cloud Security Alliance, London, UK

Nigel McKelvey MSc, BSc, PGCE, MIEEE, MICS is a lecturer at the Letterkenny Institute of Technology within the Computing Department specialising in secure programming, performance based programming as well as legal studies and ethics. Nigel is currently pursuing a Doctorate in Education looking at the holistic and heuristic programming techniques adopted by CoderDojos. Nigel has chaired and co-chaired multiple events aimed at promoting technology and programming and both primary and post-primary level.

Kevin Curran BSc (Hons), PhD, SMIEEE is a Reader in Computer Science and group leader for the Ambient Intelligence Research Group at the University of Ulster. Dr Curran has made significant contributions to advancing the knowledge of computing evidenced by over 800 publications. He is a regular contributor to BBC radio & TV news in the UK and quoted in trade and consumer IT magazines on a regular basis.

Benny Gordon recently graduated with a 2.1 Honours Bachelor of Science Degree in Applied Computing. Benny is currently employed as a Software Developer at Gartan Technologies in Letterkenny, Co. Donegal, Ireland. Benny has a keen interest in Cloud Computing and in the development of mobile first software in a wide variety of environments.

Edward Devlin has recently graduated with a first class Honours degree in Applied computing from Letterkenny IT. He is presently applying the skills he acquired as an applications developer for the logistics department of General Motors and is currently based in Limerick. John is most comfortable when coding in Java but is happy to work in almost any environment. He is a recent convert to agile development practices and tries to spread the good word at every opportunity. The little time he spends away from the keyboard is enjoyed playing darts and reading detective novels.

Kenneth Johnston is a graduate of LYIT, he has 8 years experience in industry software development. He is well travelled and enjoys learning new skills, mostly in technology. Currently, he is starting the journey of using JavaScript for both server side and front-end web development.

Part II

Application and Approaches

Security Certification for the Cloud: The CUMULUS Approach

8

Marco Anisetti, Claudio A. Ardagna, Ernesto Damiani, Antonio Maña, George Spanoudakis, Luca Pino, and Hristo Koshutanski

Abstract

This chapter presents a certification-based assurance solution for the cloud, which has been developed as part of the FP7 EU Project CUMULUS. It provides an overview of the CUMULUS certification models, which are at the basis of the certification processes implemented and managed by the CUMULUS certification framework. Certification models drive the collection of evidence used by the framework to assess whether the system under certification supports required security properties, and generate and manage certificates proving compliance to such properties (certification process). Collected evidence can be of different types (i.e., test-based, monitoring-based, and trusted computing-based evidence) and addresses the peculiarities of cloud environments. The framework also supports continuous and incremental evaluation of services in the production cloud.

Keywords

Assurance • Certification • Cloud • Security

M. Anisetti (✉) • C.A. Ardagna • E. Damiani
DI – Università degli Studi di Milano, Milano, Italy
e-mail: Marco.Anisetti@unimi.it; ClaudioA.Ardagna@unimi.it; Ernesto.Damiani@unimi.it

A. Maña • H. Koshutanski
University of Malaga, Malaga, Spain
e-mail: amg@lcc.uma.es; hristo@lcc.uma.es

G. Spanoudakis • L. Pino
City University of London, London, UK
e-mail: G.E.Spanoudakis@city.ac.uk; Luca.Pino.2@city.ac.uk

S.Y. Zhu et al. (eds.), *Guide to Security Assurance for Cloud Computing*,
Computer Communications and Networks, DOI 10.1007/978-3-319-25988-8_8

8.1 Introduction

The cloud computing paradigm supports the provision of infrastructure, platform, and software services without incurring the considerable costs and overheads of managing the computational infrastructure required for this purpose. Despite all its benefits, cloud technology still raises concerns regarding the security, privacy, governance, and compliance of the data and software services offered through it. Such concerns arise from the difficulty to prove security properties of cloud services. In this context, both service providers and cloud users are reluctant to move their service and data to the cloud and take full responsibility of their security. This creates a trust deficit that, in the past especially for software systems, has been filled through auditing and inspection schemes, as those based on ISO/IEC 27002 and Common Criteria. These schemes, however, do not fit cloud requirements, since they are manual, cost/time consuming, do not consider the continuum of service provision, and their evaluation is invalidated by dynamic changes in the infrastructure beneath cloud services.

To address the above needs, CUMULUS (http://cumulus-project.eu), an R&D project funded by the EU, has developed a certification framework, which continuously and incrementally collects evidence on the security of services deployed on cloud infrastructures. This evidence is collected by means of testing and monitoring techniques, as well as trusted platform modules, and is used to assess security properties of cloud services in certificates. The working of the CUMULUS framework is driven by certification models, which have a twofold role: (i) they describe the evidence collection process at the basis of service security property assessment and certificate release, and (ii) they specify how to manage certificate life cycle throughout service evolution. The proposed framework can be used by certification authorities and/or cloud service providers to certify cloud services according to different security properties and types of evidence and by cloud users to verify service certificates and increase their trust in the cloud.

The remaining of this chapter is organized as follows. Section 8.2 describes the overall CUMULUS certification process from certification model definition to their execution and the generation of corresponding certificates. Section 8.3 presents basic certification models. Section 8.4 illustrates advanced certification models. Section 8.5 presents the trust model at the basis of the certification processes and the certificates that may be generated by it using the CUMULUS infrastructure. Finally, Sect. 8.6 discusses related work, and Sect. 8.7 gives some concluding remarks.

8.2 Certification Process and Framework Architecture

According to [1], a certification process receives as input the Target of Certification (ToC), describing the system under certification, the security property p to be certified, and all the evaluation activities to be carried out on the ToC, and returns as output a certificate including the evidence describing the evaluation activities. The certification process is composed of two consecutive phases, each one described in machine-readable document.

- **Certification methodology specification**: the certification authority defines a set of mandatory evaluation activities to be executed on a generic class of ToC to certify a given property. It is defined as a declarative model called Certification Model (CM) Template – CMT – and is signed by the certification authority. It represents the basis for establishing a chain of trust grounded on the correctness of the methodology defined by the certification authority.
- **Certification process specification**: the CUMULUS-accredited lab together with the service provider instantiates the methodology described in a CMT on a specific ToC to evaluate the corresponding property. It is defined as a procedural model called Certification Model (CM) Instance – CMI, without direct involvement of the certification authority. It can be directly executed by the CUMULUS certification framework.

Certification models are complex documents specifying all activities of a certification process. For the sake of simplicity, in this chapter, we consider simplified CMs defined as the models driving the collection of generic evidence (see Sect. 8.2.1).

8.2.1 CM Instance and CM Template

CM Template and CM Instance are machine-readable documents associated with a pair (p, ToC) and both represent the execution flows (i.e., a path in the CM) of a ToC as the concatenation of mechanisms deployed at different layers of the cloud stack. Although they share a similar structure, they have some fundamental differences. CMT defines generic execution flows as a sequence of vertices with abstract function calls and mechanism annotations, while CMI defines real execution flows that refer to a concrete ToC, with real function calls and mechanisms. Also, the trust in CMT is given by the trust in the signature of the certification authority, while the trust in CMI inherits from a correct instantiation of the corresponding CMT [2].

Practically, CMT and CMI are defined as direct acyclic graphs, where each vertex refers to a mechanism type and models its execution, and each edge is annotated with the function call to the mechanism represented by the vertex. We note that each function call annotating an edge triggers a state transition and corresponding mechanism execution. Each vertex also includes (i) the description of the mechanism (i.e., the minimum required mechanism in CMT and the implemented mechanism in CMI), (ii) its deployment layer (i.e., service, platform, or infrastructure layer), (iii) a set of events affecting its execution, and (iv) activities to be executed to evaluate its correct behavior.

The correct instantiation of a CMT in a CMI is verified according to a *consistency check* function composed of three steps: *CM Instance Reduction*, *Graph Matching*,

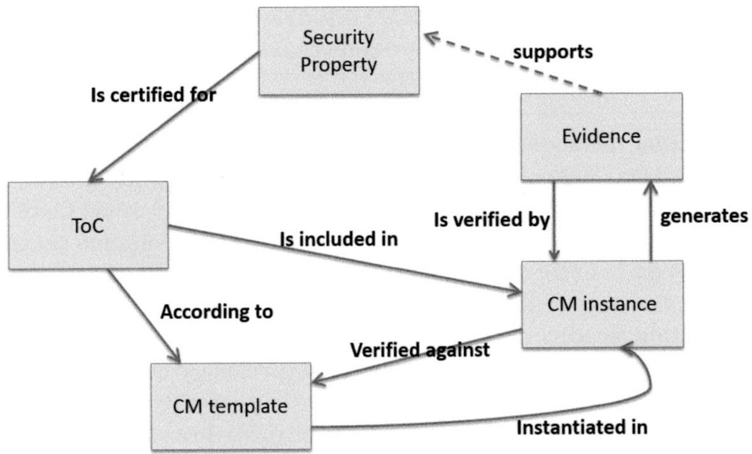

Fig. 8.1 Conceptual framework

and *Annotation Matching*. *CM Instance Reduction* includes all preparatory activities needed to compare CMT and CMI. *Graph Matching* checks whether CMI graph is a proper instantiation of the CMT graph, meaning that the two graphs are isomorphic, that is, they have the same vertices and edges, and corresponding vertices have the same type. *Annotation Matching* traverses CMI and CMT graphs using breadth-first search and, for each pair of vertices, verifies whether: (i) the implemented mechanism in CMI is at least as strong as the required mechanism in CMT, (ii) information associated with each pair of corresponding vertices in CMI and CMT must be such that the cloud layer is the same, and the events and the activities in the CMT are a subset of the events and the activities in the CMI. More details on the consistency check function can be found in [1]. We say that CMI is consistent with CMT (denoted CMI$\triangleright$CMT) according to the above three steps.

8.2.2 Certification Process

Figure 8.1 shows the conceptual framework of our certification process, as an extension of the one in [2]. The certification of the ToC for a given security property starts upon the definition of a CM Instance that is generated as a specialization of a given CM Template and continuously verified against it using the *Consistency Check* (see Sect. 8.2.1). The evidence is continuously collected and analyzed by executing the CM Instance, to verify support (dashed arrow in Fig. 8.1) for the property to be certified. The evidence, in fact, could be insufficient to prove a given security property and thus to award the corresponding certificate. The continuous check of consistency between CMI and CMT and incremental evidence collection introduce two loops in the framework, which are at the basis of the advanced certification models in Sect. 8.4 and the trust model in Sect. 8.5.

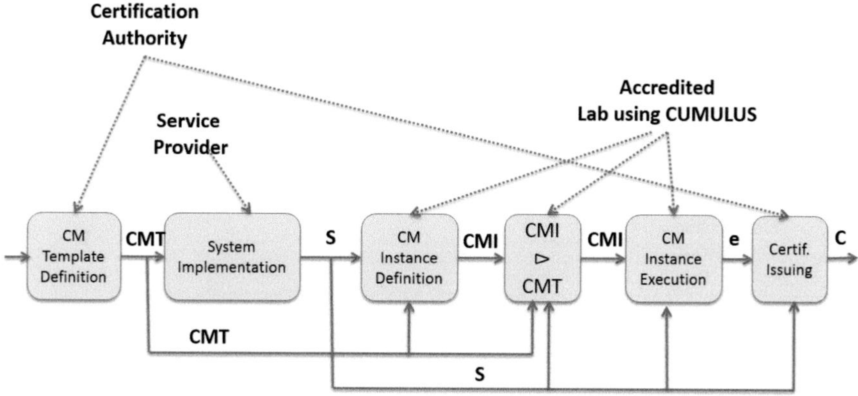

Fig. 8.2 Certification process

Based on this conceptual framework, we define the certification process in Fig. 8.2 that works as follows. First of all, independently from the certification of any specific systems, certification authorities define their CM templates for different pairs (p, ToC). Then, a service provider aiming to implement a certified cloud-based system selects a specific CMT, implements the system, and defines the CMI according to the selected CMT and implemented system. The CUMULUS-accredited lab then evaluates the consistency between CMI and CMT (CMI $\triangleright$ CMT) and, if consistent, executes CMI and collects the evidence using the functionalities offered by the CUMULUS framework (see Sect. 8.2.3). Finally, the certification authority adopting the CUMULUS framework evaluates the evidence collected and, if sufficient, releases a certificate C.

8.2.3 Architecture

Figure 8.3 shows an integrated view of the CUMULUS framework architecture [3] and its multi-layer certification assurance [4]. The architecture consists of internal components processing CUMULUS certification models, remote components residing on cloud platforms with services and applications part of the target of certification, and APIs and dashboard GUI offering retrieval and management functionality to various types of actors interacting with the framework.

Topmost part of Fig. 8.3 shows the different actors interacting with the framework. Certification authorities and accredited labs access framework's functionality for management of certification models (storage, retrieval, update, deletion) and execution of certification processes for given CMIs. Cloud service providers access framework's functionality for retrieval of certificates and CMIs issued for providers' services. The third category of actors are cloud service and application developers. This category of users interact with the framework due to their needs of consuming cloud services and resources within their applications, subject of development, in

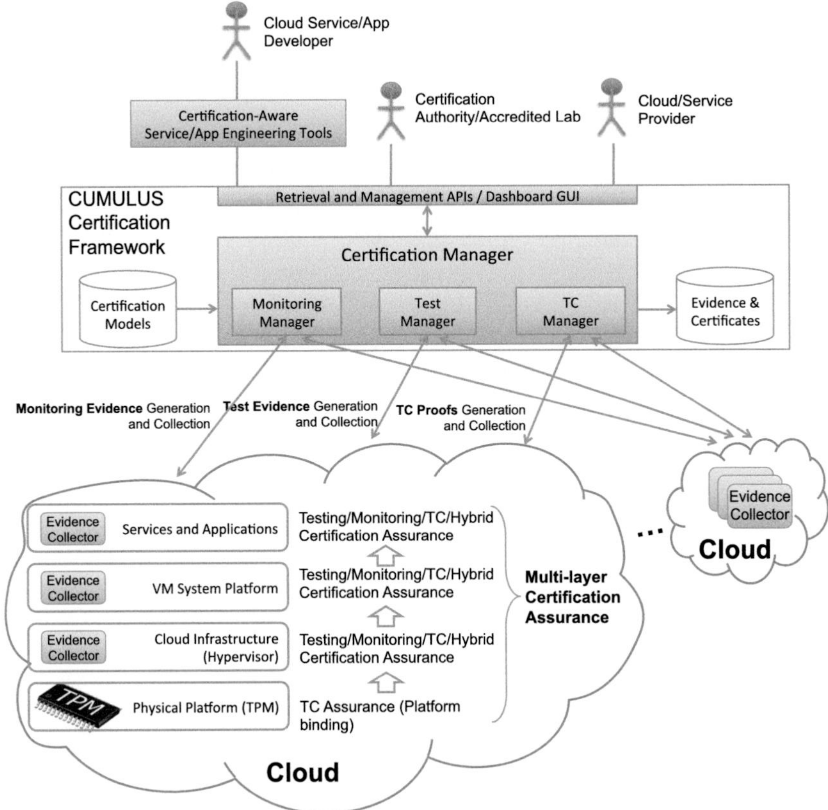

Fig. 8.3 CUMULUS certification framework architecture

order to obtain required security assurance about the security aspects and properties of those cloud resources. The central certification artifacts for this last category of actors are the certificates issued by the framework. In that direction, the CUMULUS framework provides an engineering process and toolkit for cloud application developers to facilitate certification-aware engineering of cloud applications [5]. A set of APIs and dashboard GUI are provided to enable access to the retrieval and management functionality of the framework for the different types of actors.

The central part of Fig. 8.3 shows the CUMULUS framework architecture. The main component of the framework in charge of execution of all certification processes is the Certification Manager. The CUMULUS framework triggers the execution of type-specific certification processes by submitting a CMI for execution through the framework management APIs or through the Dashboard. The framework calls the Certification Manager to handle the execution of the given CMI. The Certification Manager has three main sub-components – *Monitoring Manager*, *Test Manager*, and *TC Manager*. Each of these type-specific managers is responsible for the execution of the corresponding type-specific CMIs and for handling all related certification processes and sessions. In this way, the Certification Manager main role is to dispatch all certification requests coming from the framework actors to the corresponding type-specific certification managers and return the results of certification process executions back to the framework actors (e.g., through the dashboard).

Each type-specific certification manager implements (i) all necessary certification mechanisms and underlying certification processes and their execution, for the corresponding type-specific certification, and (ii) all interactions with the corresponding type-specific Evidence Collector. The evidence collector is a remote framework component residing on the cloud platform deploying the target of certification and is responsible for gathering type-specific evidence on the target of certification and its environment and reporting those to the corresponding type-specific certification manager. Three Evidence Collectors have been developed [6]: (i) Event Captor, gathering evidence for monitoring-based certification by capturing events on the ToC and its environment; (ii) Test Agent (TA), gathering evidence for test-based certification by executing test cases on the ToC and its environment; and (iii) TC Module, gathering evidence for TC-based certification by measuring integrity of ToC's software and its environment/platform using a Trusted Platform Module (TPM) [7].

The bottom part of Fig. 8.3 shows how CMIs relate to the different layers of the cloud computing model (SaaS/PaaS/IaaS) and provide multi-layer certification-based security assurance [4]. Depending on the ToC, its perimeter and the security property to be certified, hybrid and/or multi-layer certification models might be specified, which require the presence of different type-specific Evidence Collectors on the same or different layers of the cloud computing model to gather sufficient evidence and ensure the security property holds for the ToC. It might be also the case where a CMI requires type-specific certification on lower levels of cloud computing model in order to ensure the security property holds for the ToC.

8.3 Basic Certification Models

We first describe three basic certification models supported by CUMULUS, namely, test-based, monitoring-based, and trusted computing-based certification, and refer the reader to [8] for more details and examples. We have adopted a meta-model approach to express common elements across all CMIs. This approach ensures uniformity of high-level structural representation across different types of certification and simplifies processing of CMIs by CUMULUS infrastructure components. Each CMI includes the following main elements:

- *Security Property* defines a security property to be certified by a Certification Model. CUMULUS has defined an extensive catalog with security properties and vocabularies pertinent to cloud computing [9].

- *Target of Certification* (ToC) defines the perimeter of certification. The ToC identifies not only the instance of the service to be certified but also an instance of every cloud stack layer, including definitions of components, connections, interfaces, and the like. As a result, the ToC enables a consumer to determine whether the security property satisfies consumer's requirements, thanks to a detailed description of the certification perimeter.
- *Life Cycle* defines certificate evolution after a certificate is issued. In traditional certification, the life cycle is in the bailiwick of the Certification Authority issuing the certificate. It is executed statically looking at the produced evidence and evaluating the sufficiency conditions on the validity of the certificate (i.e., certificate issuing). Decisions like certification suspension, revocation, or expiration are normally taken asynchronously and offline by the Certification Authority, for instance, as a reaction to new discovered vulnerabilities. In a cloud scenario, where the certificate life cycle is managed at run time on the basis of evolving evidence, the static intervention of a Certification Authority is not always feasible, and high-level certificate life cycle automation is desired. The Life Cycle element defines a vocabulary of basic certificate states, such as Issued, Suspended, Revoked, and Expired, to simplify processing and comparison across life-cycle specification of different CMIs. However, for the sake of flexibility, an extended set of CM states can be defined.
- *Evidence Collection* defines entities such as *Evidence Collector*, *Evidence Aggregator*, and *Metrics/Conditions* which provide information about how evidence is collected and aggregated, how metrics are computed and compared to thresholds, and starting conditions for evidence collection activities.
- *Signature* element provides the signature of the certification framework that signed the CMI via delegation from the certification authority. The signature is necessary to establish a chain of trust grounded on the produced certificates.

In the following, we present how the above common elements have been defined in each type-specific CM.

8.3.1 Monitoring-Based Certification Models

The CUMULUS infrastructure can also be used to generate certificates based on the analysis of evidence gathered through the continuous monitoring of the operation of cloud services. To use it, in this capacity it is necessary to define a Monitoring-Based Certification Model (MBCM). An MBCM certification model specifies:

(i) The cloud service to be certified (i.e., the ToC)
(ii) The security property to be certified for ToC
(iii) The certification authority that will sign the certificates generated by the model
(iv) An assessment scheme that defines general conditions regarding the evidence that must be collected for being able to issue a certificate

(v) Additional validity tests regarding the configuration of the cloud provider that must be satisfied prior to issuing certificates
(vi) The configurations of the agents that will be used in order to collect the evidence required for generating certificates
(vii) The way in which the collected evidence will be aggregated in certificates (evidence aggregation)
(viii) A life cycle model that defines the overall process of issuing certificates

The three main elements of MBCMs, which are essential for specifying and executing MBCM, are (a) the security properties, (b) the evidence sufficiency conditions, and (c) the life cycle models. In the following, we overview each of these elements briefly.

Security property. The security property to be certified for ToC is specified by one monitoring rule and zero or more assumptions, expressed as follows:

$$\mathit{Security-property} ::= \mathit{MonitoringRule}\ [\text{“,”}\ \mathit{MonitoringAssumption}]*$$

$$\mathit{MonitoringRule} ::= [\mathit{precondition}]*\ \text{“}\Rightarrow\text{”}\ \mathit{postcondition}$$

$$\mathit{MonitoringAssumption} ::= [\mathit{precondition}]*\ \text{“}\Rightarrow\text{”}\ \mathit{postcondition}$$

Monitoring rules expressing conditions that must be satisfied during the monitoring of ToC and monitoring assumptions are assertions, which specify how to record and update state variables indicating the state of ToC during monitoring. The chunk of BNF grammar shown above is part of *EC-Assertion+*, i.e., a language for expressing monitoring conditions in the EVEREST monitoring system [10] that is used in CUMULUS. *EC-Assertion+* is based on Event Calculus [11].

To demonstrate the use of *EC-Assertion+* in specifying security properties, consider an example showing how it may be used to specify the monitoring of a security property requesting data integrity at rest. More specifically, let us assume that this property requires that any modification of data in the ToC that is carried out through an accepted request of a data update operation of ToC should be notified to required parties. This property can be expressed by the *EC-Assertion* by monitoring rule R1 listed below. The specification of this rule, as well as all models in the paper, assumes the following agents and variables denoting them: service consumers (*_sc*), target of certification (*_TOC*), authentication infrastructure (*_AI*), and certification authority (*_CA*).

Rule R1:
Happens*(e(_e1,_sc,_TOC,REQ,_updOp(_cred,_data,_auth),_TOC),t1,[t1,t1]) ^*
Happens*(e(_e2,_TOC,_AI,RES,_updOp(_cred,_data,_vCode),_TOC),*
t2,[t1,t1+d1]) ^ (_vCode ≠ Nil)
⇒ ***Happens****(e(_e3,_TOC,_A,REQ,_notifO(_cred,_data,_auth,_h),_TOC),*
t3,[t2,t2+d2])

According to R1 when a call of an update operation in a *_TOC* is detected at some time point *t1* (see event *Happens(e(_e1,_sc,_TOC,REQ,_updOp(_cred,_data,_auth), _TOC),t1,[t1,t1]))* and a response to this call occurs after it (see event *Happens(e(_e2, _TOC,_AI,RES,_updOp(_cred,_data,_verCode),_TOC),t2,[t1,t2+d1]))* indicating that the request has been granted (see condition *(_vCode* $\neq$ *Nil)* in the rule), the monitor should also check for the existence of another event showing the call of an operation in some authorization agent *_A* to notify the receipt and execution of the update request (see *Happens(e(_e3,_TOC,_CA,REQ,_notifO(_cred, _data,_auth,_h),_TOC),t3, [t2,t2+d2]))*.

Target of Certification and Assessment Scheme. The assessment scheme in an MBCM defines conditions regarding the sufficiency of evidence that must be collected in order to be able to issue a certificate. Evidence sufficiency conditions may be specified as: (a) the minimum period of monitoring ToC, (b) the minimum number of monitoring events, and/or (c) the representativeness of the monitoring events with respect to the expected behavior of ToC that should be seen by the monitor before a certificate can be issued. While the specification of (a) and (b) is straightforward, to enable checks of the representativeness of monitoring events, the certification model should include a specification of a model of the *expected behavior* of ToC. The expected behavior model for a ToC is expressed as a probabilistic state transition model, determining in which order the operations of ToC may be executed at each state in its operation and how likely each execution is.

In the case of the previous example of the integrity at rest property, an ETOCB model would determine at which stages in the operation of ToC the operation *_updOp(.)* could be executed and what would be the likelihood of it. The existence of an ETOCB model enables the CUMULUS infrastructure to check if a representative sample of the behavior of ToC has been considered before a certificate can be issued.

Life Cycle. The life cycle model (LCM) in a certification model defines the process by which certificates can be generated and managed. LCM is a compulsory element of a certification model as it enables a certification authority to specify with full precision the certification process, by defining the different states of certificates that can be generated by the certification model and which events should change it. During the operation of the CUMULUS framework, the LCM is used to monitor ongoing certification processes, determine the state at which they are (e.g., collecting monitoring evidence, check validity conditions prior to issuing a certificate), and, depending on it, update the state of the certificate that may be generated by the process.

The LCM is defined as a state transition model. An example of an LCM is shown in Fig. 8.4. The LCM in the figure has an initial state called Activated and the states *Insufficient Evidence*, *Pre-issued*, *Issued*, and *Revoked*. It also has two composite states: *Continuous Monitoring* and *Issuing*.

According to the model, after a certificate is activated, it moves to the *InsufficientEvidence* state, at which the monitoring evidence that is relevant to it starts getting

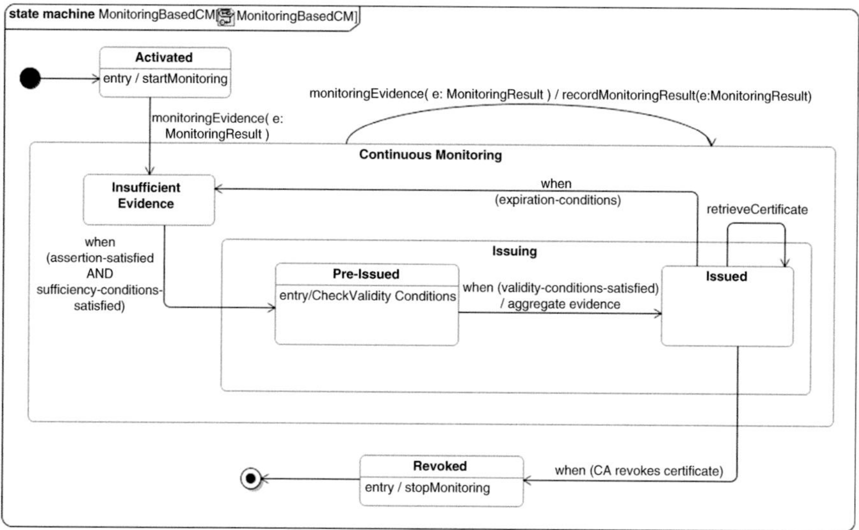

Fig. 8.4 UML diagram of life-cycle model

accumulated. When the accumulated evidence becomes sufficient according to the *EvidenceSufficiencyConditions* specified in the MBCM and there have been no violations of the monitoring rule that defines the security property (i.e., the security property of the MBCM is satisfied), the certificate moves to the state *Pre-issued.* At this state, the certification infrastructure will check if the extra validity conditions for the certificate type (if any) are satisfied, and, if they are, the certificate will move to the state *Issued.* In this state, any interested party with appropriate authority can retrieve the issued certificate from the CUMULUS infrastructure. While a certificate is at the *Issuing* state, monitoring continues and if a violation of the monitoring rule of the MBCM is detected, the certificate moves to the *Revoked* state at which it will no longer be valid and available. It should be noted, that for readability purposes, in Fig. 8.4, we have used condition labels that indicate the meaning of the relevant conditions. In the actual specification of LCM, however, conditions are declared by their unique XML level IDs, which enable condition elements to be retrieved and checked against the evidence database of the CUMULUS infrastructure. A more detailed account of monitoring-based certification models is available from [12, 13].

8.3.2 Test-Based Certification Models

The Test-Based Certification Model (TBCM) is a CM where the evidence is collected by means of testing activities. In the following, we present a detailed description of the TBCM peculiarities.

Security property. It is based on a common shared vocabulary [14–16] of abstract security properties like confidentiality, integrity, and availability, enriched with contextual attributes defining the certification scope. For instance, a test-based security property p=(*Authenticity*,{ctx=interface-level}) refers to property authenticticy (i.e., the abstract property) at ToC interface level (i.e., contextual property attribute).

***Target of Certification* (ToC).** It defines the perimeter of certification in terms of (security) mechanisms and deployment configurations, as well as the certificate binding in terms of cloud layers. For instance, let us consider security property p=(*Authenticity*, {ctx=interface-level/infrastructure-level}) for a ToC referring to a cloud service that provides functionalities to save users' data in a private folder of the file system. ToC includes two mechanisms mec_1 and mec_2 related to service layer and infrastructure layer, respectively, and its binding is defined at service layer. Mechanism mec_1 =(*authentication*, {algo=username-password, level=interface}) refers to a password-based authentication at interface level; mechanism mec_2 =(*authentication*, {algo=Linux authentication}) refers the Linux authentication mechanism at infrastructure level, that is, linux-based filesystem where the users' data are stored.

ToC includes also Targets of Test (ToTs) sub-element (the sub-element specifies the accessible APIs for testing the ToC) and the operative condition sub-elements.

- **Target of Test** (ToTs) is a set of smaller and more specific targets that compose the whole ToC. It provides general information on the type of interface (such as public interface, internal api, configuration file) and how to call it.
- **Operative condition** describes the operational conditions under which the ToC works and include all the necessary technical information (e.g., information on service vendor and release, installation constraints).

Security property p specifies the certification scope, while the ToC specifies certification perimeter in terms of involved mechanisms, their configurations, and requirements on their implementation.

Assessment scheme. The assessment scheme of TBCM defines how test-based evidence is collected and analyzed to prove properties supported by a given ToC. It is composed of the following elements.

- **Collectors**. It contains a set of sub-elements, called AbstractCollector and Collector, whose goal is to describe the test-based evidence collection process for a given property and ToC.
  - **AbstractCollector**. It describes testing activities in a generic form without the definition of the real test cases to be executed on the ToC but using the notions of test partitions [17]. It is aimed at defining a set of testing flows for specific test types (e.g., input partitioning, boundary values) and categories (e.g., functional, robustness, penetration). It is defined in CMT and inherited by CMI.

  - **Collector**. It is defined according to an element **AbstractCollector** and specifies the real test cases to be executed. **AbstractCollector** and **Collector** play a significative role in the process of instantiating a CMT into a CMI.
  - **Aggregator**. It describes how to collect the test outcomes and how the evidence must be aggregated. **Aggregator** is a sub-element of **AbstractCollector** and **Collector** elements. It also deals with criteria for interpreting test results in terms of sufficiency conditions and includes performance thresholds that are appropriately mapped on assurance levels.
- **Context**. It details the test agent (see Sect. 8.2.3) required for executing all test cases. Each test agent defines a specific deployment over a specific cloud or address test cases to an already deployed test agent.

Life cycle. It is modeled as a deterministic finite state automaton with each vertex representing a possible state of the certificate with label (e.g., issued, suspended, revoked, expired) and each edge representing a transition between two states. Each edge is labeled with a condition over certificate's evidence that regulates the transition. For instance, a transition from Issued state to Suspended state can be triggered by a condition saying that the amount of positive evidence in a certain period of time is going under a predefined threshold. Specifically in the case of test-based life cycle, the transitions are expressed as Boolean formulas in terms of aggregators.

Multi-layer certification. Test-based CM is natively multi-layer since it may refer to ToC having mechanisms at different layers. The testing architecture supports the definition and deployment of test agents suitable for every cloud layer.

8.3.3 TC-Based Certification Models

Trusted Computing-Based Certification Models (TCCMs) represent how a ToC, residing on a TC-enabled cloud platform, can be certified based on TC mechanisms, namely, the TPM [7] and the required hardware and software for that.

Security property. The security property supported by the CUMULUS TC certification is *software integrity* with subject of the property the software or application running on a cloud platform. Given the nature of TC, the trust chain for software integrity measurement and validation is bottom-up, starting with the trust on the TPM and physical platform hosting the TPM chip (i.e., the motherboard) and building up the chain by measuring and reporting the integrity of the firmware and software upper in a platform stack reaching the application layer on the top. In that case, integrity of applications (software) running on a platform (regardless if physical or virtual in case of cloud) is in *function* of the integrity state of the underlying platform. The security property supported by CUMULUS TC certification approach is called *software integrity bound to platform state*. We say

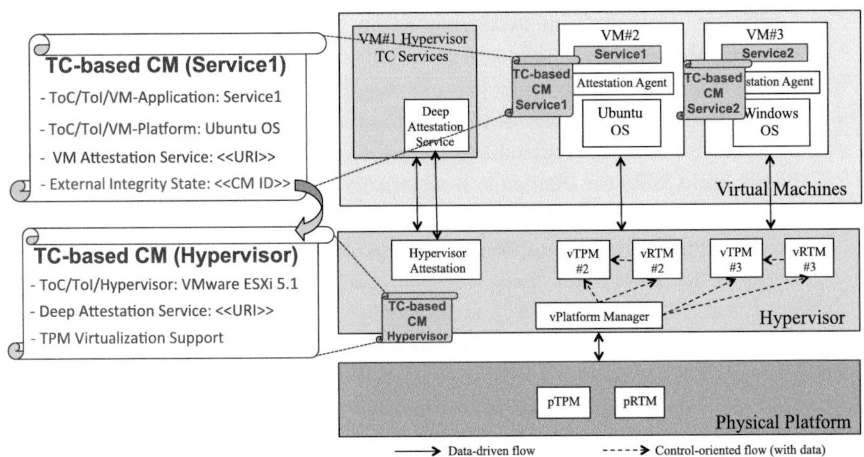

Fig. 8.5 TC-based multi-layer certification

"bound" because the software integrity is assured only for a given integrity state of the underlying platform.

Target of Certification and assessment scheme. The assessment scheme of TC-based certification is based on *remote attestation* of ToC integrity, a core functionality provided by trusted computing platforms [7]. A remote attestation process underpins any CUMULUS TC certification process, i.e., we perform attestation of ToC and its underling platform layers to certify integrity of a ToC. The outcome of such integrity attestation is a TC-based certificate. Correspondingly, an attestation process is also used to validate the ToC's TC-based certificate and determine if the current ToC's integrity state matches the one at the time the ToC was certified.

TC-based certification requires TPM virtualization on the corresponding Cloud platform [18]. Figure 8.5 shows the reference TC-aware cloud computing architecture and layers to be reflected by a TCCM:

- *Physical Platform Layer*. The bottom layer comprises the physical platform and associated to that physical hardware TPM (pTPM) and physical Root of Trust for Measurement (pRTM). The pRTM is responsible for measuring integrity of software (e.g., hypervisor) running on a physical platform and reports those measurements into pTPM's Platform Configuration Registers (PCRs).
- *Hypervisor Layer*. The software layer running on top of the physical (hardware) platform. Importantly, upon creation of a new VM, the hypervisor creates also an instance of a virtual TPM (vTPM) associated to that VM and triggers virtual RTM (vRTM), which in turn measures the first code execution of a VM and reports that to vTPM's PCRs. The hypervisor is in charge of creation and destruction of vTPM and vRTM instances for each VM. The vTPM component

is defined as hardware and/or software realization of the functionality described in the TPM specification [7]. The goal of the instantiated vRTM and vTPM is to make those appear the same as their physical equivalents (pRTM, pTPM).

- *Virtual Machine Layer*. The top layer of the cloud architecture where VMs reside. Each VM runs an attestation agent serving (remote) attestation requests from challengers by following a specific attestation protocol, the same as in the case of a non-virtualized platform. The attestation agent in a VM provides attestation evidence about the state of the VM, i.e., about the state of the VM's system platform and applications running on it by using the vTPM.

There is a dedicated service on the hypervisor layer, called *Deep Attestation Service*, used to create attestation evidence about the state of the hypervisor [18]. For instance, after an attestation of a VM has succeeded, a Remote Challenger might wish to attest the hypervisor below the VM to determine if it is trustworthy enough to not modify the VM behavior and attestation reporting. Because the hypervisor (the layer below VMs) might also be operating on top of a virtualized platform, the concept of iteratively attesting each individual lower virtualization layer in order to establish the trustworthiness of a VM (and applications running in the VM) is known as a "deep attestation." In that case, the remote challenger may need to repeatedly attest virtualization layers down until it reaches the bottom-most layer operating on top of a physical trusted platform (with pTPM).

An important aspect of a TCCM is the representation of the available TC support by the underlying to the ToC cloud infrastructure. In fact, such representation is crucial to allow the ToC integrity be properly measured and validated following the TC-specific bottom-up chain of trust (of integrity measurements). To do so, we defined a specific data structure as part of ToC definition, called *Target of Integrity* (ToI). The role of ToI is to represent all necessary information about the ToC and its underlying platform and cloud infrastructure layers down to a physical platform with a physical TPM.

Important and complementary artifacts to the ToI are the *Evidence Collector* and *Evidence Aggregator*. An Evidence Collector is defined per each layer of the ToI, and its role is to represent all necessary information about how software integrity of a given ToI layer is to be attested (collected). An Evidence Aggregator defines how to perform the complete ToI integrity attestation process starting *top-down* from the top-level application components of a ToI (located in a VM) down through all layers to a physical platform.

Life cycle. There are three main life cycle states defined for TC certificates – "Issued," "Expired," and "Revoked." The state "Issued" is defined by having evidence collection for ToC integrity and all layers down the cloud stack to the physical layer. The transition from state "Issued" to "Expired" is defined when the certificate is expired according to its time validity period. The transition from "Issued" to "Revoked" is defined by having a contradictory evidence either of ToC integrity or integrity states of any of the virtualization layers down the cloud stack.

Multi-layer certification. TC-based certification for SaaS-level services requires that a CA/Evaluation Lab must ensure not only the integrity state of all layers down the cloud stack but also must recognize that all virtualization layers down the stack provide correct TPM virtualization (e.g., according to TCG specification [18]). Given that a cloud provider may need to offer several thousands of VMs for customers' needs, it may become impractical to manage TCCMs if for each SaaS-level service requesting certification the CA/Evaluation lab has to explicitly recognize the hypervisor's state and its correct TPM virtualization. To address that issue, TC-based certification allows a CA/Evaluation lab to certify services at SaaS level without the need to recognize hypervisor integrity state supporting TPM virtualization but instead to express external integrity state condition to a TCCM certifying the hypervisor state. In that way, the CA/evaluation lab issuing a TCCM for a SaaS-level service does not need privileged access to the hypervisor layer but instead would only need to examine the TCCM of the hypervisor and indicate in the TCCM of the SaaS-level service an external integrity state dependence on the hypervisor's TCCM. In other words, multi-layer TC-based certification provides *layered assurance* for cloud services and platforms based on the assurance of the integrity states of lower layers of the cloud stack as provided by the relevant TC-based certification processes for those layers. Figure 8.5 illustrates the main aspects of TC-based multi-layer certification.

A TC-based certificate states the TC proofs (integrity evidence) of the ToC's software and all layers below. Given the multi-layer certification, upon certificate generation, the TC certification manager component (see Fig. 8.3) will first check if a certificate exists for the referenced hypervisor's TCCM and will then validate the hypervisor's certificate (i.e., whether the hypervisor integrity state still holds according to the certificate-stated evidence). If successful validation, the certification manager will generate the corresponding TC-based certificate for the SaaS-level service 1 and will include in the certificate an external integrity state condition pointing to the corresponding hypervisor's certificate. In that way, each time the TC-based certificate of service 1 is validated, the certification manager will first validate the corresponding hypervisor certificate to ensure the referenced hypervisor state holds.

8.4 Advanced Certification Models

CUMULUS provides advanced certification models to deal with (i) evidence of different nature supporting specific properties (Hybrid CM in Sect. 8.4.1), (ii) reuse of already issued certificates and processes (Compositional CM in Sect. 8.4.2), and (iii) certification process adaptation to changes reducing the need of unnecessary, time-consuming re-certification from scratch (Incremental CM in Sect. 8.4.3).

8.4.1 Hybrid Certification Models

Our discussion so far has covered different types of certification models that are supported by the CUMULUS framework. All these models have a common characteristic: they carry out assessments of security properties based on single types of evidence (e.g., testing or monitoring). In some cases, however, relying solely on such evidence is not sufficient. Considering the data integrity at rest property that was discussed in Sect. 8.3.1, for example, the assessment of the property through monitoring data updates executed via the update operations of ToC may be insufficient if there is a possibility of updating ToC data through other means (e.g., by modifying the files in which data are stored directly). To cope with such cases, the CUMULUS framework supports also *hybrid certification models*.

Hybrid certification models are used to define schemes for assessing the satisfaction of security properties by a ToC through the aggregation and cross-checking of different types of evidence, namely, testing and monitoring evidence. The combination of monitoring and testing evidence in a hybrid model can be carried out in two basic modes:

1. The *dependent mode* – In this mode, a security property is assessed for a ToC by a *primary assessment* (i.e., monitoring or testing), and depending on the outcome of it, the model may trigger a *subordinate assessment* in order to confirm and/or complete the evidence required for the assessment. In models of this mode, monitoring and testing may take the roles of primary and subordinate assessment, respectively, or vice versa.
2. The *independent mode* – In this mode, the security property is assessed for a ToC by both monitoring and testing independently without any of these assessments being triggered by the outcomes of the other. Subsequently, the collected bodies of testing and monitoring evidence are correlated and cross-checked against each other; if the assessment conditions of this phase are satisfied, a certificate can be generated.

Beyond the elements of certification models that were discussed in the basic certification models, a hybrid model includes additional elements. These elements define: (a) the mode of hybrid certification; (b) the way of correlating monitoring and testing evidence; (c) conditions for characterizing these types of evidence as conflicting, and (d) the way in which a final overall assessment of the property can be generated based on both types of evidence.

As an example of a hybrid certification model, with monitoring as the primary and testing as the subordinate form of assessment, consider the case of a property of authentication. This security property requires the existence of an effective authentication mechanism to assure that for any granted request to obtain data from ToC, the user who made the request must be authenticated. This property can be assessed through a hybrid model expressed by the following monitoring rule:

Rule R2:
Happens(*e(_e1,_sc,_TOC,REQ,_updateOp(_username,_usersecret,_data,vCode), _TOE) ,t1,[t1,t1]) ^*
Happens(*e(_e2,_TOE,_sc,RES,_updateOp(_vusername,_vusersecret,_data, _authcode), _TOE),t2,[t1,t1+d1]) ^ (_authcode* $\neq$ *Nil)*
$\Rightarrow$ ***Happens***(*e(_e3,_CA,_AI,EXC,_authenticateOp(_username,_usersecret, _vCode, _authcode2),_TOE),t3,[t2,t2+d2]) ^ (_authcode2* $\neq$ *Nil)*

The above rule checks if, when request to update data is received and granted by the ToC (i.e., it is executed and a response is produced by ToC), the user who made the request had indeed the appropriate authorization rights. In the rule, the request for data update is represented by the event *Happens(e(_e1,_sc,_TOC,REQ, _updateOp(_username, _usersecret, _data, vCode),_TOE),t1,[t1,t1])*, and the successful response to it is represented by the event *Happens(e(_e2,_TOE,_sc, RES, _updateOp(_vusername, _vusersecret, _data, _authcode),_TOE),t2,[t1,t1+d1])*. When these two events occur and the condition *(_authcode* $\neq$ *Nil)* is satisfied indicating the update request was granted, the rule executes a test to ensure that the user had the appropriate authorization rights. This is expressed in the rule by the forced event *Happens(e(_e3,_CA,_AI,EXC,_authenticateOp(_username,_usersecret,_vCode, _authcode2), _TOE),t3,[t2,t2+d2])*. The latter event is triggered by the monitor, which requests the test manager of CUMULUS to execute the relevant test. Subsequently, the monitor checks if the outcome of the test satisfies the condition *(_authcode2*$\neq$*Nil)*.

A potential problem of the monitoring certification model for the data integrity at rest property shown in Sect. 8.3.1 would arise if in a ToC it was possible to update data directly, i.e., without using the data update operations in the interfaces of the ToC. To capture such cases, someone could use a hybrid certification model with testing as the dominant and monitoring as the subordinate form of assessment. The following monitoring rule would express this model:

Monitoring Rule:
HoldsAt(*LastHash(_file,_h2,t2),t1) ^ (_h1* $\neq$ *_h2)*
$\Rightarrow$ ***Happens***(*e(_e3,_TOC,_CA,REQ,_notifO(_cred,_data, _auth,_h1),_TOC), t3,[t2,t1])*

Monitoring Assumption A1:
Happens(*e(_e1,_CA,_TOC, EXC(*T_{per1}*),_getHash(_TOC,_file,_h1), _TOC), t1, [t1,t1]) ^*
HoldsAt(*LastHash(_file,_h2,t2),t1) ^ (_h1* $\neq$ *_h2)*
$\Rightarrow$ ***Terminates***(*_e1,LastHash(_file,_h2,t2),t1)) ^* ***Initiates***(*_e1,LastHash (_file,_h1,t1),t1))*

The monitoring rule in the above model executes a periodic test which retrieves the hash value of the file where the ToC data of interest are stored (see periodic executable event *Happens(e(_e1,_CA,_TOC, EXC(*T_{per}*), _getHash(_TOC,_file,_h1),_CA), t1, [t1,t1])*) and checks if this value is equal to the last hash value of this file (i.e., the value represented by the fluent *HoldsAt(LastHash(_file,_h2,t2),t1)*). In cases where the two hash values are different, the monitor checks if a notification event (see event *Happens(e(_e3,_TOC,_CA,REQ,_notifO(_cred,_data,_auth,_h1),_TOC), t3,[t2,t1]))* has occurred between the time that the current hash value was retrieved (*t1*) and the time on which the last update of the hash value took place (i.e., *t2*). In this case, the certification model includes also a monitoring assumption that is used to update the record of the last hash value of a file every time that an update to it occurs. This is expressed in the formula by terminating the last value of fluent (see predicate *Terminates(_e1,LastHash(_file,_h2,t2),t1)*) and initiating the same fluent with a new value (see predicate *Initiates(_e1,LastHash(_file,_h1,t1),t1)*) through a periodic check of the hash value of the file (see predicate *Happens(e(_e1,_CA,_TOC, EXC(*T_{per1}*),_getHash(_TOC,_file,_h1),_TOC),t1,[t1,t1]))*. A more detailed account of hybrid certification models is available from [19].

8.4.2 Compositional Certification Models

Certificate composition is a concept already introduced in SOA environment by Anisetti et al. [20]. It is aimed at re-using evidence in existing certificates of component services to issue a new certificate for a composite service. In Anisetti et al. [20], the certification process is not formally represented as a machine-readable document supporting the certificate (i.e., no declarative description in the form of a CM Template is available); thus, the composition requires an orchestration managed by the CA that selects candidates based on existing evidence and testing models. CUMULUS proposes a simpler approach for the composition of certificates, which relies on their multi-layer and hybrid nature, and the concept of CM Template.

CUMULUS certificate composition is based on a special type of test-based CM Template (Compositional CM Template), where certification requirements on component services are expressed in terms of required certificates (i.e., Component Certificates) instead of required evidence. The abstract collectors of such templates directly refer to certificates (for a specific property and ToC) and require testing their status (i.e., if the certificate is valid or not). Consequently, the compositional Life Cycle is a standard Test-Based Life Cycle where the evidence relates to the validity of the required certificates. CA defines a compositional CM Template to guarantee that the certified property is supported by the composition of certificates addressing requirements in the CM Template itself. We note that each CUMULUS Certificate requires a valid and running CMI, and thus the certificate status may change depending on the results of the corresponding CMI execution, its Life Cycle, and the changing scenario. In other words, each certificate is the expression of the corresponding certification process.

The CUMULUS certification Framework executes the instantiation of the Compositional CM Template for certificate issuing as a normal test-based CM as follows: (i) valid CM Instance of the given Compositional CM Template is produced, where collectors refer to the status of certificates, (ii) a Test Agent is deployed for each collector, (iii) every Test Agent is responsible for collecting evidence inspecting each certificate Life Cycle status, (iv) the evidence is aggregated depending on the compositional life cycle, (v) Test Manager collects the aggregated values and eventually issues a compositional certificate.

8.4.3 Incremental Certification Models

To support the dynamics of the cloud, the certification process must be able to constantly verify the validity of a certificate in the production environment. An incremental certification process is aimed at providing such ability, avoiding as much as possible time-consuming re-certification. This can be achieved by adapting the process to cloud events (e.g., service migration), changes of the mechanisms in the ToC, and configuration changes on custom or cloud stack mechanisms while proving a comparable level of assurance for the ToC. Monitoring-based certification is incremental by definition, as it continuously checks for a property to be valid. For instance, certification of a ToC migrated to a different stack is automatically supported by moving also the event captors in the new stack. TC-based certification is based on discrete evidence collection due to the nature of TC concept and TPM technology. As such, incremental certification models are not considered by TC-based certification. It is precisely the goal of TC-based certification to provide means to assure that a service/software integrity state collected at a given point in time (discrete evidence collection) remains the same over a time period with strong assurance. Test-Based Certification Model is not incremental by definition and requires a specific process to deal with incremental certification. We consider two main incremental scenarios as follows:

- *CM Instance adaptation* allowing to react to new versions of service, platform, or infrastructure, or any changes in the configurations at all cloud layers specified in the ToC.
- *CM Template adaptation* allowing the adaptation to new conditions and requirements for the validity of a property. For instance, a bug in a mechanism/algorithm is found or a new attack discovered. We note that any change to CMT also triggers an adaptation process on CMI.

In both scenarios the incremental certification process provides the ability to re-execute (part of) the process in Fig. 8.2, according to changes in the CM Template, the CM Instance, and the system implementation. We remark that any adaptation produced by the incremental process must satisfy the consistency check in Sect. 8.2.1. In the following we denote as CMT′ any possible adaptation of a given CMT and as CMI′ any possible adaptation of a given CMI.

8.4.3.1 CM Instance Adaptation

CM Instance adaptation focuses on the reuse of available evidence and follows four different approaches.

- **Partial re-evaluation**: where evidence is still sufficient. The adapted CMI′ is verified positively against CMT but it has minor differences with the original CMI. Some of the testing flows in CMI′ are updated with respect to the corresponding testing flows in CMI requiring one of the following actions: (i) re-execution of the relative test cases because they might be affected by cloud events, (ii) execution of additional test cases reflecting additional features introduced in an existing testing flow (not impacting on the flow sequence), and (iii) re-execution of all the test cases executed on the modified flow due to changes in mechanism under test. We note that partial re-evaluation can be executed by CUMULUS incremental certification process at runtime, according to CMI′, and without requiring any certificate authority intervention.
- **Partial re-certification**: where evidence is no more sufficient but not contradictory. The adapted CMI′ is not consistent with CMT, but it exists a consistent CMT′ (CMI′$\triangleright$CMT′). A re-certification process is instantiated for new execution flows of CMI′ that do not exist in the original CMI. The accredited lab then evaluates only those additional flows rather than implementing a complete re-certification. It generates and executes new test cases to collect the evidence needed to award a certificate for a new property according to the new instance CMI′. With the new CMI′, the evidence becomes sufficient again and the certificate status is moved back to issued. A lightweight degeneration of the general case of partial re-certification that do not require new testing activities but a little involvement of the certification authority is obtained via Certificate upgrade and downgrade [1].
- **Full re-certification**: where evidence is contradictory. It is applied when changes in CMI cannot be managed by the above approaches.
- **Component substitution**: where evidence is contradictory. It is applied only in the case of Compositional Certification model (see Sect. 8.4.2), where changes to a component service leads to revocation of component service certificate. The component service is therefore not suitable for composition, and therefore another component service with a suitable certificate in *issued* state is searched and integrated. We note that this substitution is completely transparent from the certification authority point of view.

8.4.3.2 CM Template Adaptation

CM Template adaptation focuses on changes at certification methodology level. It is driven by a certification authority, releasing a refined version CMT′ of a given CMT, for instance, if new conditions and requirements for the validity of the methodology are discovered. This adaptation at methodology level may trigger instance level adaptations for all instances CMI referring to CMT.

The incremental process first verifies the consistency of CMI with the adapted CMT′; if CMI⊳CMT′ the differences between the CMT′ and CMT are used for the identification of the portion of CMI that requires re-evaluation. Otherwise (i.e., CMI ⋫CMT′) the system under certification must be adapted and a new instance CMI′, which is consistent with CMT′, is defined.

8.5 Trust Model

Cloud and its peculiarities require a new trust model based on a novel chain of trust between all involved parties: the service provider, the customer, the certification authority, and the CUMULUS certification framework. Traditional approaches to SOA certification (e.g., [17]) assumes a CA in charge of all certification activities including certificate signature. This approach is not anymore valid in a cloud scenario, when a certificate is first issued at deployment time and then renewed when needed.

Figure 8.6 shows our chain of trust [2], identifying with rectangles the roles and with rounded rectangles the artifacts. The certification activities are represented by black arrows, while the trust relations are represented using dashed arrows. The chain of trust is based on the trust user c has on the CM Instance $CMI_{F,ws}$, on the evidence $E_{F,ws}$ generated by F according to CMI ($Tr(c, E_{F,ws})$), and assertions $A_{F,ws}$ made by CUMULUS framework F on a service ws ($Tr(c, A_{F,ws})$). The latter is based on (i) the reputation of the certification authority defining the CM template and the CUMULUS framework managing the overall process and (ii) the methodology discussed in Sect. 8.2.

The basic chain of trust in Fig. 8.6 can also be applied for hybrid and multi-layer certification. In the first case, the trust model is recursively applied to slave CMs; in

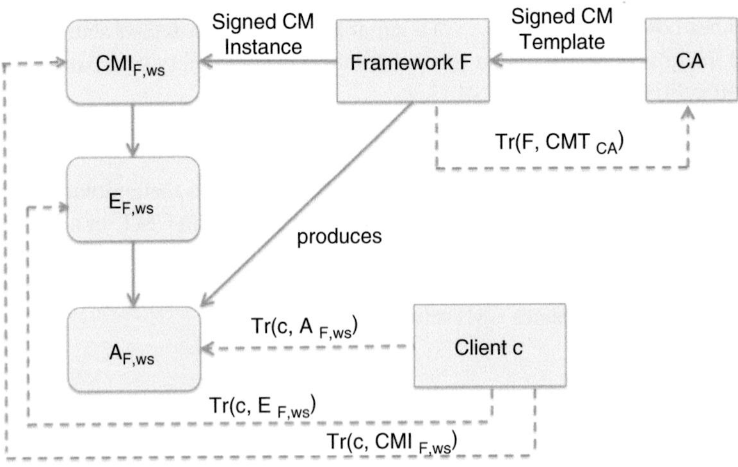

Fig. 8.6 Chain of trust

the second case, multi-layer ToC is treated as a single-layer ToC and therefore the basic chain of trust in Fig. 8.6 used.

A change to the basic trust model is instead needed for incremental certification. With incremental certification, the service is first certified in a laboratory environment, and then the validity of the awarded certificate is continuously verified in the production environment. In the laboratory certification, the basic certification and trust model still apply. Upon certificate release, the service is deployed on the cloud and an incremental certification starts. In this case, the trust in an incremental process is based on the trust user c has in the continuous evidence collection process and in the CM Instance possibly adapted according to the incremental process in Sect. 8.4.3.

8.6 Related Work

Lack of trust in cloud paradigm and technology is one of the main issues limiting their adoption in security- and privacy-critical domains. In the past, assurance techniques have been proposed for software/service systems to increase the confidence of users that such systems are behaving correctly and as expected. Developed techniques usually fall under three main classes, namely, audit, certification, and SLA.

Audit techniques are usually adopted to evaluate the properties of a system after its execution to identify unexpected behaviors. Several effort has been put on defining audit solutions for the cloud both from a research and industrial point of view (e.g., [21–27]). Given their nature, audit techniques provide powerful approaches but cannot be applied for a priori, continuous, and incremental evaluation of cloud service properties. SLA techniques define the basis to establish agreements between service providers and users on the Quality of Service. Different approaches have been provided both for SOA and cloud such as [28–31]. SLA-based approaches are similar to certification schemes, though they do not provide verifiable evidence and are usually based on self-assessment. Today, this techniques are usually adopted by cloud service provider, though they do not contribute to increase the transparency of and trust in the cloud environment. Finally, certification schemes have been at the basis of software/service evaluation of non-functional properties since 1985 with the TCSEC standard in USA (aka Orange book) for security certification of software [32]. Following several national efforts, Common Criteria [33] is the first international standard for software certification and is today the most used certification approach. Software certification approaches, however, consider manual inspection, monolithic services, and static evaluation, making them not suitable for cloud-based and service-based environments. More recently, different approaches to certification of SOA and web service have been proposed (e.g., [17, 34–36]) and some approaches to cloud certification discussed (e.g., [2, 37–40]). Although they represent an important starting point for cloud certification, none of the above approaches provide a complete and semi-automatic certification framework for the cloud, which accomplishes the peculiarities of the cloud.

8.7 Conclusions

In this chapter, we have presented an overview of the CUMULUS framework and how it can be used to automate the process of certifying security properties of cloud services. The CUMULUS framework supports the automated and continuous certification of security properties of cloud services through different types of certification models. These models can be basic or advanced. The former include models using monitoring, test, and TC evidence, and the latter include models relying on multiple types of evidence (hybrid) as well as models supporting incremental certification.

The CUMULUS framework has been realized through a prototype whose architecture is described in the chapter and has been tested in a series of scenarios involving applications in the domains of eHealth and smart cities.

8.8 Review Questions

1. Which are the major artifacts driving a CUMULUS certification process?
2. Which are the key aspects enabling CUMULUS certification process automation?
3. Which are the main elements underpinning any CUMULUS certification model?
4. Which are the main differences between basic certification models (monitoring-based, test-based, and TC-based certification models) in terms of evidence collection and life cycle?
5. Sketch multi-layer TC-based certification for the case of nested virtualization.
6. Discuss a use case of hybrid certification between test-based and monitoring-based certification models.
7. Which are the main differences between hybrid and incremental certification in terms of evidence collection, assurance, and trust?

Acknowledgements The work presented in this chapter has been partially funded by the EU FP7 project CUMULUS (grant no 318580).

References

1. Anisetti M, Ardagna CA, Damiani E (2015) A test-based incremental security certification scheme for cloud-based systems. In: Proceedings of the 12th IEEE international conference on services computing (SCC 2015), New York, June–July 2015
2. Anisetti M, Ardagna CA, Damiani E (2014) A certification-based trust model for autonomic cloud computing systems. In: Proceedings of the IEEE conference on cloud autonomic computing (CAC 2014), London, Sept 2014
3. CUMULUS Consortium (2015) Deliverable D5.3 – CUMULUS framework architecture v2. Available at http://www.cumulus-project.eu/index.php/public-deliverables
4. Harjani R, Arjona M, Espinar J, Maña A, Muñoz A, Koshutanski H (2014) An integrated framework for multi-layer certification-based assurance. In: Proceedings of the 8th layered assurance workshop (LAW 2014), New Orleans, Dec 2014

5. CUMULUS Consortium (2015) Deliverable D4.3 – CUMULUS-aware engineering process specification v2. Available at http://www.cumulus-project.eu/index.php/public-deliverables
6. CUMULUS Consortium (2015) Deliverable D3.3 – certification mechanisms for incremental and hybrid certification. Available at http://www.cumulus-project.eu/index.php/public-deliverables
7. Trusted Computing Group, TPM main specification. http://www.trustedcomputinggroup.org/resources/tpm_main_specification
8. CUMULUS Consortium (2015) Deliverable D2.4 – final CUMULUS certification models. Available at http://www.cumulus-project.eu/index.php/public-deliverables
9. CUMULUS Consortium (2013) Deliverable D2.1 – security-aware SLA specification language and cloud security dependency model. Available at http://www.cumulus-project.eu/index.php/public-deliverables
10. Spanoudakis G, Kloukinas C, Mahbub K (2009) The serenity runtime monitoring framework. In: Spanoudakis G, Kokolakis S (eds) Security and dependability for ambient intelligence. Springer, New York/US, pp 213–237
11. Shanahan M The event calculus explained (1999) In: Wooldridge MJ, Veloso M (eds) Artificial intelligence today. Springer, Berlin Heidelberg, Germany, pp 409–430
12. Krotsiani M, Spanoudakis G, Mahbub K (2013) Incremental certification of cloud services. In: Proceedings of the 7th international conference on emerging security information, systems and technologies (SECURWARE-2013), Barcelona, Aug 2013
13. Krotsiani M, Spanoudakis G (2014) Continuous certification of non-repudiation in cloud storage services. In: Proceedings of the 4th IEEE international symposium on trust and security in cloud computing (IEEE TSCloud 2014), Beijing, Sept 2014
14. Irvine C, Levin T (1999) Toward a taxonomy and costing method for security services. In: Proceedings of the 15th annual conference on computer security applications (ACSAC 1999), Phoenix, Dec 1999
15. Chung L, Nixon BA (1995) Dealing with non-functional requirements: three experimental studies of a process-oriented approach. In: Proceedings of the 17th international conference on software engineering (ICSE 1995), Seattle, Apr 1995
16. Chung L, Leite JCP (2009) Conceptual modeling: foundations and applications. chapter on non-functional requirements in software engineering. Springer, Berlin/Heidelberg, pp 363–379
17. Anisetti M, Ardagna CA, Damiani E, Saonara F (2013) A test-based security certification scheme for web services. ACM Trans Web (TWEB) 7(2):1–41
18. Trusted Computing Group (2011) Virtualized trusted platform architecture specification, Sept 2011. http://www.trustedcomputinggroup.org/resources/virtualized_trusted_platform_architecture_specification
19. Katopodis S, Spanoudakis G, Mahbub K (2014) Towards hybrid cloud service certification models. In: Proceedings of the IEEE international conference on services computing (SCC 2014), Anchorage, June–July 2014
20. Anisetti M, Ardagna CA, Damiani E (2013) Security certification of composite services: a test-based approach. In: Proceedings of the 20th IEEE international conference on Web services (ICWS 2013), San Francisco, June–July 2013
21. Pearson S (2011) Toward accountability in the cloud. IEEE Internet Comput 15(4):64–69
22. Rasheed H (2013) Data and infrastructure security auditing in cloud computing environments. Int J Inf Manag 34(3):364–368
23. Doelitzscher F, Reich C, Knahl M, Passfall A, Clarke N (2012) An agent based business aware incident detection system for cloud environments. J Cloud Comput 1(1):1–19
24. Rajkumar MN, Kumar VV, Sivaramakrishnan R (2013) Efficient integrity auditing services for cloud computing using raptor codes. In: Proceedings of the ACM international conference on research in adaptive and convergent systems (RACS 2013), Montreal, Oct 2013
25. Yang K, Jia X (2013) An efficient and secure dynamic auditing protocol for data storage in cloud computing. IEEE Trans Parallel Distrib Syst 24(9):1717–1726
26. Wang B, Li B, Li H (2014) Oruta: privacy-preserving public auditing for shared data in the cloud. IEEE Trans Cloud Comput 2(1):43–56

27. CSA (2014) CloudAudit: automated audit, assertion, assessment, and assurance. https://cloudsecurityalliance.org/research/cloudaudit/
28. Wieder P, Butler JM, Theilmann W, Yahyapour R (2011) Service level agreements for cloud computing. Springer, Dortmund, Germany
29. Ye L, Zhang H, Shi J, Du X (2012) Verifying cloud service level agreement. In: Proceedings of IEEE GLOBECOM 2012, Anaheim, Dec 2012
30. Casalicchio E, Silvestri L (2013) Mechanisms for sla provisioning in cloud-based service providers. Comput Netw 57(3):795–810
31. Marinescu DC, Paya A, Morrison JP, Healy PD (2013) An auction-driven self-organizing cloud delivery model. CoRR, abs/1312.2998
32. USA Department of Defence (1985) Department Of defense trusted computer system evaluation criteria, Dec 1985
33. Herrmann DS (2002) Using the common criteria for IT security evaluation. Auerbach publications/CRC press, London
34. Kourtesis D, Ramollari E, Dranidis D, Paraskakis I (2010) Increased reliability in SOA environments through registry-based conformance testing of web services. Prod Plan Control 21(2):130–144
35. Ryu SH, Casati F, Skogsrud H, Betanallah B, Saint-Paul R (2008) Supporting the dynamic evolution of Web service protocols in service-oriented architectures. ACM Trans Web 2(2):13:1–13:46
36. Papazoglou MP, Andrikopoulos V, Benbernou S (2011) Managing evolving services. IEEE Softw 28(3):49–55
37. Grobauer B, Walloschek T, Stocker E (2011) Understanding cloud computing vulnerabilities. IEEE Secur Priv 9(2):50–57
38. Sunyaev A, Schneider S (2013) Cloud services certification. Commun ACM 56(2):33–36
39. Khan KM, Malluhi Q (2010) Establishing trust in cloud computing. IT Prof 12(5):20–27
40. Bertholon B, Varrette S, Bouvry P (2011) Certicloud: a novel tpm-based approach to ensure cloud iaas security. In: Proceedings of the 4th IEEE international conference on cloud computing (CLOUD 2011), Washington, July 2011

Marco Anisetti is an Assistant Professor at the Università degli Studi di Milano. He received the PhD degree in computer science from the Università degli Studi di Milano in 2009. His research interests are in the area of Computational Intelligence and its application to the design of complex systems and services. Recently, he has been investigating the adoption of Computational Intelligence techniques in the area of security mechanisms for distributed systems, with particular consideration of Cloud and SOA security and software/service certification. The URL for his web page is http://www.di.unimi.it/anisetti.

Claudio A. Ardagna is an Associate Professor at the Dipartimento di Informatica, Università degli Studi di Milano, Italy. His research interests are in the area of cloud security and certification. He is the recipient of the ERCIM STM WG 2009 Award for the Best PhD Thesis on Security and Trust Management. He has co-authored the Springer book "Open Source Systems Security Certification." He has been a Visiting Researcher at George Mason University (2008–2010) and EBTIC-Khalifa University (2014). The URL for his web page is http://www.di.unimi.it/ardagna.

Ernesto Damiani is a Full Professor at Università di Milano, the director of the Università degli Studi di Milano's PhD program in computer science, and the leader of the Big Data Initiative at the Etisalat British Telecom Innovation Center in Abu Dhabi, UAE. He was a recipient of the Chester-Sall Award from the IEEE IES Society (2007). He is a senior member of the IEEE, was named ACM Distinguished Scientist (2008), and received the IFIP TC2 Outstanding Contributions Award (2012). He is the Vice-Chair of the IEEE Technical Committee on Industrial Informatics. The URL for his web page is http://www.di.unimi.it/damiani.

Antonio Maña received his PhD degree in Computer Engineering from the University of Malaga, where he is currently an Associate Professor of Software Engineering in the Computer Science Department. His current research activities include security and software engineering, information and network security, ubiquitous computing and ambient intelligence, application of smart cards to digital content commerce, software protection, DRM, and mobile applications. The URL for his web page is http://www.lcc.uma.es/~amg/eng/.

George Spanoudakis is a Professor of Computer Science at City University London and member of the Council of the University of Piraeus in Greece. His research focuses on cloud computing and software systems security. In these areas, he has published extensively and attracted significant research funding from the EU, national research councils and directly by the industry. Currently, he is the technical coordinator of the F7 EU project CUMULUS (2012–15). He served in the program and organization committees of several international conferences and workshops and the editorial boards of several journals. The URL for his web page is http://www.city.ac.uk/people/academics/george-spanoudakis.

Luca Pino is a senior software engineer and research assistant at City University London. He is working in the EU FP7 project CUMULUS, developing automated security certification processes for clouds, and in the EU project EMBalance, developing a decision support system to help physicians in the diagnostic evaluation of balance disorders. His research interests are in the area of cloud and web service security and assurance.

Hristo Koshutanski is a postdoctoral fellow in Proteus Research Lab at the University of Malaga. He received his PhD degree from the University of Trento in 2005 and held a postdoctoral research fellowship Marie Curie EIF for 2007–2009. His research interests are in the areas of security architectures for distributed, federated and cloud-based systems, security assurance, certification and digital security certificates of cloud and Web services, and identity management in federated systems. The URL for his web page is http://www.koshutanski.net.

Improving Cloud Assurance and Transparency Through Accountability Mechanisms 9

Siani Pearson, Jesus Luna, and Christoph Reich

Abstract

Accountability is a critical prerequisite for effective governance and control of corporate and private data processed by cloud-based information technology services. This chapter clarifies how accountability tools and practices can enhance cloud assurance and transparency in a variety of ways. Relevant techniques and terminologies are presented, and a scenario is considered to illustrate the related issues. In addition, some related examples are provided involving cutting-edge research and development in fields like risk management, security and Privacy Level Agreements and continuous security monitoring. The provided arguments seek to justify the use of accountability-based approaches for providing an improved basis for consumers' trust in cloud computing and thereby can benefit from the uptake of this technology.

Keywords

Accountability • Assurance • Cloud computing • Continuous monitoring • Privacy level agreement (PLA) • Service level agreement (SLA) • Transparency

---

S. Pearson (✉)
Security and Manageability Lab, Hewlett Packard Labs, Long Down Avenue, Bristol BS34 8QZ, UK
e-mail: siani.pearson@hpe.com

J. Luna
Cloud Security Alliance, 34 Melville Street, Scotland EH3 7HA, UK
e-mail: jluna@cloudsecurityalliance.org

C. Reich
Furtwangen University, Robert-Gerwig-Platz 1, Furtwangen 78120, Germany
e-mail: christoph.reich@hs-furtwangen.de

S.Y. Zhu et al. (eds.), *Guide to Security Assurance for Cloud Computing*,
Computer Communications and Networks, DOI 10.1007/978-3-319-25988-8_9

9.1 Introduction

The National Institute of Standards and Technology (NIST) defines cloud computing as "a model for enabling ubiquitous, convenient, on-demand network access to a shared pool of configurable resources (e.g., networks, servers, storage, applications, and services) that can be rapidly provisioned and released with minimal management effort or service provider interaction" [34]. This model enables a very significant change in the information technology (IT) landscape that can allow benefits to organisations including economies of scale, reduced spending on technology infrastructure and improved accessibility and flexibility. As a result, more and more organisations, in particular small- and medium-sized enterprises (SMEs), are using the cloud, either as end users or in order to become part of the service supply chain.

However, major perceived barriers to cloud usage are still the lack of transparency and assurance of the cloud service providers (CSPs). The lack of transparency can arise due to different reasons and be compounded by lack of knowledge and action by data controllers and data processors (e.g. about the chain processing, inadequate levels of data protection or illegality of transfers or the law applicable to data protection disputes) [17]. This is one aspect of the lack of accountability in the data protection context [18]: Accountability was seen in a recent report by the International Data Corporation (IDC) as the most important action that business users thought would help improve cloud adoption [27]. In order for potential cloud customers to make appropriate assessments about the suitability in a given context of using the cloud, and indeed particular cloud service providers, it is very important that these customers are provided with both the relevant information about the cloud service providers and an awareness of the type of things they should be assessing, which include not only organisational security risk aspects but also consideration of potential harm to data subjects and how that might be avoided, as well as wider regulatory and contractual compliance aspects. Furthermore, in the case of data breaches, notifications must be provided to a number of parties that may include data subjects, cloud customers and regulatory authorities, and enhanced transparency in this respect may affect not only follow-up actions relating to remediation and redress but also enhance future decision-making processes.

In this chapter we argue that more transparency and assurance can be achieved through an accountable-based approach where new processes, mechanisms and tools can be put in place. After assessing the state-of-the-art and current inadequacies in this regard in Sect. 9.2, we consider in Sect. 9.3 how accountability relates to transparency and assurance. In Sect. 9.4 we present a motivating cloud scenario with reference to which further discussions will be made. In Sects. 9.5, 9.6 and 9.7, we explain how greater transparency and assurance may be achieved via three core elements: a *risk assessment* approach adapted to cloud service providers (CSPs); improved levels of assurance through *Service Level Agreements* (SLAs) and Privacy Level Agreements (PLAs); *transparency* during the service provision, including usage of continuous monitoring. Furthermore, in Sect. 9.8, we present novel mechanisms that can be provided at different phases of an accountability lifecycle.

These demonstrate how risk management and transparency can be enhanced in the provisioning for accountability phase, how continuous monitoring can be utilised in an operational phase and how audit and certification can be linked to policies such as PLAs. Finally, we present conclusions.

9.2 State of the Art

In this section we provide a brief introduction to related work in order to frame the context and contribution of our chapter.

Security information and event management (SIEM or SIM/SEM) solutions have a critical role in monitoring operational security and supporting organisations in decision making. They provide a standardised approach to collect information and events, store and query and provide degrees of correlations, usually driven by rules. The leading SIEM solutions in the market, as analysed by Gartner [32], are:

1. *HP ArcSight*[1]: This is oriented to large-scale security event management and offers appliance-based preconfigured monitoring of log data, management functions and reporting.
2. *IBM Security QRadar*[2]: This provides log management, event management, reporting and behavioural analysis for networks and applications.
3. *LogRhythm*[3] and *McAfee Enterprise Security Manager*[4]: This can be deployed in smaller environments, supporting log management and network forensic capabilities.
4. *EMC Corp. RSA Security Analytics*[5]: This provides log and full packet data capture, security monitoring forensic investigation and big data analytic methods.

SIEM solutions do not cover business audit and strategic (security) risk assessment but instead provide inputs that need to be properly analysed and translated into a suitable format to be used by senior risk assessors and strategic policymakers. Risk assessment standards such as ISO 2700x,[6] NIST [35], etc. operate at a macro level and usually do not fully utilise information coming from logging and auditing activities carried out by information technology (IT) operations. Similarly, there exist a number of frameworks for auditing a company's IT controls, most notably COSO[7] and COBIT.[8]

Other types of detective mechanism are concerned with cloud service usage rather than security and information monitoring. There exists a class of

[1] http://www8.hp.com/us/en/software-solutions/siem-security-information-event-management/

[2] http://www.ibm.com/software/products/en/qradar-siem/

[3] https://www.logrhythm.com/

[4] http://www.mcafee.com/us/products/enterprise-security-manager.aspx

[5] http://uk.emc.com/security/security-analytics/security-analytics.htm

[6] http://www.27000.org/

[7] http://www.coso.org

[8] http://www.isaca.org

evidence-related cloud technologies that provide generic mechanisms supporting basic logging and monitoring. Examples are:

- *Sumo Logic*[9]: This is a log management platform that allows a cloud provider to collect log data from applications, network, firewalls and intrusion detection system.
- *Amazon Web Services (AWS) CloudTrail*[10]: This is a Web service that records AWS API calls for a customer's account and delivers log files to the customer. CloudTrail records important information about each API call, including the name of the API, the identity of the caller, the time of the API call, the request parameters and the response elements returned by the AWS service. This information helps to track changes made to your AWS resources and to troubleshoot operational issues. The main purpose of CloudTrail is to make it easier to ensure compliance with internal policies and regulatory standards.
- *Logentries*[11]: This collects and analyses logs across software stacks using a preprocessing layer to filter, correlate and visualise log data.

Different security controls can be identified that organisations need to implement in the cloud (see, e.g. [37]). From a management viewpoint, it is possible to identify critical processes (e.g. security risk assessment and privacy management) that address the mitigation of security and privacy threats [40], and the essential elements of a good organisational privacy management programme have been defined [42]. Furthermore, an accountability framework for the cloud context has been described [44, 45], in which different types of accountability tools (usable either individually or in combination) may be provided for cloud users, providers and governance entities, ranging from preventive tools that aid informed choice, control and decision making upfront and thereby can reduce privacy and security risk, to detective tools that monitor for and report policy violations, to corrective tools that ameliorate remediation and redress in case of failure. Certification can be an important aspect of such frameworks. ENISA has developed a Cloud Certification Schemes Metaframework (CCSM) that classifies different types of security certification (which are aligned with specific standards) for cloud providers [22]. This meta-framework is used to compare a number of different certifications identified within the Cloud Certification Schemes List (CCSL). The overall objective of this framework is to make the cloud more transparent for cloud customers, in particular, in the way cloud providers meet specific security objectives.

In general, technical security measures (such as open strong cryptography) can help prevent falsification of logs, and privacy-enhancing techniques and adequate access control should be used to protect personal information in logs. Relevant techniques that can be used include non-repudiable logs, backups, distributed logging, forward integrity via use of hash chains and automated tools for log

[9]http://www.sumologic.com

[10]http://aws.amazon.com/cloudtrail/

[11]https://logentries.com/

audits. More specifically, in the work of [51], a collaborative monitoring mechanism is proposed for making multitenant platforms accountable. A third-party external service is used to provide a "supporting evidence collection" that contains evidence for Service Level Agreement (SLA) compliance checking (defined distinctively from runtime logs). This type of service is presented as an *accountability service*, in other words one that offers "a mechanism for clients to authenticate the correctness of the data and the execution of their business logic in a multitenant platform". The external accountable service contains a Merkle B-tree structure with the hashes of the operation signatures concatenated with the new values of data after occurrence of state changes. This work includes algorithms for logging and request processes and an evaluation of a testing environment implemented in Amazon EC2. Furthermore, Butin et al. [5] propose a framework for accountability of practice using privacy-friendly logs. They take the approach of using formal methods to define the "accounts" and the accountability process to analyse these accounts. In the accountability process, the abstract events and logs are related, and the correctness is proved such that an abstract event denotes a concrete log, thus allowing analysis of the abstract events for compliance instead of a log. The compliance with respect to policies were formally checked and proved. One of the concerns as identified by the authors is to verify that the logs, which are the basis of any accountability system, reflect the actual and complete activities of the data controller. In general, their work models an accountability framework that is formally proved and verified which is in contrast to the approach described in this chapter, which is an implementation solving the problem of collecting evidence, analysing it, generating policy-based notifications/violations and generating audit reports.

9.3 The Relationship Between Accountability and Assurance

Accountability is the state of accepting allocated responsibilities (including usage and onward transfer of data to and from third parties), explaining and demonstrating compliance to stakeholders and remedying any failure to act properly. Responsibilities may be derived from law, social norms, agreements, organisational values and ethical obligations. Furthermore, accountability for complying with measures that give effect to practices articulated in given guidelines has been present in many core frameworks for privacy protection [43]. Within cloud ecosystems, accountability is becoming an important (new) notion, defining the relations between various stakeholders and their behaviours towards data in the cloud.

Specifically, an *accountor* is accountable to an *accountee* for:

- **Norms:** the obligations and permissions that define data practices
- **Behaviour:** the actual data processing behaviour of an organisation
- **Compliance**: entails the comparison of an organisation's actual behaviour with the norms

By the accountor exposing the norms it subscribes to and its behaviour, the accountee can check compliance. Norms can be expressed in policies and they derive from law, contracts and ethics. We consider further the definition and exposure of certain types of norms in a cloud context in Sect. 9.6 (focusing on SLAs).

Accountability and good systems design (in particular, to meet privacy and security requirements) are complementary, in that the latter provides mechanisms and controls that allow implementation of principles and standards, whereas accountability makes organisations responsible for providing an appropriate implementation for their business context and addresses what happens in case of failure (i.e. if the account is not provided and is not adequate; if the organisation's obligations are not met, e.g. there is a data breach; etc.). Section 9.5 further elaborates the cloud-adapted risk assessment methodology targeting the elicitation of controls from an accountable perspective. Part of the justification that appropriate measures have been use comes from an enhanced risk assessment process. The role of a risk-based approach in data protection has been considered by a number of parties, including: as an assessment of the relative values of such an approach [4], modifying the data protection principles to take this into account [41], analysing the relationship with accountability [24] and recent regulatory analysis [7, 19].

Typically in a cloud ecosystem in a data protection context, the accountors are cloud actors which are organisations (or individuals with certain responsibilities within those) acting as a data steward for other actors' personal data or business secrets. The accountees are other cloud actors, which may include private accountability agents, consumer organisations, the public at large and entities involved in governance. In addition, a connection between appropriateness and effectiveness can be made through the agreed SLA, which will contain committed security and privacy values relating to each metric selected, as discussed further in Sect. 9.6.

A core attribute of accountability is transparency, which is "the property of a system, organisation or individual of providing visibility of its governing norms, behaviour and compliance of behaviour to the norms" [23]. A distinction can be made between ex ante transparency, which is concerned with "the anticipation of consequences before data is actually disclosed (e.g. in the form of a certain behaviour)" [26] and ex post transparency, which is concerned with informing "about consequences if data already has been revealed" [26]. Being transparent is required not only with respect to the identified objects of the cloud ecosystem (i.e. norms, behaviour and compliance) but also with respect to remediation. In Sect. 9.7, we consider further how transparency may be provided during cloud service provision.

Although organisations can select from accountability mechanisms and tools in order to meet their context, the choice of such tools needs to be justified to external parties. A strong accountability approach would include moving beyond accountability of policies and procedures, to accountability of practice giving accountability evidence. Accountability evidence can be defined as "a collection of data, metadata, routine information, and formal operations performed on data and metadata, which provide attributable and verifiable account of the fulfilment (or not) of relevant obligations; it can be used to support an argument on the validity of claims about appropriate functioning of an observable system" [52].

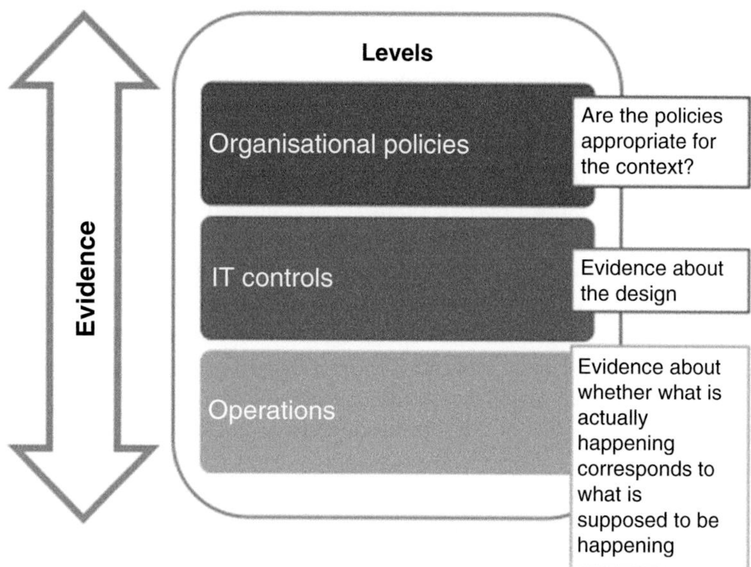

Fig. 9.1 Accountability evidence

Accountability evidence, as illustrated in Fig. 9.1, needs to be provided at a number of layers. At the organisational policy level, this would involve provision of evidence that the policies are appropriate for the context, which is typically what is done when privacy seals are issued. But this alone is rather weak; in addition, evidence can be provided about the measures, mechanisms and controls that are deployed and their configuration, to show that these are appropriate for the context. For example, evidence could be provided that privacy-enhancing technologies (PETs) have been used, to support anonymisation requirements expressed at the policy level. For higher-risk situations, continuous monitoring may be needed to provide evidence that what is claimed in the policies is actually being met in practice; even if this is not sophisticated, some form of checking the operational running and feeding this back into the accountability management programme in order to improve it is part of accountability practice, as described above, and hence evidence will need to be generated at this level too. In particular, technical measures should be deployed to enhance the integrity and authenticity of logs, and there should be enhanced reasoning about how these logs show whether or not data protection obligations have been fulfilled. The evidence from the above would be reflected in the account and would serve as a basis for verification and certification by independent, trusted entities. As we shall consider further in Sect. 9.7, the actual assessment of the effectiveness of the IT controls is performed during the service's operation.

Accountability evidence contributes towards the more general concept of assurance, which can be viewed as "Grounds for confidence that the other four security goals (integrity, availability, confidentiality, and accountability) have been adequately met by a specific implementation. "Adequately met" includes (1) functionality that performs correctly, (2) sufficient protection against unintentional errors (by users or software), and (3) sufficient resistance to intentional penetration or bypass" [48]. Different kinds of assurance need to be provided during the accountability lifecycle described in Sect. 9.8. In particular, as we shall consider further in Sect. 9.8, in an initial phase of provisioning for accountability, assurance (based, e.g. on assessment of capabilities) needs to be provided about the appropriateness and effectiveness of the cloud service providers under consideration; from an operational perspective, there needs to be both internal and external demonstration (to relevant stakeholders) that the organisation is operating in an accountable manner (e.g. built on monitoring evidence and via accounts); external parties will be involved in audit and validation based on information made available to them.

Before moving on to consider these aspects in more detail, we present an illustrative cloud scenario that will be used as a reference point.

9.4 Case Study

This section describes a scenario to motivate the main transparency-/assurance-related issues that confront cloud customers, in particular small- and medium-sized enterprises (SMEs) embracing the cloud.

"Wearable Co" is a manufacturer of wearable devices that needs to select a CSP to build a Web-based service on its behalf. This service should facilitate processing and storing wearable data while providing user-level functionalities, which will be consumed by the Wearable customers via a Web user interface (UI). The wearable data will be collected in two ways: automatic collection via the wearable devices and manual input from the customer via the Web application/UI. Part of the application will involve visualisation of aggregated statistics on maps. The service should be realised through one or more CSPs (i.e. a cloud service supply chain).

Wearable Co has concerns with respect to the implementation of the Wearable service in the cloud. These concerns are driven by the Data Protection Authority (DPA) observing the fulfilment of the legal framework and the type of personal data that should be collected. In this case, Wearable Co should ensure that all the personal data collected by the Wearable customers (either automatically or manually) is protected at all phases on their processing, while a specific set of geographical data centres should be considered for storing. At the same time, this SME should apply specific data access and data handling rules that should be enforced at runtime by all the involved stakeholders in this Wearable service.

Let us also consider CardioMon, which is a software-as-a-service (SaaS) CSP offering a complete solution by means of providing features for collecting, managing, storing and processing wellbeing data. CardioMon is doing business with many other customers with similar functional/business requirements as the Wearable Co and has an existing business agreement with DataSpacer, an infrastructure-as-a-service (IaaS) cloud provider, who offers advanced security and privacy

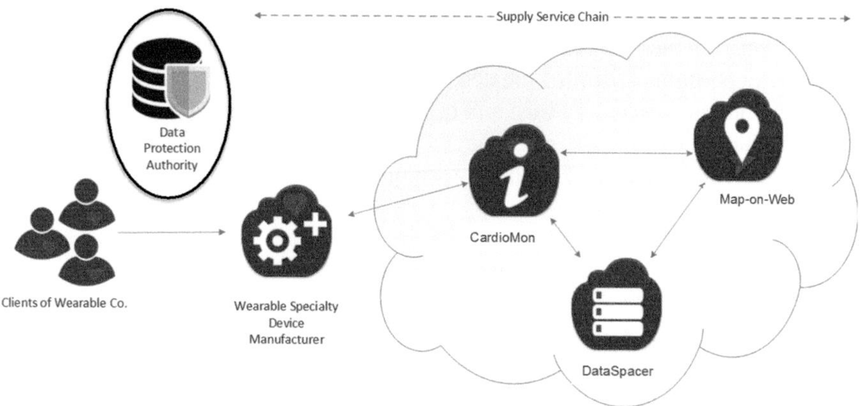

Fig. 9.2 Use case scenario – system model and involved actors

mechanisms for the protected storage and retrieval of personal and sensitive information. Furthermore, the CardioMon service allows for the core functionality to be expanded via third-party services to enrich the experience of the users. Such an expansion is provided by Map-on-Web, which is a separate SaaS cloud provider, with expertise on map visualisations for big data sets. Thus, Map-on-Web complements CardioMon by expanding on the available data visualisation features.

The scenario of this use case assumes that (after a period of researching the market) Wearable Co selects CardioMon as the provider of the software service that it will make available to its customers. A high-level system model of the described case study is shown in Fig. 9.2.

The next three sections of the chapter will elaborate on the assurance and transparency issues related to this use case along with the proposed solutions from the risk assessment (Sect. 9.5), Service Level Agreement (Sect. 9.6) and operational provisioning of assurance (Sect. 9.7) perspectives.

9.5 Risk Assessment

Organisations aiming to use the benefits of the cloud (like the Wearable Co introduced in Sect. 9.4) are in need of mechanisms to implement good-enough information security and data protection. These SMEs often find it convenient to start with an introspective view that identifies both the assets to protect and the risks to consider when migrating to the cloud. Risk, as explained in risk management frameworks (RMFs) such as NIST SP 800-30 [35], is strictly tied to uncertainty, and most approaches to manage risk are based on the probability of an event happening. However, cloud security/privacy requirements reflect intrinsic security problems not seen in regular IT security scenarios. Current risk assessment methods are not tailored to cloud computing: The lack of transparency about how cloud service ecosystems are composed prevents the seamless application of traditional methodologies and standards. While the future Internet creates new business opportunities, it also creates a variety of new risks as connectivity and the multidomains created by trust and organisational boundaries increase. Because of its set-up, scenarios like the one shown in Fig. 9.2 create several types of technical, organisational and regulatory "complexities" and risks. Take, for example, the following:

- Availability issues in any of the involved CSPs, resulting in the full/partial unavailability of the Wearable service
- Insider attacks on the IaaS provider (DataSpacer) resulting on the customers' personal identifiable information (PII) being leaked
- Vendor lock-in issues forbidding Wearable Co to migrate their business to a different cloud supply chain
- Lack of service transparency (in particular related to data handling), resulting in customers being unaware of where their (own) data is being stored and processed

As IT functions are spread across the cloud, companies like Wearable Co will need not only event monitoring systems that cross cloud boundaries but also assurance systems that demonstrate that each CSP is enforcing their required policies and that the combination adequately manages risk. However, the missing link amongst these objectives is a common model to allow assessment of risk based on some trust assumptions and how to use such representations to derive contracts, policies and security/privacy controls that will enable accountability.

The type of cloud delivery model and the service type that are chosen for adoption, in association with security controls selected for the ecosystem, need to be chosen in such a way that the system preserves its security posture. Therefore, a properly performed risk management cycle should ensure that the residual risk remaining after securing the ecosystem is minimal and that the system achieves a security posture equivalent to that of an on-premise technology architecture or solution (in-house Wearable solution). Conversely, the type of selected deployment model has an impact on the distribution of security responsibilities amongst the cloud actors, as related to the security conservation principle [37].

Despite the variety of approaches in cloud risk management derived from relevant works [36], the challenges associated with complex supply chains (from a risk management perspective) have only recently resulted in new initiatives to address them. The key element for the successful adoption of assurance and transparency in a cloud-based system solution is the cloud consumers' full understanding of the cloud-specific traits and characteristics, the architectural components for each cloud service type and deployment model, along with each cloud actor's precise role in orchestrating a secure ecosystem. How confident cloud customers feel if the risk related to using cloud services is acceptable depends on how much trust they place in those involved in the surrounding cloud ecosystem's orchestration. The risk management process ensures that issues are identified and mitigated early on in the investment cycle and followed by periodic reviews. Since cloud customers and other cloud actors involved in securely orchestrating a cloud ecosystem (cf. Fig. 9.2) have differing degrees of control over cloud-based IT resources, they need to share the responsibility of implementing and continuously assessing the security requirements.

Furthermore, it is essential for the cloud consumers' business and mission-critical processes that they be able to identify all cloud-specific risk-adjusted security and privacy controls. Cloud consumers need to leverage their contractual agreements to hold the CSPs accountable for the implementation of the security and data protection controls. They also need to be able to assess the correct implementation and continuously monitor all identified security controls. But what are the elements of a successful cloud risk management strategy in order to enable transparency and assurance? The draft NIST SP 800-173, *Cloud-Adapted Risk Management Framework (CRMF)* [39], is one of the most relevant works addressing this issue.

The CRMF was first highlighted in NIST SP 500-299, *Cloud Computing Security Reference Architecture* [37]. This specification discusses several key aspects of managing risks associated with a cloud environment while stressing the importance of adhering to the security conservation principle. CRMF is a cyclically executed process composed of a set of coordinated activities for overseeing and controlling risks. This set of activities consists of:

- Risk assessment
- Risk treatment
- Risk control

These activities collectively target the enhancement of strategic and tactical cloud security and privacy in scenarios like the Wearable Co. The NIST Cloud-Adapted Risk Management Framework (CRMF) provides a consumer-centric approach while closely following the original RMF, identifying the six steps shown in Table 9.1.

The described risk-based approach to managing information systems is a holistic activity that should be fully integrated into every aspect of the Wearable Co scenario, from planning and system development lifecycle processes (Steps 1–2) to security/privacy controls allocation (Steps 3–5). The selection and specification of security and privacy controls support effectiveness, efficiency and constraints via appropriate laws, directives, policies, standards and regulations. The resulting set of security and privacy controls (baseline, tailored controls, controls inherited from the supply chain and under customer's direct implementation and management) derived from applying the CRMF (Steps 1–4) lead gradually to the creation of the applicable cloud SLA in the CRMF's Step 5, as explained next.

9.6 Service Level Agreements

A lack of assurance and transparency, along with the current paucity of techniques to quantify security and privacy levels, often results in cloud customers (in particular SMEs like the Wearable Co in Fig. 9.2) being unable to assess the security of the

Table 9.1 Managing risks in the Wearable Co scenario

CRMF activity	CRMF step	Wearable Co. implementation
Risk assessment	Step 1 – Conduct an impact analysis to categorise the information system that has been migrated to the cloud and the information that is processed, stored and transmitted by that system	This is carried by the Wearable Co itself, usually during the design phase of the service. The customers' PII must be clearly identified in accordance to applicable regulations
	Step 2 – Identify the security and privacy requirements of the system by performing a risk assessment. Select the baseline and tailored supplemental security and privacy controls	Wearable Co might decide to perform the assessment considering the risk classification proposed by ENISA [21]. Security and privacy controls can be mapped to the Cloud Security Alliance (CSA) Cloud Control Matrix (CCM [9]) and Privacy Level Agreements (PLAs [12]) best practices
Risk treatment	Step 3 – Select the cloud ecosystem architecture that best suits the assessment results for the system	Wearable Co should decide on both the cloud deployment and cloud service model to use (i.e. the supply chain shown in Fig. 9.2)
	Step 4 – Assess the service provider options. Identify the security controls needed for the system the cloud provider has implemented. Negotiate the implementation of any additional security controls that are identified. Identify any remaining security controls that fall under the cloud consumer's responsibility for their implementation	In order to make a well-informed decision based on elicited security and privacy controls (cf. Step 2), the Wearable Co might decide to search and compare CSP offers based on publicly available information. Repositories like the CSA STAR [11] and information contained in applicable certifications and Service Level Agreements (SLAs) will prove useful during this stage. Section 9.6 will further expand on these topics
Risk control	Step 5 – Select and authorise a cloud provider to host the cloud consumer's information system. Draft a Service Level Agreement that lists the negotiated contractual terms and conditions	Wearable Co agrees on the SLAs with the different CSPs participating in the supply chain, i.e. CardioMon, Map-on-Web and DataSpacer, in Fig. 9.2. Assurance and transparency in relationship to cloud SLAs will be further explained in the next section
	Step 6 – Monitor the cloud provider to ensure that all Service Level Agreement terms are being met. Ensure that the cloud-based system maintains the necessary security and privacy posture. Monitor the security controls that fall under the cloud consumer's responsibility	This is an essential stage to fully close the assurance and transparency lifecycle. Wearable Co (and also other CSPs) should need to deploy the required continuous monitoring/certification mechanisms to guarantee the fulfilment of its security and privacy requirements during the service operation. This will be further analysed in Sect. 9.7

CSPs they are paying for. Despite the advocated economic and performance related advantages of the use case presented in Sect. 9.4, two issues arise:

1. How can the (non-security expert) Wearable Co meaningfully assess if the CSPs in the supply chain fulfil their security/privacy requirements?
2. How do all CSPs (including the Wearable Co itself) provide assurance and transparency during the full cloud service lifecycle?

This section will focus on exploring the first issue and how it is being solved using the state of the art through the use of security and privacy parameters in cloud SLAs. Operational assurance/transparency will be discussed in Sect. 9.7.

With regard to the implementation of the elicited security and privacy controls (cf. Step 1 in Table 9.1), the CSPs within the supply chain can only assume the type of data the Wearable Co customer will generate and use during the operational phase of the cloud service; therefore, the CSPs are not aware of the additional security and privacy requirements and tailored controls deemed necessary to protect the Wearable Co's customer PII. Customers require the mechanisms and tools that enable them to understand and assess what "good-enough security" means in the cloud. This requirement is critical when assessing if, for example, the Wearable Co security and privacy requirements are being fulfilled by the controls and certifications implemented by the selected CSPs.

Fortunately, stakeholders in the cloud community have identified that specifying security and privacy parameters in Service Level Agreements (termed as secSLA and PLA, respectively, in the rest of this chapter) is useful to establish a common semantics to provide and manage security assurance from two perspectives, namely, (i) the security/privacy level being offered by a CSP and (ii) the security/privacy level requested by a cloud customer.

In order to develop the full context of the value of secSLAs and PLAs for our case study, we introduce next the rationale of SLA usage along with the basic vocabulary.

9.6.1 Importance of secSLAs and PLAs for Cloud Transparency

Contracts and Service Level Agreements (SLAs) are key components defining cloud services. According to the ETSI Cloud Standards Coordination group [20], SLAs should facilitate cloud customers in understanding what is being claimed for the cloud service and in relating such claims to their own requirements. Naturally, better assessments and informed user decisions will also increase trust and transparency between cloud customers and CSPs.

A recent report from the European Commission [15] considers SLAs as the dominant means for CSPs to establish their credibility, attract or retain cloud customers since they can be used as a mechanism for service differentiation in the CSP market. This report suggests a standardised SLA specification aiming to achieve the full potential of SLAs, so all cloud customers can understand what is being claimed for the cloud service and relate those claims to their own requirements.

At the SecureCloud 2014 event [13], the Cloud Security Alliance (CSA) compiled and launched an online survey to better understand the current usage and needs of European cloud customers and CSPs related to SLAs. Almost 200 equally balanced cloud customer and CSP responders (80 % from the private sector, 15 % from the public sector and 5 % from other backgrounds) provided some initial findings on the use of standardised cloud SLAs. Respondents ranked the two top reasons why cloud SLAs are important as (1) being able "to better understand the level of security and data protection offered by the CSP" (41 %) and (2) "to monitor the CSP's performance and security and privacy levels" (35 %). Furthermore, based on the respondents' experiences, the key issues needed to make cloud SLAs "more usable" for cloud customers highlighted (1) the need for "clear SLO [Service Level Objective] metrics and measurements" in first place (66 %), (2) "making the SLAs easy to understand for different audiences (managers, technical legal staff, etc.)" in second place (62 %), (3) "having common/standardised vocabularies" (58 %) in third place and (4) "clear notions of/maturity of SLAs for Security and Privacy" (52 %) in fourth place. These responses are empirical indicators of the need to develop the field of cloud secSLAs and PLAs and the techniques to reason about them.

9.6.2 How Are secSLAs and PLAs Structured?

This section summarises the basic cloud secSLA/PLA terminology, based (where applicable) on the latest version of the relevant ISO/IEC 19086 standard [28] and the CSA PLA initiative [12]. A cloud SLA is a documented agreement between the CSP and the customer that identifies cloud services and SLOs, which are the targets for service levels that the CSP agrees to meet. If a SLO defined in the cloud SLA is not met, the cloud customer may request a remedy (e.g. financial compensation). If the SLOs cannot be (quantitatively) evaluated, then it is not possible for customers or CSPs to assess if the agreed SLA is being fulfilled. This is particularly critical in the case of secSLAs and PLAs, but there is also an open challenge on how to define useful (and quantifiable) security and privacy SLOs.

In general, a SLO is composed of one or more metrics (either quantitative or qualitative), where the SLO metrics are used to set the boundaries and margins of errors CSPs have to abide by (along with their limitations). Considering factors such as the advocated familiarity of practitioners with security/privacy control frameworks (e.g. ISO/IEC 27002 [29], CSA CCM [9] and CICA [3]), the relevant workgroups (e.g. the European Commission (EC) Cloud Select Industry Group on Service Level Agreements (C-SIG SLA) [16]) have proposed an approach that iteratively refines individual controls into one or more measurable security SLOs. The elicited SLO metrics can then be mapped into a conceptual model (such as the one proposed by the members of the NIST Public RATAX Working Group [38]), in order to fully define them. Cloud secSLAs and PLAs are typically modelled using the hierarchical structure shown in Fig. 9.3. The root of the structure defines the main container for the secSLA/PLA. The second and third levels represent the

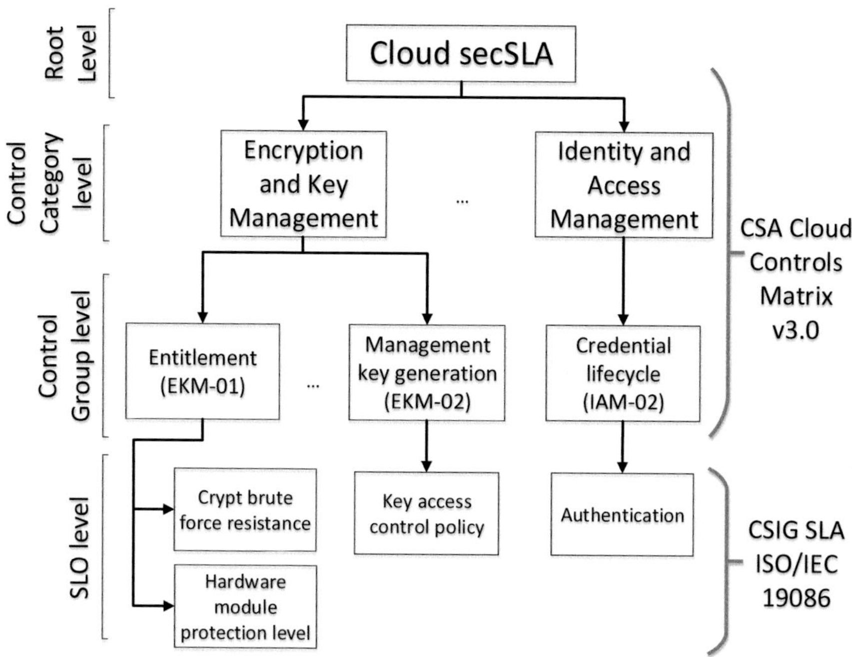

Fig. 9.3 Example of a cloud secSLA being derived from a security control framework

control category and control group, respectively, and they are the main link to the security/privacy framework used by the CSP. The lowest level in the SLA structure represents the actual SLOs committed by the CSP, in which threshold values are specified in terms of security and privacy metrics.

Next we will develop an example related to secSLAs, but the same methodological approach is also applicable to PLAs. In Fig. 9.3, let us suppose that a CSP implements the secSLA Control "Entitlement (i.e. EKM-01)" from the CSA CCM [9]. As observed in the figure, this control is actually contained within the group "Encryption and Key Management (i.e. EKM)". After selecting EKM-01, the same CSP then refers to the SLO list provided on the C-SIG SLA report [16] (or any other relevant standard) and finds out that two different SLOs are associated with control EKM-01, i.e. "cryptographic brute force resistance" and "hardware module protection level". Both SLOs are then refined by the CSP into one of more security metrics, which are then specified as part of the secSLA offered to the cloud customer. For example, a CSP can commit to a "cryptographic brute force resistance" measured through security levels such as *level1–level8* or through a metric called "FIPS compliance" defined as Boolean YES/NO values. Therefore, the secSLA could specify two SLOs: (cryptographic brute force resistance = level4) and (FIPS compliance = YES). If any of these committed values is not fulfilled by the CSP, then the secSLA is violated, and the customer might receive some compensation (this is the so-called SLA remediation process).

Using the presented approach, the security and privacy SLOs proposed by the CSP can be matched to the cloud customer's requirements before acquiring a cloud service. Actually, these SLOs provide a common semantics that both customers and CSPs can ultimately use to automate the management of cloud secSLAs and PLAs during the service provision. This will be further elaborated in the next section.

In our Wearable Co scenario, it is important to highlight that it does not suffice to understand how the Wearable service may affect its own customers, but one also needs to consider how the sub-services in the supply chain (i.e. CardioMon, Map-on-Web and DataSpacer in Fig. 9.2) contribute to the overall security and privacy levels. Hence, there is a distinct need for aggregation of metrics guaranteed by individual cloud services in order to get the values for a composite one. While practitioners have acknowledged the challenges associated with the composition of security (and privacy) metrics long before the "cloud times" [30], nowadays this topic is still mostly unexplored in cloud systems.

9.7 Continuous Assurance During Service Provision

The CRMF process shown in Table 9.1 highlights the fact that better levels of transparency can be achieved if the CSP continuously provides the expected assurance levels to the customer, during the whole provision of the cloud service. Based on the discussion presented in Sect. 9.6, the notion of continuous assurance can be related to reassessing the risk levels achieved during the operation of the service through analysing the compliance with agreed secSLAs and PLAs.

Let us take as a starting point the use case presented in Fig. 9.2, supposing that Wearable Co has agreed and signed SLAs (i.e. secSLAs and PLAs) with all the CSPs in the supply chain (i.e. CardioMon, Map-on-Web and DataSpacer). According to current practice, SLAs are signed by peers, which means that in our use case Wearable Co should have signed three different SLAs. However, in a real-world scenario, it might be also common for involved CSPs to sign SLAs, e.g. one SLA between CardioMon and DataSpacer and other between Map-on-Web and DataSpacer. This discussion is important to establish the way in which signed SLAs will be continuously assessed during the operation of the Wearable service. In Fig. 9.2, despite the fact that the security and privacy levels depend on several components of the supply chain, the responsibility of reporting these levels of overall service remains that of the "primary" CSP at the end of the supply chain: the CSP that directly faces the customer (i.e. Wearable Co). It is the responsibility for this "primary" CSP to gain assurance about the "secondary" CSPs involved in the supply chain. If the "primary" CSP uses a continuous monitoring mechanism to exchange information with customers, and if this "primary" CSP uses the same mechanism to exchange data with "secondary" CSPs, then it may choose to "proxy" some information originating from the supply chain back to the customer. This proxy approach is useful to automate the discovery of all entities in the supply chain. Providing visibility on the supply chain is often considered as a compliance requirement for CSPs with regard to EU data protection rules. Later on this section, we will discuss the CSA Cloud Trust Protocol (CTP), a mechanism than can be implemented to automate this process.

However, which elements should be assessed on a secSLA/PLA? Which mechanisms are available to continuously monitor cloud assurance? Once a cloud secSLA/PLA is built and agreed with the CSP, the customer now has a baseline to monitor the fulfilment of the agreed SLOs. The SLA can be evaluated through (i) the analysis of the fulfilment of agreed security SLOs and (ii) the identification of potential deviations from expected values (i.e. SLA violations). Intuitively, these violations can be managed by the CSP through actions ranging from changes to the current secSLA/PLA to termination of the agreed cloud service. Continuous assessment of agreed SLAs should consider on the one hand the hierarchical organisation of the SLOs (cf. Fig. 9.3) and their quantitative/qualitative nature. Both challenges have just started to be studied by the academic community [33], and we foresee the midterm adoption of these approaches in real-world deployments.

From the continuous monitoring mechanism perspective, despite the apparent feasibility of the control/monitoring approach, to the best of our knowledge, there are very few efforts exploring this area. One of the recent developments in the area of continuous monitoring is CSA's Cloud Trust Protocol (CTP) [10] which is an open API to enable cloud customers to query CSPs about the security/privacy levels of their services. A key design choice that has shaped CTP is the focus on the monitoring of secSLAs/PLAs, rather than the pure monitoring of security/privacy controls. The CTP API is designed to be a RESTful protocol that cloud customers can use to query a CSP on current security/privacy attributes related to a cloud service such as the current level of availability or information on the last vulnerability assessment. This can be done in a classical query-response approach, but the CTP API also has the ability to specify event triggers on the CSP that may optionally be reported in push mode to a specific customer. These triggers allow the cloud customers to be notified of important security/privacy events that occurred in near real time. The CTP API additionally provides access to a log facility that can be used to store and access security events generated by triggers.

It is important to emphasise that CTP mainly proposes a unified standardised API to present measurement results to improve cloud transparency and assurance. As such, the CTP API does not cover the actual monitoring infrastructure and related technologies that are used to gather, store and analyse events in order to produce these measurement results. A high-level view of CTP's system model is shown in Fig. 9.4.

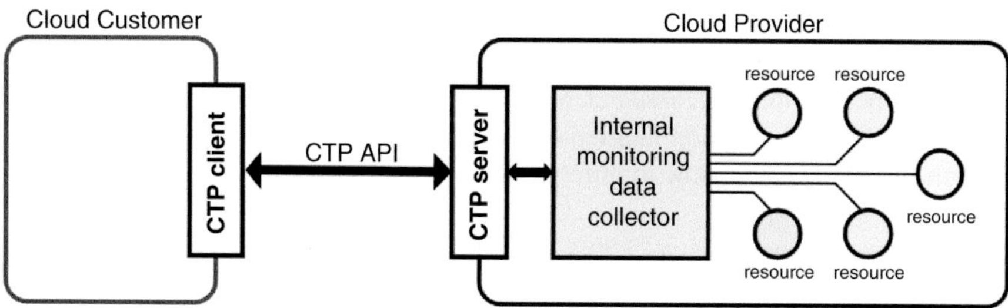

Fig. 9.4 Simplified system model of the CSA Cloud Trust Protocol

At the state of the art, CSA CTP is the main enabler of the upcoming continuous monitoring procedure to be implemented by the certification scheme called the Open Certification Framework (OCF) [11].

9.8 Example Tools

In this section we present how some of our tools developed within the Cloud Accountability Project [8] have been implemented to solve part of the identified issues, linking to phases within the accountability lifecycle. The organisational lifecycle for accountability as described in the A4Cloud Reference Architecture [25] can be summarised into three major accountability lifecycle phases:

- *Phase 1 – Provisioning for Accountability*: works on risk identification (based on business impact, not just technology), control identification, control implementation design and control implementation through technology and processes. Examples include the Cloud Offerings Advisory Tool (COAT) and Data Protection Impact Assessment Tool (DPIAT) described in Sect. 9.8.1.
- *Phase 2 – Operating in an Accountable Manner*: corresponds to the operational (production) phase of the solution and includes all the associated management processes. The Audit Agent System (AAS) monitors the infrastructure and collects policy-based evidence to prove that the cloud provider operates the infrastructure in an accountable manner. This tool is presented in Sect. 9.8.2.
- *Phase 3 – Audit and Validate*: corresponds to the assessment of the effectiveness of the controls which have been deployed, the necessary reporting, and paves the way to the tuning (adaption) of the measures deployed to ensure that obligations are being met. Based on the evidence collection, the Audit Agent System (AAS) generates policy violations and audit reports, as discussed in Sect. 9.8.3.

9.8.1 Phase 1: Provisioning for Accountability

The A4Cloud toolkit contains tools which address the need for support in managing risk and cloud service contract selection in the context of accountability for data stewardship in the cloud. Tools in this area serve a *preventive* role, by means of:

1. Evaluation of cloud offerings and contract terms with the goal of enabling a more educated decision making on which service and service provider to select
2. Assessment of the risks associated with the proposed usage of cloud computing, involving personal and/or confidential data and elicitation of actionable information and guidance on how to mitigate them

These two mechanisms are being developed as the following distinct tools that may be used separately or in combination.

9.8.1.1 Cloud Offerings Advisory Tool (COAT)

COAT is a cloud brokerage tool that allows potential cloud customers (with a focus on end users and SMEs) to make informed choices about data protection, privacy, compliance and governance, based upon making the cloud contracts more transparent to cloud customers. A number of related factors vary across cloud providers and are reflected in the contracts, for example, subcontracting, location of data centre, use restriction, applicable law, data backup, encryption, remedies, storage period, monitoring/audits, breach notification, demonstration of compliance, dispute resolution, intellectual property rights on user content, data portability, law enforcement access and data deletion and retention. The focus of the tool is on providing feedback and advice related to properties that reflect compliance with regulatory obligations rather than providing feedback on qualitative performance aspects (such as availability), although potentially the tool could be integrated with other tools that offer the latter.

A Web user interface enables interaction with the target users. During this interaction, potential cloud customers can provide as input to the graphical interface a collection of answers to a questionnaire, but most of this information is optional and need not be provided although the interactions help guide the users as to their needs and provide a more targeted output. Such information includes the data location, the roles involved in the scenario to be built on the cloud, contact details of those responsible for defining the purpose of use for the involved data, contextual information about the environment setting and the user needs and requirements. Other knowledge used by the system includes the cloud service offerings in structured form, models of cloud contracts and points of attention and reputation information with respect to the agents involved in the offering process. During this process of interaction, guidance is provided on privacy and security aspects to pay attention to when comparing the terms of cloud service offerings. The outcome of COAT is an immediate and dynamically changeable report, including an overview of compatible service offerings matching the user requirements and links to further information and analysis. See Fig. 9.5 for an example.

Ongoing research involves usage of ontologies for more sophisticated reasoning and linkage to PLA terms and usage of maturity and reputational models to optimise ordering of the outputs. For further information about the system, see [1].

9.8.1.2 Data Protection Impact Assessment Tool (DPIAT)

DPIAT is a tool that assesses the proposed use of cloud services, helping users to understand, assess and select CSPs that offer acceptable standards in terms of data protection. The tool is tailored to satisfy the needs of SMEs that intend to process personal data in the cloud; it guides them through the impact assessment and educates them about personal data protection risks, taking into account specific cloud risk scenarios. The approach is based on legal and socio-economic analysis of privacy issues for cloud deployments and takes into consideration the new requirements put forward in the proposed European Union (EU) General Data Protection Regulation (GDPR) [14], which introduces a new obligation on data

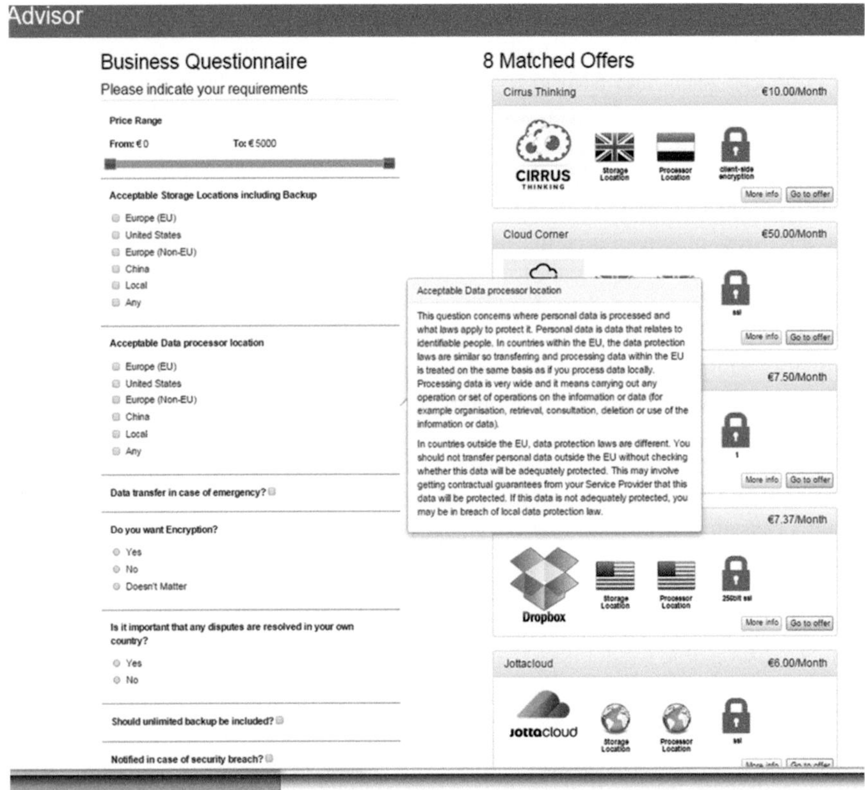

Fig. 9.5 Example COAT screenshot

controllers and/or processors to carry out a Data Protection Impact Assessment prior to risky processing operations (although the requirements differ slightly across the various drafts of the regulation).

Figure 9.6 shows the high-level approach of DPIAT. The assessment is based on input about the business context gathered within successive questionnaires for an initial screening and for a full screening for a given project, assessed using Drools rules [31], combined with risk assessment of cloud offerings [6] based upon information generated voluntarily by CSPs, and collected from the CSA Security, Trust and Assurance Registry (STAR) [11]. This risk assessment approach is aligned to the methodology presented in Sect. 9.5.

The output of the first phase of the DPIAT reflects advice about whether to proceed to the second phase of assessment. The second phase questionnaire contains a set of 50 questions. The output of this phase is a report that includes: the data protection risk profile, assistance in deciding whether to proceed or not and the context of usage of this tool within a wider DPIA process. Amongst other things, the

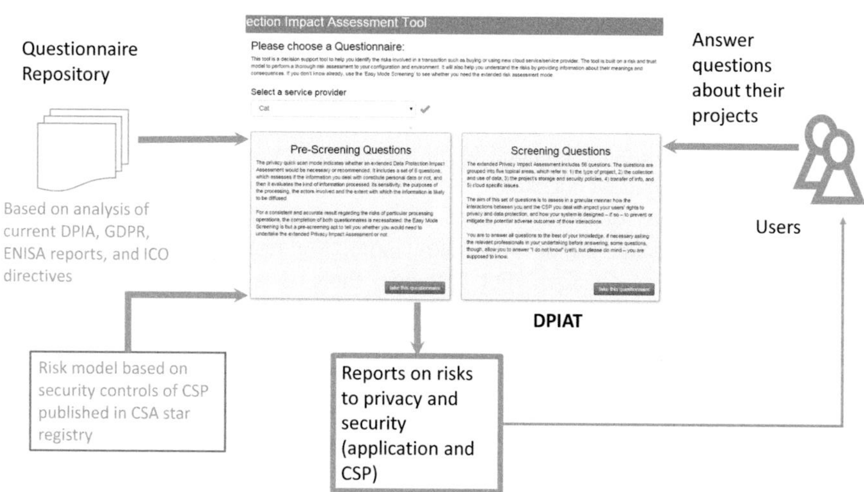

Fig. 9.6 The high-level approach of the Data Protection Impact Assessment Tool

tool is able to demonstrate the effectiveness and appropriateness of the implemented practices of a cloud provider helping him to target resources in the most efficient manner to reduce risks. The report from this phase contains three sections. The first, *project-based risk assessment*, is based on the answers to the questionnaire and contains the risk level associated with sensitivity, compliance, transborder data flow, transparency, data control, security and data sharing. The second part displays risks associated with the *security controls used by the CSP*. It contains the 35 ENISA risk categories [21] with their associated quantitative and qualitative assessments. The last section highlights additional information that the user needs to know related to requirements associated with GDPR article 33 [14]. The system also logs the offered advice and the user's decision for accountability purposes. For further information about the system, see [2].

9.8.2 Phase 2: Operating in an Accountable Manner

The Audit Agent System (AAS) is used to prove that the cloud infrastructure is operated in an accountable manner, by collecting evidence to capture the relevant information for proving accountability. The AAS is associated with policy monitoring, which sniffs the cloud ecosystem transactions to verify that policy configuration is followed in the service chain and appropriate notifications are alerted when data usage is not compliant to contracts.

The evidence collection process builds an information base, which includes the collection of operational evidence (how data is processed in the system demonstrated by logs and other monitoring information), documented evidence (documentation for procedures, standards, policies), configuration evidence (are systems configures as expected), accountability controls, deployed accountability tools and correct implementation of an accountability process. Evidence is not collected purposelessly but requires a distinct reason. This reason is defined in a policy, which is directly mapped to an accountability obligation for which the compliance status shall be checked.

There are various evidence sources to be considered, such as logs, cryptographic proofs, documentation and many more. For each, there needs to be a suitable collection mechanism. For instance, there is a log parser for logs, a cryptographic tool for cryptographic proofs or a file retriever for documentation. This is done by the AAS software agent called the Evidence Collection Agent that is specifically developed for data collection from the corresponding evidence source. Another type of collection agent has client APIs implemented to interface with more complex tools, such as Cloud Management Systems (CMS), that is, one of the major evidence collection sources for cloud resource usage, access rights, configurations, resource provisioning, virtual machine (VM) locations, etc. Evidence Collection Agents can be deployed at different cloud architectural layers (i.e. network, host, hypervisor, IaaS, platform-as-a-service (PaaS), SaaS), with the purpose of collecting, processing and aggregating evidence for enabling validation of the account. Generally, these agents receive or collect information as input and translate that information into an evidence record, before storing it in the Evidence Store. Agent technology helps to ensure extensibility by allowing easy introduction of new evidence sources by adding new collection agents. This approach also allows AAS to address rapid infrastructure changes, which are very common in cloud infrastructures by easily deploying and destroying agents when needed.

Remediation actions that have to be performed after some policy has been violated, for instance, often rely on fine-grained monitoring facilities and extensive analysis capabilities of the resulting evidence.

The AAS tool provides suitable means for the runtime monitoring of cloud applications and infrastructures, the verification of audit policies against the collected data and the reporting of policy violations along with the evidence supporting it (for more details about the architecture, see Sect. 9.8.4).

9.8.3 Phase 3: Audit and Validate

The cloud audit process implemented by AAS is comprised of two main processes: First evidence has to be collected, as described in the previous section, which includes required information to conduct audits. Second, audits in general can be performed periodically, on-demand or continuously. One of the major problems of periodical audits in cloud computing is the dynamic change of the infrastructure, and therefore there is a risk of missing critical violations or incidents if the interval is too big.

With respect to cloud audits, we have implemented the following audit processes:

1. *Planning Phase*: Audit policies are derived from the input policy (e.g. an A-PPL policy), which form an automatic audit plan. Audit tasks define the evidence collection and steps for analysis, i.e. whose evidence has to be collected and how it should be analysed.
2. *Securing Phase*: Installation of evidence collection for audit trail collection. Evidence is collected from the evidence sources according to what has been defined in phase 1.
3. *Analysis Phase*: Automatic evaluation of the collected evidence according to the defined policies, which results in a statement about (non)compliance with supporting evidence for that claim.
4. *Presentation Phase*: Presentation in an audit dashboard and/or generation of a human-readable document, which includes all processed audit tasks including their results.

Figure 9.7 depicts these different phases of auditing. An audit policy serves as the main input to the audit process, where collected evidence is analysed. As a result, an audit report is generated, which can take the form of a Web-based dashboard presenting policy violations or a notification of other components about policy compliance and violations. AAS is used by auditors, who may act on behalf of the cloud customer/data subject (external view) or the cloud provider (internal view) to perform continuous and periodic audits. The goals and nature of policies which are audited may differ depending on the view. The view may also differ in case of a trusted third-party auditor (TPA), who is independent from the customer and provider, but acting on behalf of any of those.

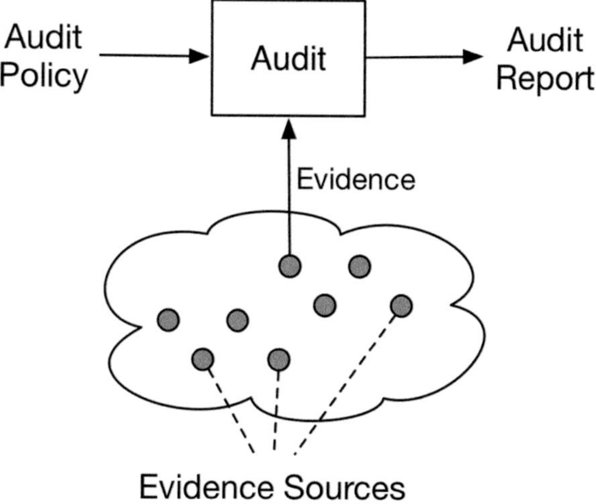

Fig. 9.7 Audit process

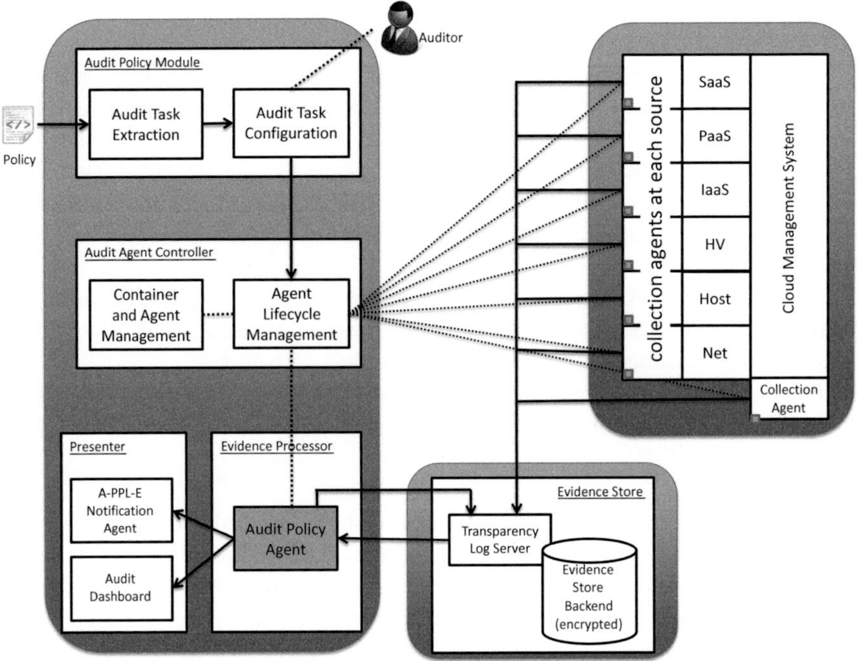

Fig. 9.8 Audit agent system architecture overview

9.8.4 Architecture of the Audit Agent System

The AAS architecture comprises the six major modules shown in Fig. 9.8.

The six AAS modules can roughly be divided into four major parts:

1. *Input*: Audit Policy Module (APM)
2. *Runtime Management*: Audit Agent Controller (ACC)
3. *Collection and Storage*: Evidence Collection Agents, Evidence Store
4. *Processing and Presentation*: Evidence Processor, Presenter

These are now considered in turn.

9.8.4.1 *Input*: Audit Policy Module (APM)

The Audit Policy Module (APM) is the main component for handling input to the AAS. Typically, obligations, access control requirements and other types of policies define how a cloud service is supposed to handle data. To gather evidence about the compliance with or violation of these policies is part of the AAS. In the APM, machine-readable input policies are parsed, and evidence collection tasks and evidence-processing tasks are extracted. The main assumption in this parsing process is that this will not be fully automatable. Therefore, additional information is provided by the auditor. Depending on the actual audit task, this includes infrastructure-specific information such as:

- Specifics of the evidence source (IP addresses, Java Agent Development Environment (JADE) agent platform [49], REST endpoints)
- Specifics of the monitored service (path to log files, files to monitor for changes)
- Required credentials (authentication strings, usernames, passwords)
- Audit type (periodic, continuous, one-time)

9.8.4.2 *Runtime Management*: Audit Agent Controller (AAC)

The Audit Agent Controller (AAC) is the main runtime management component. At the core of AAS, it is responsible for orchestrating audits and agents according to what has been previously defined in the APM. The typical audit lifecycle is as follows:

1. According to the input provided by the APM, AAC creates and configures audit policies, its tasks and corresponding collection and processing agents.
2. Agents are migrated between the core platform and target platforms (near the evidence source).
3. During the agents' lifetime, the AAC monitors registered platforms and registered agents, handles exceptions and manages the creation, archival and deletion of evidence stores.

The AAC uses the JADE Agent Communication Language (ACL) [50] for internal communication between agents. Therefore, the AAC sits at the core of the AAS and manages all operations regarding the orchestration of collection and processing agents, as well as maintaining the Evidence Store. Most notably, the AAC uses UDP-based monitoring of the various agents to ensure a consistent and smooth operation of the AAS.

9.8.4.3 *Collection and Storage*: Evidence Collection Agents and Evidence Store

The Evidence Collection Agent reads raw evidential data from the source and generates evidence records that are sent to the Evidence Store. The Evidence Store is implemented using transparency log (TL) [46, 47]. Since TL functions as a key-value store for storing evidence records (encrypted messages identified by a key), NoSQL or RDBMS-based back ends for persisting evidence records can be used. All data contained in the Evidence Store is encrypted. The evidence records are encrypted on a per audit task basis, which means only the Audit Policy Agent corresponding to the collection agents is able to decrypt the evidence records for further processing. Isolation between tenants in a single Evidence Store is achieved by providing one container for each tenant where his evidence records are stored.

However, even stronger isolation by providing a separate Evidence Store hosted on a separate VM is also possible with this approach.

9.8.4.4 *Processing and Presentation*: Evidence Processor and Presenter

The processing or analysis of evidence consists of two steps:

1. Retrieval of the appropriated collected information from the Evidence Store (which must be policy/audit task based)
2. A verification process, which checks the correctness of recorded events according to defined obligations and authorisations

These procedures are inherently dependent on the type of audit task. There can be specific audit tasks defining a single or a small set of checks to be performed (e.g. availability of VMs, results of a proof of retrievability (PoR), etc.) or more complex compliance over time periods (e.g. monthly checks of policy compliance). According to the complexity of the task, due to the number of obligations, or the volume of evidence to analyse, different verification processes may need to be considered, ranging from log mining, checking for predefined tokens or patterns, to automated analysers and automated reasoning upon the audit trail.

For the situations where the audit task consists of defined checks, the Evidence Store is accessed, and the required logs (or other elements) are identified in the related evidence records. More complex compliance checks will involve the retrieval of evidence records covering given periods of time or specifically related to a policy identifier.

The outputs of any audit, including report, notification alerts and messages of non-compliance, are then processed for presentation.

There are two main ways of evidence presentation in AAS. The A-PPL-E Notification Agent is designed to generate violation notification messages, which are consumed by other A4Cloud tools, to reported violation according to what is defined in the A-PPL policy.

The second presenter in AAS is the Web-based dashboard (see Fig. 9.9). The auditor uses the dashboard as the main way of interaction with AAS. Most importantly, audit results are displayed to the auditor, which provides an immediate overview of the current compliance status. The main contact point with the system is the audit dashboard which is a Web application implemented using Bootstrap.

Automated Incident Detection: Collected evidence serves as the basis for policy violation detection in AAS. Audit agents monitor collected evidence records and generate violation or compliance notifications. There are three modes an audit agent can run in:

1. *Continuous*: In continuous mode, the audit agent evaluates evidence records as soon as they are generated by the collection agent. The continuous audit mode is very similar to monitoring with immediate notification if a violation is detected. The time between evidence about a violation or incident being recorded and

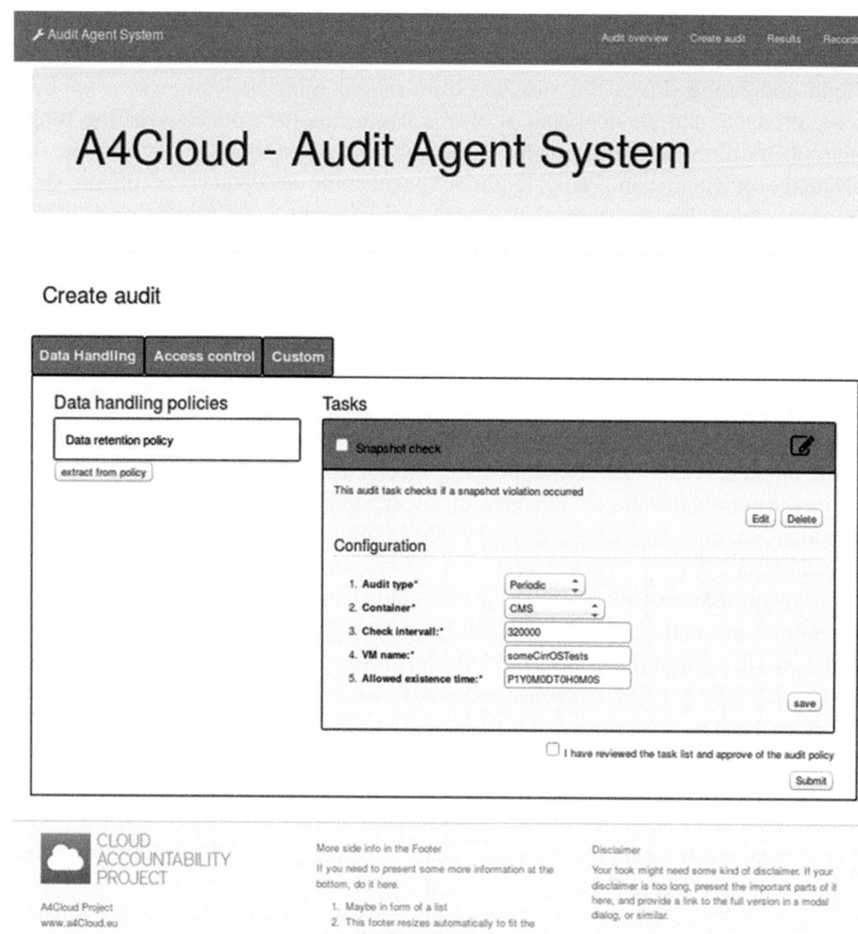

Fig. 9.9 AAS dashboard

actual detection and notification is minimal in this scenario. However, since evidence is analysed on the fly, more complex evidence analysis that relies on taking a whole series of records into account is generally harder to implement.

2. *Periodic*: In periodic mode, the audit agent evaluates evidence records at specific intervals (e.g. hourly, daily, weekly, etc.).
3. *One-time*: In one-time mode, the audit agents, collection agents and the corresponding evidence records are archived immediately after the audit result has been generated.

9.9 Conclusions

Cloud computing drives the vast spectrum of emerging and innovative applications, products and services and is also a key technology enabler for the future Internet. Its direct economic value is unambiguously substantial, but taking full advantage of cloud computing requires considerable acceptance of off-the-shelf services, which directly impacts the customer's perception of transparency in this technology. Through a hypothetical use case, this chapter presented some of the main transparency and assurance barriers that (prospective) customers might find when migrating to the cloud, with a particular focus on SMEs. Furthermore, this chapter described three promising state-of-the-art mechanisms aimed to improve the levels of trust that customers can have in cloud systems, namely, (i) specific risk management frameworks, (ii) security and privacy specification in SLAs and (iii) the assessment of achieved security and privacy levels during the operation of the cloud service. The choice of these mechanisms is not accidental: All three are incrementally developed and have strong dependencies amongst each other. For example, associated risks are continuously monitored through the assessment of agreed SLAs.

However, the analysis presented in this chapter acknowledges that prior to any meaningful use and standardisation of the proposed mechanisms by the academic or industrial communities, effort should be invested into empirical validation of the security and privacy elements composing these SLAs. In particular we refer to the evaluation of their feasibility in real-world scenarios. An entire research agenda should be developed by cloud stakeholders to guarantee the creation of standards and best practices reflecting Cloud-Adapted Risk Management Frameworks, secSLA/PLA elements that are feasible to deploy and trade-offs associated to continuous monitoring mechanisms. These efforts will pave the road for the broad adoption of tools like the ones presented in this chapter.

Finally, we have illustrated a variety of accountability mechanisms that provide novel ways of improving cloud assurance and transparency, at various stages of an organisational lifecycle for accountability.

9.10 Review Questions

1. What is accountability?
2. How can an accountability-based approach improve cloud assurance and transparency?
3. Explain how risk assessment, SLAs and certification relate to accountability-based approaches.
4. What is the need for specific Cloud-Adapted Risk Management Frameworks?
5. Mention some advantages related to the use of security and privacy SLAs with respect to security and privacy certification.
6. Give some examples of accountability mechanisms for the cloud.

Acknowledgements This work is supported in part by EC FP7 SPECS (grant no. 610795) and by EC FP7 A4CLOUD (grant no: 317550). We would like to acknowledge the various members of these projects who contributed to the approach and technologies described.

References

1. Alnemr R, Pearson S, Leenes R, Mhungu R (2014) COAT: cloud offerings advisory tool. In: Proceedings of CloudCom, IEEE, pp 95–100
2. Alnemr R et al (2015) A data protection impact assessment methodology for cloud. In: Proceedings of Annual Privacy Forum (APF), LNCS, Springer, October 2015 (to appear)
3. American Institute of Certified Public Accountants and Canadian Institute of Chartered Accountants (AICPA-CICA) (2015) Privacy maturity model. Available via http://www.cica.ca/resources-and-member-benefits/privacy-resources-for-firms-and-organizations/item47888.aspx. Cited 1 June 2015
4. Bennett CJ, Raab CD (2006) The governance of privacy: policy instruments in global perspective. MIT Press, Cambridge, MA
5. Butin D, Chicote M, Le Metayer D (2013) Log design for accountability. In: Proceedings of IEEE CS Security and Privacy Workshops (SPW), pp 1–7
6. Cayirci E, Garaga A, Santana de Oliveira A, Roudier Y (2014) A cloud adoption risk assessment model. In: Proceedings of Utility and Cloud Computing (UCC), IEEE/ACM, pp 908–913
7. Centre for Information Policy Leadership (CIPL) (2014) A risk-based approach to privacy: improving effectiveness in practice. Available via http://www.hunton.com/files/upload/Post-Paris_Risk_Paper_June_2014.pdf. Cited 1 June 2015
8. Cloud Accountability Project (A4Cloud). www.a4cloud.eu
9. Cloud Security Alliance (CSA): Cloud Controls Matrix (CCM). Available via https://cloudsecurityalliance.org/research/ccm/
10. CSA: Cloud Trust Protocol (CTP). Available via https://cloudsecurityalliance.org/research/ctp/
11. CSA: Open Certification Framework (OCF). Available via https://cloudsecurityalliance.org/star/
12. CSA: Privacy Level Agreement (PLA). Available via https://cloudsecurityalliance.org/research/pla/
13. CSA: Secure Cloud (2014). Available via https://cloudsecurityalliance.org/events/securecloud2014/
14. European Commission (EC) (2012) Proposal for a regulation of the European Parliament and of the Council on the protection of individuals with regard to the processing of personal data and on the free movement of such data (General Data Protection Regulation), Brussels, January 2012
15. EC (2013) Cloud computing service level agreements: exploitation of research results
16. EC (2014) Cloud service level agreement standardisation guidelines. C-SIG SLA
17. European DG of Justice (Article 29 Working Party) (2010) Opinion 03/2010 on the principle of accountability (WP 173), July 2010
18. European DG of Justice (Article 29 Working Party) (2012) Opinion 05/2012 on cloud computing
19. European DG of Justice (Article 29 Working Party) (2014) Statement on the role of a risk-based approach in data protection legal frameworks (WP218). Available via http://ec.europa.eu/justice/data-protection/article-29/documentation/opinion-recommendation/files/2014/wp218_en.pdf
20. European Telecommunications Standards Institute (ETSI) Cloud Standards Co-ordination Group (2013) Cloud standards coordination final report

21. European Union Agency for Network and Information Security (ENISA) (2009) Cloud computing – benefits, risks and recommendations for information security
22. ENISA (2014) Cloud certification schemes metaframework. Version 1.0, November 2014
23. Felici M, Pearson S (eds) (2014) Report detailing conceptual framework. Deliverable D32.1, A4Cloud
24. Felici M, Pearson S (2014) Accountability, risk, and trust in cloud services: towards an accountability-based approach to risk and trust governance. In: Proceedings of Services, IEEE, pp 105–112
25. Gittler F et al (2015) Initial reference architecture. Deliverable 42.3, A4Cloud
26. Hildebrandt M (ed) (2009) Behavioural biometric profiling and transparency enhancing tools, D 7.12, FIDIS
27. International Data Corporation (IDC) (2012) Quantitative estimates of the demand of cloud computing in Europe
28. International Organization for Standardization (ISO) (2014) (Draft) Information technology – cloud computing – service level agreement (SLA) framework and terminology. ISO/IEC 19086
29. ISO (2014) Information technology – security techniques: guidelines on information security controls for the use of Cloud computing services based on ISOIEC 27002. ISOIEC 27002
30. Jansen W (2010) Directions in security metrics research. TR-7564. NIST
31. JBoss: Drools business rules management system solution. Available via http://www.drools.org/
32. Kavanagh KM, Nicolett M, Rochford O (2014) Magic quadrant for security information and event management. Gartner
33. Luna J, Langenberg R, Suri N (2012) Benchmarking cloud security level agreements using quantitative policy trees. In: Proceeding of the Cloud Computing Security workshop, ACM
34. Mell P, Grance T (2011) The NIST definition of cloud computing, NIST Special Publication 800-145, September 2011
35. National Institute of Standards and Technology (NIST) (2002) Risk management guide for information technology systems. SP 800-30. NIST
36. NIST (2010) Guide for applying the risk management framework to federal information systems. SP 800-37. NIST
37. NIST (2013) Cloud computing security reference architecture. NIST SP 500-299, vol 1
38. NIST (2014a) (Draft) Cloud computing: cloud service metrics description. Public RATAX WG, NIST
39. NIST (2014b) Cloud-adapted risk management framework. Draft NIST SP 800-173
40. Nymity Inc (2014) Privacy management accountability framework
41. Organisation for Economic Co-operation and Development (OECD) (2013) Guidelines concerning the protection of privacy and transborder flows of personal data
42. Office of the Information and Privacy Commissioner of Alberta, Office of the Privacy Commissioner of Canada, Office of the Information and Privacy Commissioner for British Colombia (2012) Getting accountability right with a privacy management program, April 2012
43. Pearson S (2011) Toward accountability in the cloud. IEEE Internet Comput 15(4):64–69, IEEE Computer Society
44. Pearson S (2014) Accountability in cloud service provision ecosystems. In: Secure IT systems, LNCS, vol 8788, Springer, pp 3–24
45. Pearson S, Wainwright N (2013) An interdisciplinary approach to accountability for future internet service provision. IJTMCC 1(1):52–72
46. Pulls T, Martucci L (2014) User-centric transparency tools. D-5.2, vol 1, A4Cloud
47. Ruebsamen T, Pulls T, Reich C (2015) Secure evidence collection and storage for cloud accountability audits. In: Proceedings of CLOSER 2015, Lisbon, Portugal, 20–22 May 2015
48. Stoneburner G, Hayden C, Feringa A (2004) Engineering principles for information technology security (A baseline for achieving security). SP800-27, NIST
49. Telecom Italia: Java Agent Development Environment (JADE). http://jade.tilab.com
50. Telecom Italia: JADE Agent Communication Language (ACL) (2005). Retrieved from http://jade.tilab.com/doc/api/jade/lang/acl/package-summary.html

51. Wang C, Zhou Y (2010) A collaborative monitoring mechanism for making a multitenant platform accountable. In: Proceedings of HotCloud. Available from https://www.usenix.org/legacy/event/hotcloud10/tech/full_papers/WangC.pdf
52. Wlodarczyk, Tomasz et al (2014) A4Cloud project: DC-8.1 framework of evidence. A4Cloud

Siani Pearson is a principal research scientist in the Security and Manageability Lab at Hewlett Packard Labs (Europe). She is a fellow of the British Computer Society, associate editor of *IEEE Transactions on Cloud Computing* and scientific coordinator of a major European research project on *Accountability for the Cloud* (*A4Cloud*). Her current research focuses on accountability, privacy and cloud computing.

Jesus Luna is the research director at Cloud Security Alliance (Europe). He obtained his Ph.D. degree from the Technical University of Catalonia in Spain. He is also affiliated with TU Darmstadt (Germany) with his main research interests on security quantification, cloud security and security policies.

Christoph Reich is a professor at the faculty of computer science at the University of Applied Science in Furtwangen (HFU) and teaches in the field of network technologies, programming, IT management, middleware and IT security. He leads scientific management of the HFU Information and Media Center, which consists of the Information Technology, Online Systems, Learning Systems and HFU library departments. His research focus is cloud computing, QoS, virtualization and IT security.

DDoS Protection and Security Assurance in Cloud

10

Gaurav Somani, Manoj Singh Gaur, and Dheeraj Sanghi

Abstract

DDoS attacks have become a big concern for enterprises in the era of Internet computing. DDoS attacks have gained large attention from the community due to numerous fatal incidents in the last one decade. In particular, incidents on cloud services and cloud infrastructures have triggered anticipations related to heavy, longer, and hazardous attacks in near future. Additionally, economic losses due to these attacks, have given rise to Economic Denial of Sustainability (EDoS) attacks that exploit the on-demand resource provisioning feature of cloud computing. As attack strikes a service hosted on a cloud platform, the resource bottleneck would occur. Consequently, the ambiguity and inability to differentiate between legitimate and attacker traffic would lead to acquiring or buying more and more resources on the go. These fake resource claims would lead to a heavy economic burden, unnecessary downtime, power consumption, and migrations. This chapter targets at detailing the insights into the DDoS and EDoS attacks in cloud computing. Additionally, this chapter provides a comprehensive sketch of the present state of the art, recent incidents, their impact, cloud pricing and accounting mechanism, and its readiness for these attacks.

G. Somani (✉)
Department of Computer Science and Engineering, Central University of Rajasthan, Ajmer, Rajasthan, India
e-mail: gaurav@curaj.ac.in

M.S. Gaur
Department of Computer Science and Engineering, Malaviya National Institute of Technology, Jaipur, India
e-mail: gaurms@mnit.ac.in

D. Sanghi
Computer Science and Engineering, Indian Institute of Technology, Kanpur, India
e-mail: dheeraj@iitk.ac.in

S.Y. Zhu et al. (eds.), *Guide to Security Assurance for Cloud Computing*, Computer Communications and Networks, DOI 10.1007/978-3-319-25988-8_10

Through this chapter, we argue that the present solution stack is not sufficient enough to deter or defend DDoS attack on cloud services. The major emphasis of the proposed chapter would be towards security assurance, loss sharing, and providing a detailed guideline about the ideal solutions.

Keywords
Cloud computing • DDoS attacks • EDoS attacks • Attack mitigation • Security assurance

10.1 Introduction

Cloud computing, as an emerging technology paradigm, has changed the enterprise IT planning. Even government services and public utilities have shifted their IT implementations from traditional fixed on-site infrastructure to on-demand cloud computing infrastructure. Cloud computing provides many features including better resource utilization, pay-as-you-go accounting, on-demand resource allocation, no maintenance overhead, no depreciation of resources, fault tolerance, minimum downtime, and many such similar features. DDoS attacks have been proven fatal for many websites. Recently, this has attracted the security community to find solutions to detect, prevent, and mitigate the attack. Importantly, DDoS attackers have reportedly shifted their interest from the traditional web services and started targeting cloud-based web services. This is necessary due to two important reasons, one, large number of cloud-based services or their versions of popular services and, two, it is easy for attackers to achieve the goals of the attack, which have turned it into EDoS (Economic Denial of Sustainability) attack. DDoS in cloud is effective due to the on-demand availability of profound resources. Many recent incidents of DDoS in cloud have shown enormous costs resulted due to a DDoS attack on a cloud-based web service [41]. This chapter aims at providing a detailed discussion about the DDoS attack in cloud, their attack and threat model, characterization, modeling, and solutions. In order to motivate readers to the developments and open areas of research, a comprehensive survey space is also provided with effective solution guidelines in the form of security assurance.

10.2 DDoS in Cloud Computing

A typical DDoS scenario in cloud is as shown in Fig. 10.1. Cloud will typically have multiple high-capacity servers connected using a high-speed network. Each of these servers is virtualized using hypervisors or virtual machine monitors (VMM). Virtualization enables these servers to run multiple guest operating systems on top of the virtual machines. One of these VMs is the victim VM, which is running a web server which has been targeted by attackers. These attackers may range from a single node to a large network of nodes which are also termed as Bot-nets. Bot-nets and their availability as hired services have led a completely new dimension of DDoS

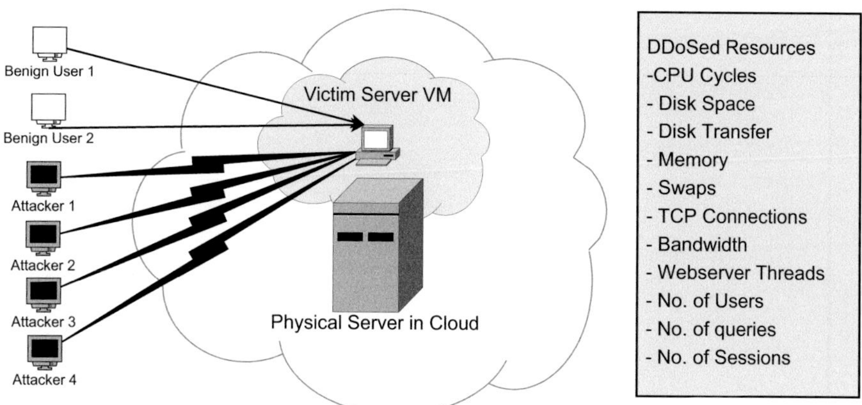

Fig. 10.1 DDoS scenario: cloud computing

attacks. Anybody having intentions to stop the web services of its competitors may hire services from a Bot-net provider on hourly basis and use thousands of nodes to flood the competitor servers. The attack packets may be of any type ranging from TCP SYN, ICMP, FTP or HTTP GET requests, etc. The aim of the attacker is to send more and more requests as to consume the usable resources on the server, in a manner such that the legitimate users would not get services with required quality or any service at all. Resources which may be exhausted by such requests may range from any of the resources listed in Fig. 10.1. Attackers may choose to exhaust one or more resources to get the desired success. Few of the resources are considered as easy resources to attack on, such as number of connections or sessions. If an attacker is successful in establishing the maximum connections, the server will not be able to serve legitimate clients anymore. The most important resource to consider from the perspective of cloud is CPU cycles. Attackers may plan to send a large number of requests in such a manner that the CPU utilization reaches the maximum (100 %), resulting in service denial. Now, let us take insight into cloud specifics which change the attack consequences differently. While the attack forces the virtualized server to reach maximum utilization of its resources, on-demand cloud which owns a huge amount of resources may add more resources to the virtualized server. This is because of the nature of the resource allocation and accounting models used in cloud. Cloud computing is a paradigm popularly known for the on-demand resource allocation and "pay-as-you-go" accounting model. In the absence of any DDoS protection mechanism, the cloud resource allocation algorithm would see a resource surge of victim server which is under attack. As per the allocation policy (usually termed as "auto-scaling"), cloud will automatically add resources to the victim server on the go. Theoretically, this may continue to large resource additions on regular intervals, in a hope that the increased resource utilization is due to the good users, e.g., flash sale on an e-commerce site. Inadvertently, this would enable the attackers to become successful in a fatal version of DDoS, EDoS, which is

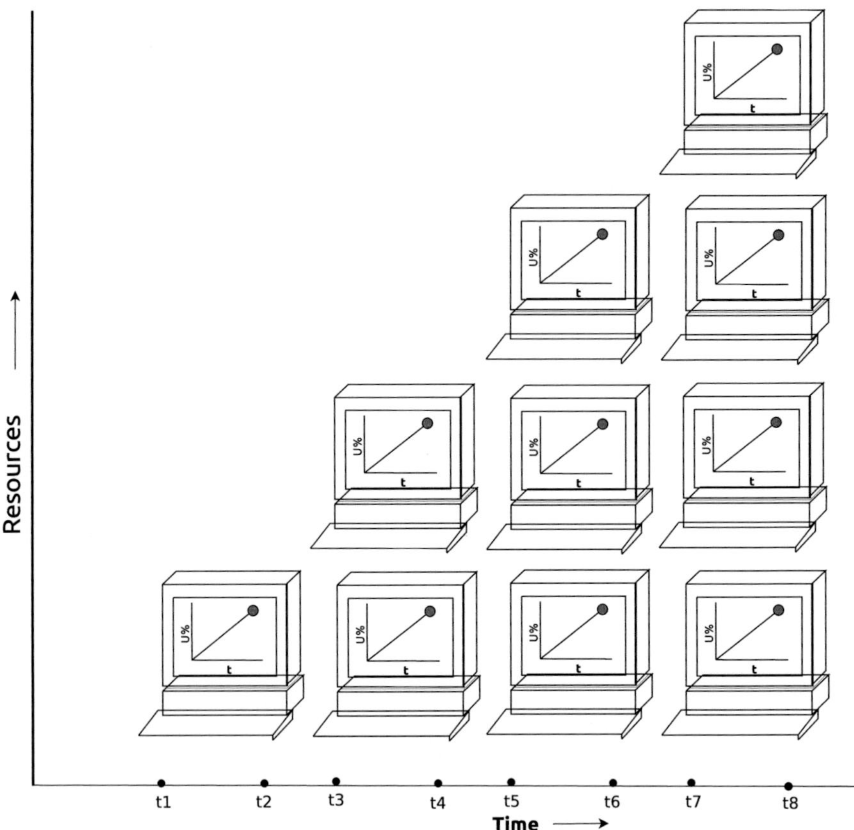

Fig. 10.2 DDoS in the form of EDoS in cloud

Economic Denial of Sustainability attack. This attack has attracted a large number of resource additions/buying from cloud, resulting into an enormous usage bill. There are instances where this attack has lead to thousands of dollars per hour to few popular services on Amazon EC2 Cloud. Though the shift of enterprises from fixed infrastructure on-site/hosted servers to on-demand remote cloud servers is happening for many good reasons, however, this has taken a shape of attackers' shift from fixed infrastructure servers to cloud-based servers. Behavior of cloud server and its allocation, in the presence of attack, is shown in Fig. 10.2. This figure shows a typical behavior, where a VM instance running in cloud is attacked by a DDoS attack at time $t1$. Due to the attack, the resource utilization starts rising, which, soon, results in to the maximum utilization of one or more resources of the VM. These resources may be any of the listed in Fig. 10.1. Generalizing the resource allocation strategies to the pure "on-demand" resource allocation, the auto-scaling feature of cloud would add more VM instances on the same or the other servers in cloud. In vertical scaling, the resource addition is done by adding more resources on the VM placed on the same physical server. In horizontal scaling, the resources are added in the form of additional VM instances on same or the other server in the cloud. Hybrid approaches can also be used having both vertical and horizontal scaling. As the attack continues with its request flood, more and more VM instances will be added and started to share the increased load. Based on the pricing and resource allocation model the consumer has opted, it will keep on adding resources, till it attains the maximum resources available or allowed based on the limits posed by the provider or consumer. Each time the resources (VM instances or resources) are added, the resource usage bill is increased. This resource bill may be enormous and as high as few thousand dollars per day [41]. After adding the maximum resources, the attack strength may result into the "service denial." Points between $t1$ and $t8$ show the attack consequences in cloud. This starts in the form of EDoS, continues as EDoS, and finally converges into DDoS. Economic harms are usually additional than the usual harms of DDoS attacks. The following are the major players, which either affects or gets affected in the whole DDoS scenarios [55]. This is very important for the aim of this chapter, as the security assurance is required to be adopted at each one of these players.

1. Victim server: This server is the direct victim of DDoS attack.
2. Attackers: One (DoS) or more nodes (DDoS) sending large number of requests. Spoofing may also be used.
3. Cloud as an entity: Cloud provider doing business by proving resources as a service.
4. Physical server hosting the victim server: This server is hosting multiple VMs in a multi-tenant environment. There is high possibility that this server will also be affected in addition to the cohosted VMs due to performance isolation aspects. Real resource demands will also be affected due to the fake allocation to the DDoSed VM.
5. Cohosted VMs: Mainly due to performance isolation aspects and unnecessary migrations/instance creation due to fake resource consumption by DDoSed VM which is subsequently into no resource availability.
6. Other physical servers: Other physical servers may be affected due to incoming migrated VMs and effects due to continuous DDoS attack.
7. Consumers to victim servers: Users of applications/services running on victim servers will be affected. The end users may be some other applications which are partially dependent upon the services of the victim web service. This results into business, rating, and reputation losses which are fatal for any organization.
8. Consumers to other VMs: Though indirectly affected, cohosted VMs user may also face service quality issues with the web service the victim web server is running.

Table 10.1 DDoS on fixed infrastructure vs. DDoS on cloud infrastructure

	DDoS on fixed infrastructure	DDoS on cloud infrastructure
Attack mechanism	Sending large number of requests by large number of nodes or Bot-nets	Similar to fixed infrastructure
Attack consequences	Service denial	Service degradation, economic losses due to resource buying and may finally result into service denial
Resource requirement at attacker side	Large	May even have effects on smaller number of resources
Effects on end users of the service under attack	Service denial	Service degradation and service denial on resource limit or exhaustion
Mitigation methods	Application layer or network layer mitigations	Additional mitigation required at cloud level or resource allocation level

10.2.1 History and Recent Incidents

DDoS attacks have been a center point of attraction in the security research and IT security planning for any enterprise. It is important to know and quantify the effects of DDoS on cloud infrastructures. DDoS attacks on fixed capacity (on-premise or hosted) are discussed. After that, recent DDoS attacks on cloud computing platforms are discussed to give an idea about their presence and nature. Table 10.1 shows the difference between "DDoS in Cloud" and "DDoS in fixed infrastructure." How the attack is being applied, its consequences, resource requirement while the attack occurs, and mitigation methods are the parameters, on which this comparison is made.

10.2.2 DDoS on Fixed Infrastructure

It is said that the first known DDoS attack was targeted to the University of Minnesota on their IRC servers in 1999 [20]. This attack had affected many machines in the campus and lasted for days. Similarly, Worldpay's payment and other services were affected by a DDoS attack in 2004, stopping its services which used to serve its clients spread to around 70 countries [44]. Subsequent to many of the similar attack incidents, various governments like the UK and Sweden had come up to legally ban DDoS attacks in 2006–2007 [35, 48]. The motives behind DDoS attacks have ranged from beating business competitions to political rivalry to cyber wars between countries. Massive DDoS attack was planned on Estonian websites in 2007 which resulted into a shutdown of major websites of the country [9]. A large DDoS attack had chocked the whole virtual gaming industry in Korea [4], costing it losses of more than $1 billion. Almost all the countries in the world have faced one or more similar attacks on their state infrastructures. Every country has large number of official websites which provide information and services for the public, defense services, intelligence services, and other information repositories for many other services. A large number of attacks have been reported on news websites [45, 58], e-commerce sites [59], and content provider websites [19].

10.2.3 DDoS on Cloud Infrastructure

DDoS attacks and their special version, EDoS, was first coined by Chris Hoff of Unisys in 2009. DDoS attacks in cloud are also termed as fraudulent resource consumption (FRC) attacks by Idziorek et al. in [22]. Authors have done characterization experiments to understand the impact of DDoS attacks on cloud infrastructure. Authors have shown that even sending mere 1 request/minute for a month from a single source results into an extra $2 bill on Amazon EC2 cloud. Authors have also calculated costs for heavy DDoS attacks where an attack of 5.2 Gbps would cost more than $6000 per day. This characterization can be extended and used for cost calculations with extensive usage of different resources. Looking at the recent attack in late 2014 and Q1 and Q2 of 2015, it is quite visible that cloud infrastructure-based services have become an easy target for DDoS attackers with effective results. A report by Alcatel-Lucent [42] signifies this argument by providing three important cases to this shift of attacker's mind. The first reported incident was on Sony and Microsoft gaming servers on Christmas day 2014. These servers provide popular gaming services for Xbox and playstation and were hosted on cloud servers. This gives a sign that multimedia and entertainment sites are among the favorites for a DDoS attack. Another attack targeted the cloud service provider Rackspace on its DNS services which disrupted the services around half of the day. Another notorious cloud-targeted DDoS was on Amazon EC2 servers, attacking it for on-line currency mining in 2014. This report had also highlighted the growth and possibilities to use cloud's profound and cheap resources in place of bots to plan DDoS attacks. In another report by Arbor Networks [43], there were attacks of the range of up to 154 Gbps in 2014 [6]. Similarly, the reports from Verisign [53] for Q1 of 2015 were threatening, as more than one third of the attacks mitigated by them were on cloud-based services/SaaS services. Reports in [47] have shown an attack cost rise of more than 400 % than the last year's data. This has been evident by the attack on GreatFire (www.greatfire.org), where the website faced a loss of more than $30 K/day on cloud-based operations [41]. There are multiple similar reports by industry which may be found out in [33, 46, 51, 57].

10.3 Attack Model and Threat Model

In this section, attack model and threat model for DDoS attacks in cloud computing platform are discussed. For better comprehension of these models, Tables 10.2 and 10.3 are given for attack model and threat model respectively. Attack model details about the features of a DDoS attack in cloud. On the other hand, threat model

Table 10.2 Attack model: DDoS in cloud

Features	Details
Attack packets	HTTP GET, TCP SYN, ICMP, HTTP POST, etc.
Attack frequency	Typically >500 requests/s, depends upon resources at both the ends [39]
Attack bandwidth	1–300 Gbps [6]
Typical attackers	A single source, a network, and bot-nets with or without spoofing
Attack methods	Low rate, flood, or flash mimic
Attack repetition	In many cases, repetition is done from different sources
Attack duration	Minutes to hours (average 72 min in [6])
Attack targets	Multimedia, government, e-commerce, cloud services, and many other targets
Attack motives	Competition, rivalry, cyber war between countries

Table 10.3 Threat model: DDoS in cloud

Threats to	Details
Victim server	Economic losses, service denial/downtime, unnecessary resource addition, VM instance creation, migrations, business and reputation losses
Cohosted VMs	Performance interference, resource race, and extra migrations due to resource exhaustion on physical server
Host physical server	Extra migrations and it would not be able to fulfill the requirements of cohosted VMs due to resource consumption by victim VM
Victim server owner	Downtime, economic losses, short-term and long-term business losses
Cloud provider	Extra migrations, performance interference to other VMs, large bandwidth bottleneck, downtime, and higher energy consumption
Other physical servers	Incoming migrations, VM instance creation, and consequent issues due to those VM instances under attack
Service end users	Poor service quality, downtime, and problems to other dependent services

illustrates various possible threats on attack targets and other elements and losses. Security literature uses both the models to provide better defensive solutions to various attacks. Though the literature uses both the terms interchangeably, however, here it would be better to comprehend in the present manner.

10.3.1 Attack Model

Based on the available literature [42] and recent incidents, it is clear that the attackers have shifted their attack targets from normal web services to cloud-based web services. This has resulted into happiness for cloud users that it will be easier to defeat the attack due to the availability of profound resources in cloud. On the other hand, attacker's joy cannot be ignored due to the easier- and difficult-to-detect

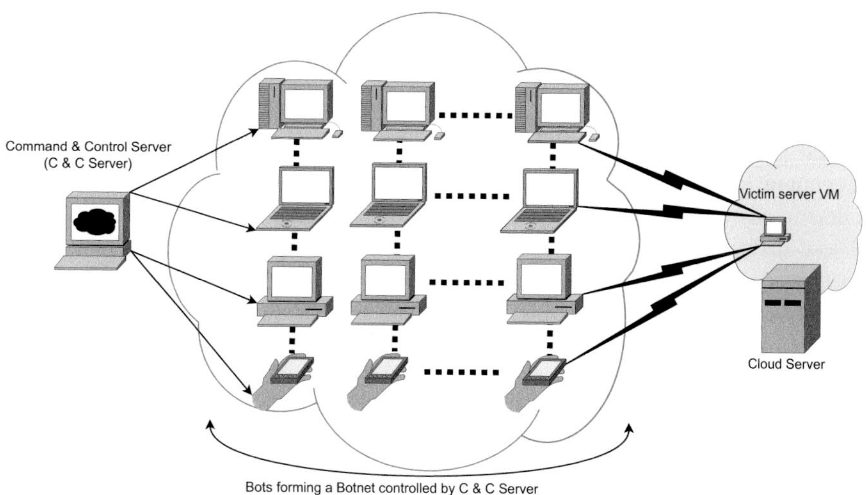

Fig. 10.3 Bot-net and C & C server

consequences of DDoS in the form of EDoS. Additionally, attackers may use cloud-based, profound resources-enabled bots to plan the attack [34]. It is important to note that the attack model is the same for both fixed infrastructure and cloud infrastructure. This is one interesting point to note that the methods of attack remains the same, while at the same time, the security community is required to spend efforts on devising new methods to circumvent and mitigate the attack in cloud platform as the consequences of the attack are different. "Bots on rent" has become quite a business these days, and there are multiple fatal stories in the recent past. Bots are typical malware programs, unknowingly installed by machines while on Internet. These bots are then controlled and used by Command & Control (C & C) servers to plan an attack (Fig. 10.3). There are reported incidents where the number of bots even ranged between 10,000 and 30,000 in number [26, 49]. These services are available on hourly basis charges on per hundred/thousand nodes. As success of DDoS attacks depends upon winning the "arms race," which is basically the resource race between attackers and victim servers, attackers are getting large number of cheap attack resources in the form of bots, while, on the other hand, victim server has dedicated resources on cloud to fight with the attackers. Bandwidth is the most important and costly resource these days, however, attacks consuming enormous bandwidth up to 300 Gbps have been observed in recent past. These sort of attacks change the whole scenario as they will consume and stress almost all the costly resources listed in Sect. 10.2. Attack duration is the most important factor while planning the mitigation. There are attack instances which last many hours to some lasting only few seconds. Average duration of these attacks have increased to 72 min from 60 min in 2014 [6].

10.3.2 Threat Model

Threat model gives the picture of how a variety of DDoS attacks result into various threats to different targets and stakeholders of cloud. In addition to service denial possibilities, economic sustainability issues are also important to ponder. Economic losses are mostly due to incorrect decisions made by on-demand resource allocation in cloud, which is also termed as "auto-scaling" (discussed in Sect. 10.2). These decisions are due to the resource utilization surge which results into the resource/VM instance addition which involves a cost. Performance isolation is one of the desired features of virtualization. However, performance interference and resource contention is still an issue in multi-tenant cloud. According to a detailed experimental and simulations study conducted by authors in [55], performance isolation and resource contention have been shown while DDoS attack is occurring on a cloud platform. In addition to losses to victim server, most of the other stakeholders in cloud environment are also affected. These indirect effects on nontargets are considerable in heavy attack DDoS scenarios. Stakeholders with various possible threat or effects on them are listed in Table 10.3. It is important to note that most of these effects are not available in the case of DDoS attack in non-cloud environment, except the service denial effects. Increased number of migrations, performance interference, short-term business losses (monetary) and long-term losses (business value), and higher energy consumption are important consequences of DDoS attacks in cloud which are also bothering nontargets. Proper isolation and DDoS protection is needed for all the VMs in multi-tenant environment as they are indirectly affected. Additionally, these effects should account to all the loss calculations and its sharing among these stakeholders.

10.4 System Model

In order to understand the DDoS attack, its impact, and relationship with the cloud resource allocation methods, a system model is presented. For more details on these models, readers are advised to contributions in [63] and [55]. A cloud will have the following components which are important for our discussion. There will be n physical servers.

$$P_i, i = 1, 2, ...n \tag{10.1}$$

and m VMs,

$$V_j, j = 1, 2, ...m \tag{10.2}$$

For resource accounting and billing, the resource items with each one of the physical servers and VM would be the following. Here, CPUs (C), memory (M), disk space (D), and bandwidth (B) are represented.

$$P_{i1} = C_i, \qquad P_{i2} = M_i, \qquad P_{i3} = D_i \qquad P_{i4} = B_i \tag{10.3}$$

Similarly, a VM V_j will have

$$V_{j1} = C_j \qquad V_{j2} = M_j \qquad V_{j3} = D_j \qquad V_{j4} = B_j \tag{10.4}$$

Capacity of physical server would be

$$Cap(P_i) = (C_i, M_i, D_i, B_i) \tag{10.5}$$

Capacity of a VM would be

$$Cap(V_j) = (C_j, M_j, D_j, B_j) \tag{10.6}$$

Cloud provides a feature of on-demand resource addition. The additional resource requirement would be

$$Require(V_j) = (C_j', M_j', D_j', B_j') \tag{10.7}$$

Each physical server has a limit on number of VMs it can host (r VMs). From V_j, few VMs as set V_s, s=1, 2,......r, can be hosted if on P_i,

$$Cap(P_i) \geq \sum_{s=1}^{r} Cap(V_s) \tag{10.8}$$

and following all should also hold.

$$C_i \geq \sum_{s=1}^{r} C_s \tag{10.9}$$

$$M_i \geq \sum_{s=1}^{r} M_s \tag{10.10}$$

$$D_i \geq \sum_{s=1}^{r} D_s \tag{10.11}$$

$$B_i \geq \sum_{s=1}^{r} B_s \tag{10.12}$$

After successful placement of VMs of subset V_s on P_i, the idle resources on the server would be

$$Idle(P_i) = Cap(P_i) - \sum_{s=1}^{r} Cap(V_s) \tag{10.13}$$

While a VM is facing a DDoS attacks, the resource requirements will increase. This will trigger the auto-scaling algorithm, and resource requirement will be met by available free resources (from Eq. 10.13) which is only possible if

$$Idle(P_i) \geq \sum_{s=1}^{r} Require(V_s) \tag{10.14}$$

If one or more of the four equations (Eqs. 10.9, 10.10, 10.11, and 10.12) does not hold for a VM, it would require the auto-scaling to either for VM migration to another physical server which has required resources available. Another option is horizontal scaling which would add another VM instance (of the VM under attack) on another physical server. This would lead to the scenario shown in Fig. 10.2. As DDoS will stress resources, the auto-scaling will be misused by it to harm the server economically.

10.5 DDoS Protection in Cloud

In the previous section, we have built a model which tries to comprehensively detail the requirements of a DDoS mitigation system. In this section, we shall focus on the state-of-the-art literature on DDoS mitigation in cloud computing. There are large numbers of surveys published in the area of traditional non-cloud infrastructures which provide methods to overcome DDoS attacks. Some of them are in [12,13,50]. Though very few DDoS mitigation methods prove to be fit for cloud, still, following are the three broad sets of solutions which will make us aware about the present state of the art in the cloud space.

10.5.1 DDoS Prevention Methods

As shown in Fig. 10.4, the entry level methods, where the user request first arrives, can be tested to prevent the DDoS attack to occur. Challenge-response protocols have been the core part of many solutions in the DDoS mitigation area. These tests allow the system to identify whether the requester is a bot or a normal human being. Generally, most of the solutions follow the Turing test approach to validate this. A simple text problem, graphical puzzle, or a game-based problem is used to allow user to prove whether it is a human being. These problems will be generated in such a manner that it would be difficult for an automated bot/machine to generate answers. There are large numbers of solutions which are partially or fully implemented on the fundamentals of Turing tests [1,3,40,40,62]. CAPTCHAs are one of the most popular implementation of this approach. In one of the initial solutions to EDoS, authors in [56] have provided a Turing test-based system, which is known as EDoS-Shield. This system only provides access to clients which pass the graphical Turing tests. Similarly, text-based puzzles have been used by [27] and [21]. In addition to the puzzles, sometimes, the system also

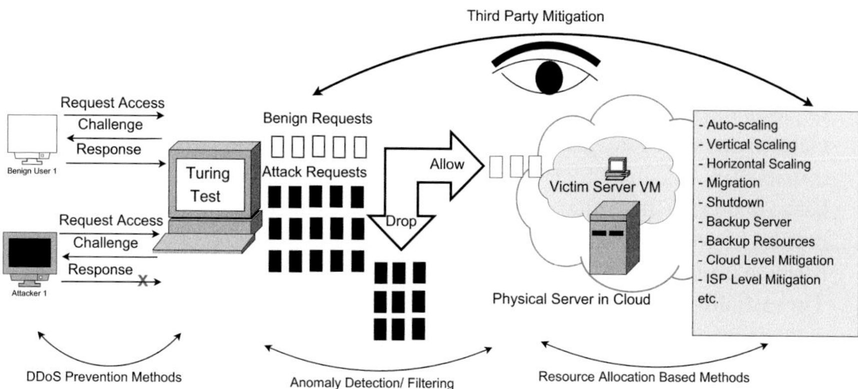

Fig. 10.4 DDoS protection in cloud at various levels

keeps a timer, in which the response should reach the server to stop computation of answers automatically. A different dimension to challenge response protocols is crypto puzzles, which are used to evaluate the compute power of clients. Many implementations have used them in [10, 28, 32]. At times, these puzzles have also been used as proof-of-work (PoW) approaches which shift the computation load on client and requires a response within a stipulated time to evaluate the capability of the clients. In addition to puzzle-based entry, there are approaches which have restrictive access policies. These policies take Turing tests as the first test, and after a suspected access, instead of dropping/blocking the requester, they would restrict for sometime/delay the requests [5, 28, 52]. Approaches exist which provide the access to "good" users on hidden servers or ports like hidden proxy servers in [61], ephemeral servers in [28], and hidden ports in [37]. In another approach, dynamic shuffling between clients and servers have been proposed to provide quality service to benign users [25]. Similarly, selective and goodwill-based access have been provided in the approached proposed by [28, 37].

10.5.2 Anomaly Detection

Anomaly detection is a major class of DDoS protection methods which are there to detect any anomaly pointing towards the occurrence of a DDoS attack. Many of these methods are based upon filtering the traffic on the basis of the phenomenon of natural traffic and its profile based on history. Time, frequency, access pattern, and count are few parameters which define the web behavior of a user which differentiates it from the other users. The second stage in Fig. 10.4 represents mitigations based upon these techniques. Techniques which are used in anomaly detection in fixed infrastructures have been listed in detail in [38]. The following are the four important categories of approaches which come under anomaly detection-based DDoS mitigation.

1. **Statistical pattern detection:** These approaches are based upon web access logs and features extracted from it. These features are compared with the features, and the deviation between them is used to detect the anomaly. Legitimate web requests have been modeled as "Zipf" distribution in [23], where authors have claimed to segregate good and bad traffic on the basis of the properties of distribution. Shamsolmoali et al. [54] have used a filtering method, which is based upon statistical filtering in which they have calculated the distance between profiles of good and bad traffic using Jensen-Shannon divergence [16]. Similarly, baseline profiling of TCP and IP flags have been used by [15].
2. **Threasholds** Thresholds or counts are quickest anomaly detection methods without much calculations. Number of requests in a specific period or request frequency is a common method to segregate traffic. This is mostly successful as the request count by a normal user can't match the frequency of attackers. Approaches in [24, 27, 52] used this method of anomaly detection. Similarly, hop-count-based filtering is used by [27] and [2] where the major assumption is towards IP spoofing. As per this assumption, the TTL or hop-count of spoofed IP addresses will be the same and can be used to detect the attackers.
3. **Sessions and Web Behavior** Time spent on a web page has been used as a metric in the contributions of [31], where authors have claimed that the attackers do not spend any time on the requested page. Similarly, Idziorek et al. [22] have proposed methods, where they could identify the web session from web logs. Differed sessions from the natural sessions would be filtered by the authors. Many approaches have used different ideas of web behavior of users in their detections. Authors in [7] and [11] have used the packet headers to identify the web behavior. Similarly, in [37], e-commerce website has been modeled for user behavior on various pages. Similar contributions exist in approaches [60], where authors have used HTTP and XML header in creating web behavior profiles.

10.5.3 Resource Allocation-Based Methods

As we have seen in the last two categories of DDoS mitigation systems, none of those methods target the cloud side of solution space. Additionally, most of those methods are similar to the ones which were there for detection in fixed infrastructure. In the system model, it has come up that the major emphasis of a mitigation solution should be towards minimizing the costs and resources. Following are some of the state-of-the-art approaches which have been proposed in the recent past after emergence of stable cloud services.

1. **Auto-scaling:** Auto-scaling being the core feature of cloud and major reason behind the success of DDoS in cloud requires major effort. Authors in [55] have proven the fatal behavior of auto-scaling approaches under attack. Methods are needed to be devised to have correct auto-scaling decisions under attack [36].
2. **Migration:** These methods are primarily used by horizontal scaling methods where the VM under attack is migrated from the bottleneck server to other

resourceful server. Many times, once the attack gets over, the VM under attack is again placed at its initial place. Authors in [64] and [34] have used backup servers and migration as their core approach while DDoS occurs.

3. **Resource usage-based detection:** The utilization matrices of VMs can be used to detect the possible attack scenarios. Virtual machine monitors can watch these activities and act accordingly. Authors in [64] and [34] used similar approaches. Shui et al. have used resource utilization of the servers in their mitigation methods.
4. **Backup servers and resources:** At the time of attack presence, some backup servers can be kept where the victim server can be migrated. Once the attack is mitigated or is over, the server can be placed back. Backup resources, their cost and migration costs are important factors to be considered while designing these methods. Authors in [63] and [34] have used this approach.
5. **Shutdown:** Shutdown of the server during the attack duration is another method to indirect mitigation but costs downtime. Shutdown-based ideas are used in [61].

10.6 DDoS Security Assurance in Cloud

This section includes the security assurance framework for DDoS attacks on cloud-based services. This framework is the gist of solutions available on each level of protection. Importantly, this framework also highlights the requirement to think in the direction of multilevel DDoS protection mechanisms as the traditional methods are not sufficient. Among the three categories of solutions presented in the previous section, most of the contributions concentrate on the solutions which work at the application layer or at the level of victim server. Research contribution like [55] and [63] have also argued to work at other levels of protection outside the victim server. A set of guidelines are provided with respect to each administrative or control level in Table 10.4.

1. **Victim level/application-level defense:** This is the level at which the server under attack has local control over application and its resources. This allows the application and the underlying middle ware and operating system to look at the

Table 10.4 Assurance at various levels

Assurance/defense level	DDoS assurance methods
Victim/application	Turing tests, Anomaly detection using web behavior and QoS monitoring, participation in auto-scaling
VMM	Resource usage-based detection
Cloud/network	Traffic monitoring, resource allocation pattern, resource limits (caps), migrations, attacks from cloud
ISP	Traffic segregation, ISP-level mitigations
Third party	Forwarding/intermediate server-based detection, cloud-based mitigation services, DDoS mitigation as a service

unusual patters in traffic, application usage and other locally available resource usage pattern. The minimum requirement for the prevention mechanism is a Turing test based on many of the challenge-response protocols. This allows the initial protection on the authentication-based websites. Even the first page, which is the home page of the website enabled with a Turing test, is prone to the DDoS attack. This requires efforts on the part of victim server to rely on other factors, like traffic patterns, transaction patterns, business value generation pattern, and the web behavior of users. This is important, in the sense that these patterns will get an insight into the real business or work the server is aiming to produce. The definition of work will always be different from application to application. This work may be a total number of buys or total sales amount for an e-commerce site, number of unique surveys filled on a survey site in some unit time.

2. **VMM/hypervisor-level defense:** Defense or detection at the level of hypervisor provides the additional outer view of the attack. After the victim server, hypervisor is the entity which can monitor the VM activities and provide necessary support for mitigation. This mitigation support requires additional information from application layer to understand whether the usage surge is due to an attack or there is really a great rewarding benign traffic which has come (which happens in the case of flash sales or large number of train reservations in the case of holidays or the visit at the FIFA site during tournament finals).
3. **Cloud-level/network-level defense:** Cloud-level defense can play a significant role in the case of DDoS. This is also important from the perspective of cloud as the mitigation service can be a part of cloud offerings which may attract service providers to choose the cloud. Additionally, at the level of cloud, it has full control of all the resources including the network resources, which help them to critically identify the overall resource usage, network traffic movement (inward and outward), energy consumption perspective, and migrations. These controls allow cloud to take abstract decisions to see any upcoming DDoS attack as well as resource requirement for genuine traffic. Accurate decisions can only be taken if there is a coordination between the three levels, victim, VMM, and cloud level. While we look for the industrial implementations at this level, Amazon has provided a feature to keep caps or resource limits on VMs. In addition to this, CloudWatch service [8] is provided to check and monitor many of the real-time accounting and resource usage information.
4. **ISP-level defense:** Internet service providers may also play a big role while mitigating the geographical DDoS attacks. These attacks may be originated from a specific organization or country pool and may target a similar group of servers from a different administration. ISP may collaborate and keep a high-level view of this unwanted flood and take necessary actions at networks level. Also this information in the form of alerts with attacker's information may help planning the clouds and victim servers. Solution on the similar lines are discussed in [18].
5. **Third-Party Defense:** Third-party mitigation systems are mostly onsite- or cloud service-based mitigation systems. Many of them have used the name DDoS mitigation as a service (DaaS) in cloud [14, 29, 30]. Most of these

solutions provide services as an overlay service which forwards the requests once satisfied. Many service providers have solutions in this market space [43,51,57]. Additionally, there are hybrid implementation in [17] which helps local firewall to mitigate the attack using profound cloud resources.

10.7 Chapter Summary

This chapter is aimed at providing a detailed tutorial cum open research direction guide for security enthusiasts working in the area of cloud security. Among many of the security issues studied by the community in the area of cloud computing, DDoS attack is proven to be the most fatal attack. This chapter has shown through recent incidents and cloud features that the effects of DDoS attacks are not on the same lines as it was with the traditional fixed infrastructure. A comparison of DDoS attacks, their effects, solutions, and major features have been compared between DDoS in fixed infrastructure and cloud infrastructure. A detailed and point-to-point attack model is presented to help readers understand the unique features of DDoS attack in cloud computing. The interesting part of the attack model is in its details which help the reader to understand the threat models. Threat models generally help in characterizing the effects of attacks with specific losses made by them to all the stakeholders. An effort has been made to prepare a threat model listing all the stakeholders and the impact of DDoS on them in addition to the real target. This is interesting to note that many of these stakeholders are significantly affected by the attack though not targeted directly.

A theoretical system model is also presented in the chapter detailing the cloud infrastructure, physical servers, virtual servers, and individual resources. Requirements of a good DDoS mitigation system have been established using the system model in addition to the important aspects. DDoS protections are surveyed and comprehensively discussed in three major categories including the most popular solutions. DDoS security assurance solutions at each level has been summarized in a manner such that to give detailed ideas to upcoming solutions in the space. DDoS attacks, their characterization, and mitigation solutions have become a vibrant area in the security space with large demands for solutions. This chapter has highlighted many of the open research problems in the space and possible solution pointers to readers.

10.8 Review Questions

1. What are the major differences between DDoS and EDoS attacks? Highlight the differences from the perspective of how the attack is planned and its consequences.
2. What are the important factors, which are considered by attackers to plan a quick and effective DDoS attack, without investing much of the resources?

3. What are the important effects of DDoS attacks to cloud and other stakeholders? Why the consequences are different as compared to traditional fixed infrastructures?
4. What are the attack and threat models of DDoS attacks in cloud infrastructures? Detail them.
5. What is the role of ISPs in mitigation of DDoS attacks? Discuss a typical example case of ISP role in DDoS Mitigation.
6. How DDoS security assurance can be guaranteed at various levels of mitigation?
7. How can a multilevel and multipoint mitigation system help in designing better solutions to defend against DDoS attacks?
8. Resource allocation in cloud is termed as a major cause for success of DDoS attacks in cloud. Why and how?

References

1. Abliz M, Znati T (2009) A guided tour puzzle for denial of service prevention. In: Annual computer security applications conference (ACSAC '09), Honolulu, pp 279–288, Dec 2009
2. Al-Haidari F, Sqalli MH, Salah K (2012) Enhanced EDoS-shield for mitigating EDoS attacks originating from spoofed IP addresses. In: Min G, Wu Y, (Chris) Liu L, Jin X, Jarvis SA, Yassin Al-Dubai A (eds) 11th IEEE international conference on trust, security and privacy in computing and communications (TrustCom 2012), Liverpool, 25–27 June 2012, pp 1167–1174. IEEE Computer Society
3. Alosaimi W, Al-Begain K (2013) An enhanced economical denial of sustainability mitigation system for the cloud. In: NGMAST, Prague, pp 19–25. IEEE
4. Arakaki T (2007) Dos attack cripples $1 billion virtual games trade – blackmailers blamed. http://texyt.com/dos+attack+hack+cripples+online+games+item+trade+00119
5. Baig ZA, Binbeshr F (2013) Controlled virtual resource access to mitigate economic denial of sustainability (edos) attacks against cloud infrastructures. In: Proceedings of the 2013 international conference on cloud computing and big data (CLOUDCOM-ASIA '13), Washington, DC, pp 346–353. IEEE Computer Society
6. Burt C (2014) Large volume ddos attacks see exceptional growth in first half of 2014: Arbor networks. http://www.thewhir.com/web-hosting-news/large-volume-ddos-attacks-see-exceptional-growth-first-half-2014-arbor-networks
7. Chen Q, Lin W, Dou W, Yu S (2011) Cbf: a packet filtering method for ddos attack defense in cloud environment. In: IEEE ninth international conference on dependable, autonomic and secure computing (DASC), Sydney, pp 427–434. IEEE
8. Amazon CloudWatch (2014) Amazon cloudwatch. https://aws.amazon.com/cloudwatch/
9. Davis J (2007) Hackers take down the most wired country in europe. http://archive.wired.com/politics/security/magazine/15-09/ff_estonia?currentPage=all
10. Dean D, Stubblefield A (2001) Using client puzzles to protect tls. In: USENIX security symposium, Washington, DC, vol 42
11. Dou W, Chen Q, Chen J (2013) A confidence-based filtering method for ddos attack defense in cloud environment. Future Gener Comput Syst 29(7):1838–1850
12. Douligeris C, Mitrokotsa A (2004) {DDoS} attacks and defense mechanisms: classification and state-of-the-art. Comput Netw 44(5):643–666
13. See refrence [12]
14. Du P, Nakao A (2010) Ddos defense as a network service. In: Network operations and management symposium (NOMS), Osaka, pp 894–897. IEEE
15. Ismail MN, et al. (2013) Detecting flooding based doS attack in cloud computing environment using covariance matrix approach. In: ICUIMC, Kota Kinabalu, p 36. ACM

16. Gómez-Lopera JF, Martínez-Aroza J, Robles-Pérez AM, Román-Roldán R (2000) An analysis of edge detection by using the jensen-shannon divergence. J Math Imaging Vis 13(1):35–56
17. Guenane F, Nogueira M, Pujolle G (2014) Reducing ddos attacks impact using a hybrid cloud-based firewalling architecture. In: Global information infrastructure and networking symposium (GIIS 2014), Montreal, pp 1–6. IEEE
18. Gupta BB, Misra M, Joshi RC (2012) An ISP level solution to combat ddos attacks using combined statistical based approach. CoRR, abs/1203.2400
19. Hendrickson M (2008) Slideshare slammed with ddos attacks from china. http://techcrunch.com/2008/04/23/slideshare-slammed-with-ddos-attacks-from-china/
20. Hoffman S (2013) Ddos: a brief history. https://blog.fortinet.com/post/ddos-a-brief-history
21. Huang VS, Huang R, Chiang M (2013) A ddos mitigation system with multi-stage detection and text-based turing testing in cloud computing. In: 2013 27th international conference on advanced information networking and applications workshops (WAINA), Barcelona, pp 655–662. IEEE
22. Idziorek J, Tannian M Exploiting cloud utility models for profit and ruin. In: Proceedings of the IEEE international conference on cloud computing (4th IEEE CLOUD'11), Washington, DC, pp 33–40, July 2011. IEEE Computer Society
23. Idziorek J, Tannian M, Jacobson D (2011) Detecting fraudulent use of cloud resources. In: Proceedings of the 3rd ACM workshop on cloud computing security, Chicago, pp 61–72. ACM
24. Jeyanthi N, Mogankumar PC (2014) A virtual firewall mechanism using army nodes to protect cloud infrastructure from ddos attacks. Cybern Inf Technol 14(3):71–85
25. Jia Q, Wang H, Fleck D, Li F, Stavrou A, Powell W (2014) Catch me if you can: a cloud-enabled ddos defense. In: 44th annual IEEE/IFIP international conference on dependable systems and networks (DSN), Atlanta, pp 264–275. IEEE
26. Kandula S, Katabi D, Jacob M, Berger A (2005) Botz-4-sale: surviving organized DDoS attacks that mimic flash crowds (awarded best student paper). In: NSDI, Boston. USENIX
27. Karnwal T, Sivakumar T, Aghila G (2012) A comber approach to protect cloud computing against xml ddos and http ddos attack. In: 2012 IEEE students' conference on electrical, electronics and computer science (SCEECS), Bhopal, pp 1–5. IEEE
28. Khor SH, Nakao A (2009) spow: on-demand cloud-based eddos mitigation mechanism. In: HotDep (Fifth workshop on hot topics in system dependability), Estoril
29. Khor SH, Nakao A (2011) Daas: Ddos mitigation-as-a-service. In: 11th international symposium on applications and the internet (SAINT), Munich, pp 160–171. IEEE
30. Kim SH, Kim JH (2010) Method for detecting and preventing a ddos attack using cloud computing, and server, 12 July 2010. US Patent App. 13/386,516
31. Koduru A, Neelakantam T, Saira Bhanu SM (2013) Detection of economic denial of sustainability using time spent on a web page in cloud. In: 2013 IEEE international conference on cloud computing in emerging markets (CCEM), Bangalore, pp 1–4, Oct 2013
32. Kumar MN, Sujatha P, Kalva V, Nagori R, Katukojwala AK, Kumar M (2012) Mitigating economic denial of sustainability (edos) in cloud computing using in-cloud scrubber service. In: Proceedings of the 2012 fourth international conference on computational intelligence and communication networks (CICN '12), Washington, DC, pp 535–539. IEEE Computer Society
33. Labs K (2014) Global it security risks survey 2014–distributed denial of service (ddos) attacks. http://media.kaspersky.com/en/B2B-International-2014-Survey-DDoS-Summary-Report.pdf
34. Latanicki J, Massonet P, Naqvi S, Rochwerger B, Villari M (2010) Scalable cloud defenses for detection, analysis and mitigation of ddos attacks. In: Future internet assembly, Valencia, pp 127–137
35. Libbenga J (2007) Ddos attacks deemed illegal in sweden. http://www.theregister.co.uk/2007/02/20/ddos_attacks_illegal_in_sweden/
36. Mao M, Li J, Humphrey M (2010) Cloud auto-scaling with deadline and budget constraints. In: 2010 11th IEEE/ACM international conference on grid computing (GRID), Brussels, pp 41–48. IEEE

37. Masood M, Anwar Z, Raza SA, Hur MA (2013) Edos armor: a cost effective economic denial of sustainability attack mitigation framework for e-commerce applications in cloud environments. In: 2013 16th international multi topic conference (INMIC), Lahore, pp 37–42, Dec 2013
38. Mirkovic J, Reiher P (2004) A taxonomy of ddos attack and ddos defense mechanisms. SIGCOMM Comput Commun Rev 34(2):39–53
39. Moore D, Shannon C, Brown DJ, Voelker GM, Savage S (2006) Inferring internet denial-of-service activity. ACM Trans Comput Syst (TOCS) 24(2):115–139,
40. Morein WG, Stavrou A, Cook DL, Keromytis AD, Misra V, Rubenstein D (2003) Using graphic turing tests to counter automated ddos attacks against web servers. In: Proceedings of the 10th ACM conference on computer and communications security (CCS '03), New York, pp 8–19. ACM
41. Munson L (2015) Greatfire.org faces daily $30,000 bill from ddos attack. https://nakedsecurity.sophos.com/2015/03/20/greatfire-org-faces-daily-30000-bill-from-ddos-attack/
42. Nelson P (2015) Cybercriminals moving into cloud big time, report says. http://www.networkworld.com/article/2900125/malware-cybercrime/criminals-moving-into-cloud-big-time-says-report.html
43. Arbor Networks (2014) Understanding the nature of ddos attacks. http://www.arbornetworks.com/asert/2012/09/understanding-the-nature-of-ddos-attacks/
44. BBC News (2004) Worldpay struck by online attack. http://news.bbc.co.uk/2/hi/business/3713174.stm
45. CNN News (2008) Cnn web site targeted. http://edition.cnn.com/2008/TECH/04/18/cnn.websites/
46. Neustar News (2014) Neustar 2014 'ddos attacks and impact report' finds unpredictable ddos landscape. http://www.neustar.biz/about-us/news-room/press-releases/2014/neustar-2014-ddos-attacks-and-impact-report-finds-unpredictable-ddos-landscape#.U33B_nbzdsV
47. SPAMfighter News (2015) Survey – with ddos attacks companies lose around £100k/hr. http://www.spamfighter.com/News-19554-Survey-With-DDoS-Attacks-Companies-Lose-around-100kHr.htm
48. OUT-LAW.COM (2006) Uk bans denial of service attacks. http://www.theregister.co.uk/2006/11/12/uk_bans_denial_of_service_attacks/
49. Peng T, Leckie C, Ramamohanarao K (2007) Survey of network-based defense mechanisms countering the dos and ddos problems. ACM Comput Surv 39(1):3
50. See reference [49]
51. Prolexic (2014) http://www.prolexic.com/. http://www.prolexic.com/
52. Saini B, Somani G (2014) Index page based edos attacks in infrastructure cloud. In: Recent trends in computer networks and distributed systems security, Trivandrum, pp 382–395. Springer
53. Seals T (2015) Q1 2015 ddos attacks spike, targeting cloud. http://www.infosecurity-magazine.com/news/q1-2015-ddos-attacks-spike/
54. Shamsolmoali P, Zareapoor M (2014) Statistical-based filtering system against ddos attacks in cloud computing. In: 2014 international conference on advances in computing, communications and informatics (ICACCI), Delhi, pp 1234–1239. IEEE
55. Somani G, Gaur MS, Sanghi D (2015) Ddos/edos attack in cloud: affecting everyone out there! In: Proceedings of the 8th international conference on security of information and networks (SIN '15), New York. ACM
56. Sqalli MH, Al-Haidari F, Salah K (2011) EDoS-shield – a two-steps mitigation technique against EDoS attacks in cloud computing. In: UCC, Melbourne, pp 49–56. IEEE Computer Society
57. Technologies A (2013) Akamai's state of the internet q4 2013 executive summary volume 6 number 4. http://www.akamai.com/dl/akamai/akamai-soti-q413-exec-summary.pdf
58. Vamosi R (2008) Imdb victim of denial-of-service attack. http://www.cnet.com/news/imdb-victim-of-denial-of-service-attack/

59. Vance A (2005) Man admits to ebay ddos attack. http://www.theregister.co.uk/2005/12/28/ebay_bots_ddos/
60. Vissers T, Somasundaram TS, Pieters L, Govindarajan K, Hellinckx P (2014) Ddos defense system for web services in a cloud environment. Future Gener Comput Syst 37:37–45
61. Wang H, Jia Q, Fleck D, Powell W, Li F, Stavrou A (2014) A moving target ddos defense mechanism. Comput Commun 46:10–21
62. Yan J, El Ahmad AS (2009) Captcha security: a case study. IEEE Secur Priv 7(4):22–28
63. Yu S, Tian Y, Guo S, Wu D (2013) Can we beat ddos attacks in clouds? IEEE Trans Parallel Distrib Syst (99):1–1
64. Zhao S, Chen K, Zheng W (2009) Defend against denial of service attack with vmm. In: Eighth international conference on grid and cooperative computing, 2009 (GCC'09), Lanzhou, pp 91–96. IEEE

Gaurav Somani is an Assistant Professor at Department of Computer Science and Engineering, Central University of Rajasthan, India. He has completed his Bachelor of Engineering (BE) in Information Technology from University of Rajasthan with honors and Master of Technology (MTech) in Information and Communication Technology from DAIICT, Gandhinagar India, with distinction. He is pursuing his PhD from Malviya National Institute of Technology, Jaipur, India. His research interests include Distributes Systems and Security Engineering. He has authored a book/monograph on Scheduling and Isolation in Virtualization. He has published number of papers in various conferences and journals of international repute like ACM SINCONF, ACM CGC, IEEE CLOUD, and Elsevier FGCS. He has served as TPC member in multiple International conferences and reviewer of top journals like IEEE transactions on cloud computing. He is a member of IEEE and ACM.

Manoj Singh Gaur is Professor in the Department of Computer Science and Engineering at Malaviya National Institute of Technology Jaipur, India. He has obtained his Ph.D. from University and Southampton, UK. He has supervised research in the areas of Networks on Chip and Information Security. He has published over 150 papers in peer-reviewed reputed conferences and journals. He has coordinated national and international projects in the domains of Information Security and Networks on Chip. He is a member of IEEE and ACM.

Dheeraj Sanghi is a Professor of Computer Science and Engineering at IIT Kanpur. Since August 15, he has started working with IIIT Delhi. From 2008 to 2010, he served as the Director, LNM Institute of Information Technology (LNMIIT), a public-private partnership University in Jaipur. His research interests include network performance optimization, security, and distributed systems. He has visited about 70 colleges in India to discuss issues related to career planning, future of IT industry, curriculum, and various technical/research talks. He has published a large number of papers at reputed international conferences and journals. He regularly writes his popular ideas about higher education and learning on his blog, dsanghi.blogspot.com. Professor Sanghi has a B. Tech from IIT Kanpur and M. S. and Ph. D. from University of Maryland.

Cloud Data Auditing Using Proofs of Retrievability

11

Binanda Sengupta and Sushmita Ruj

Abstract

Cloud servers offer data outsourcing facility to their clients. A client outsources her data without having any copy at her end. Therefore, she needs a guarantee that her data are not modified by the server which may be malicious. Data auditing is performed on the outsourced data to resolve this issue. Moreover, the client may want all her data to be stored untampered. In this chapter, we describe proofs of retrievability (POR) that convince the client about the integrity of all her data.

Keywords

Cloud computing • Data auditing • Proofs of retrievability • Erasure code • Message authentication code • Bilinear maps • Oblivious RAM

11.1 Introduction

Proper storage and maintenance of data has been an important research problem in the field of computer science. With the advent of cloud computing, cloud service providers (CSP) offer various facilities to their clients. For example, clients can outsource their computational workload to the cloud server, or clients having limited storage capacity can store huge amount of data in the server. Several storage service providers (SSP) provide this type of storage outsourcing facility to their clients. Amazon Simple Storage Service (S3) [1], Google Drive [34], and Dropbox [23] are a few of them to mention. These storage service providers (we will use SSP and server interchangeably in this chapter) store clients' data in lieu of monetary benefits. The nature of the outsourced data may be *static* (never modified once they

B. Sengupta (✉) • S. Ruj
Indian Statistical Institute, Kolkata, India
e-mail: binanda_r@isical.ac.in; sush@isical.ac.in

S.Y. Zhu et al. (eds.), *Guide to Security Assurance for Cloud Computing*,
Computer Communications and Networks, DOI 10.1007/978-3-319-25988-8_11

are uploaded) or *dynamic* (clients can modify them). On the other hand, the servers can be malicious to maximize the benefits with a constant amount of storage at their end. We consider a situation as follows. Suppose, a server has 100 GB (say) of storage capability. Now, there are two clients requesting for 100 GB of storage each to the server. The server may store 50 GB data of each client and claim that it has stored 200 GB data. When any client wants to download her data from the server, she gets only half of her data. Therefore, the client needs a guarantee that her data have been stored intact by the server. In case of any modification or deletion of data, the server needs to compensate the client appropriately. Hence, the only question remains is how to guarantee the integrity of the client's data. To address the problem of checking the integrity of data, auditing comes into play. Audits may be performed as often as asked by the client. If a server can pass an audit, then the client is convinced that her file (or some part of it) is stored untampered. However, a server can pass an audit without storing the file properly, but the probability of such an event is "very small" (a negligible function in the security parameter as defined in Sect. 11.2.1).

One naive way of auditing is as follows. A client does some preprocessing on her data before uploading them to the cloud server. This preprocessing phase includes attaching some cryptographic authenticators (or tags) corresponding to segments (or blocks) of the data file. In the following section, we discuss about some cryptographic tools based on which these authenticators are designed. The idea of using these authenticators is to prevent the server from modifying the file and still passing an audit with high probability. Now, the client uploads the processed file (data file along with the authenticators) to the storage server. During an audit, the client downloads the whole file along with the tags to her end and verify the authenticity of each of the blocks. The server passes an audit if and only if each block-authenticator pair is valid.

The naive idea mentioned above suffers from severe drawbacks. Every time a client asks for an audit, she has to download all her data from the server which incurs a high communication bandwidth. To overcome this issue, researchers have come up with what is called *proofs of storage*. As before, the client computes an authenticator for each block of her data (or file) and uploads the file along with the authenticators. During an audit protocol, the client samples a predefined number of random block indices and sends them to the server (challenge). The server does some computations over the challenge, stored data, and authenticators and sends a response to the client who verifies the integrity of her data based on this response. This is an example of *provable data possession* (PDP) introduced by Ateniese et al. [5]. This work is followed by other provable data possession schemes [4, 6, 20, 25]. Though these schemes guarantee the integrity of *almost all* the blocks of the data file, PDP cannot convince the client about the integrity of *all* the blocks. The outsourced data may contain some sensitive accounting information which the client does not want to lose. On the other hand, losing the compression table of a compressed file makes the whole file unavailable. In such circumstances, the client wants a stronger notion than PDP which would guarantee that the entire file has been stored properly and the client can *retrieve* her file at any point of time.

The first paper introducing proofs of retrievability (POR) for static data is by Juels and Kaliski [38] (a similar idea was given for sublinear authenticators by Naor and Rothblum [47]). They introduce erasure coding (see Sect. 11.2.5) to the proofs of storage. The underlying idea is to encode the original file with some erasure code, compute authenticators for the blocks of the encoded file, and then upload the file along with the authenticators to the data server. With this technique, the server has to delete or modify a considerable number of blocks to actually delete or modify a data block. Thus, the probability that the server passes an audit, given some data blocks are actually deleted or modified, is "very small." This technique ensures that all the blocks of the file are correctly stored at the server's end. This notion is formalized by defining an extractor algorithm which can extract, with high probability, the original file after interacting with a server which passes an audit with some non-negligible probability. We review some of the POR schemes in this chapter.

The organization of this chapter is as follows. In Sect. 11.2, we describe some notations and tools which will be used in later sections. Section 11.3 discusses some POR schemes for static data. In Sect. 11.4, we describe some POR schemes for dynamic data. We conclude the chapter in Sect. 11.5.

11.2 Preliminaries

In this section, we briefly discuss about some backgrounds needed for understanding the following sections. The detailed discussions on these topics can be found in [3, 28–30, 39, 44, 61, 65].

11.2.1 Notation

We take λ as the security parameter. An algorithm $\mathcal{A}(1^\lambda)$ is called a probabilistic polynomial-time algorithm when its running time is polynomial in λ and its output y is a random variable which depends on the internal coin tosses of $\mathcal{A}$. We write $y \leftarrow \mathcal{A}(\cdot)$ or $y \leftarrow \mathcal{A}(\cdot, \ldots, \cdot)$ depending upon whether $\mathcal{A}$ takes one input or more inputs, respectively. Moreover, if $\mathcal{A}$ is given access to an oracle $\mathcal{O}$, we write $y \leftarrow \mathcal{A}^{\mathcal{O}}(\cdot, \ldots, \cdot)$. In this case, the Turing machine $\mathcal{A}$ has an additional query tape where $\mathcal{A}$ places its query x and calls another Turing machine $\mathcal{O}$. Then, $\mathcal{O}$ is invoked with the input x, and the output is written on the same query tape [3, 61]. An element a chosen uniformly at random from a set S is denoted as $a \xleftarrow{R} S$. A function $f : \mathbb{N} \rightarrow \mathbb{R}$ is called negligible in λ if for all positive integers c and for all sufficiently large λ, we have $f(\lambda) < \frac{1}{\lambda^c}$. We call a problem "hard" to denote that no polynomial-time algorithms exist for solving the problem.

11.2.2 Message Authentication Code (MAC)

Let $f : \mathcal{K} \times \mathcal{M} \rightarrow \mathcal{D}$ be a function, where the $\mathcal{K}$ is the key space, $\mathcal{M}$ is the message space, and $|\mathcal{D}| \ll |\mathcal{M}|$. In other words, f takes as inputs a secret key $k \in \mathcal{K}$ and a message $m \in \mathcal{M}$, and it outputs a small $d \in \mathcal{D}$. The piece of information d is a message authentication code (MAC) [65] if the following properties are satisfied.

1. Given m and d, it is hard to find another $m' \neq m$ such that $f_k(m) = f_k(m')$.
2. The value of $f_k(m)$ should be uniformly distributed in the set R.
3. The value of $f_k(m)$ should depend on every bit of the message m equally.

Message authentication codes are used as a digest to authenticate the message. MACs are defined in symmetric setting, that is, the sender and the receiver need to share a secret key. In the generation phase, the sender calculates the MAC for the message using the secret key and sends the message along with the MAC. In the verification phase, the receiver verifies, using the same key, whether the MAC is computed on the given message using the same secret key. Due to the first property mentioned above, it is hard to modify a message m, keeping the value of $f_k(m)$ unchanged.

Message authentication codes are used hugely for authentication purposes. There are several constructions for MACs. Some of the constructions are based on pseudorandom functions [28, 39, 42] (e.g., XOR MAC [7], CMAC [48]), and some of them are based on cryptographic hash functions (e.g., HMAC [49]).

11.2.3 Bilinear Maps

Let G_1, G_2, and G_T be multiplicative cyclic groups of prime order p. Let g_1 and g_2 be generators of the groups G_1 and G_2, respectively. A bilinear map [27, 40, 43] is a function $e : G_1 \times G_2 \rightarrow G_T$ such that:

1. For all $u \in G_1, v \in G_2, a, b \in \mathbb{Z}_p$, we have $e(u^a, v^b) = e(u, v)^{ab}$ (bilinear property).
2. e is nondegenerate, that is, $e(g_1, g_2) \neq 1$.

    Furthermore, properties 1 and 2 imply that
3. For all $u_1, u_2 \in G_1, v \in G_2$, we have $e(u_1 \cdot u_2, v) = e(u_1, v) \cdot e(u_2, v)$.

If $G_1 = G_2 = G$, the bilinear map is symmetric; otherwise, it is asymmetric. Unless otherwise mentioned, we consider bilinear maps which are symmetric and efficiently computable. Let BLSetup(1^λ) be an algorithm which outputs (p, g, G, G_T, e), the parameters of a bilinear map, where g is a generator of G.

11.2.4 Digital Signature

Diffie and Hellman introduce the public-key cryptography and the notion of digital signatures in their seminal paper "New Directions in Cryptography" [21]. Rivest, Shamir, and Adleman [55] propose the first digital signature scheme based on the RSA assumption. Several signature schemes are available in the literature. Several signature schemes are found in the literature [9–11, 14, 15, 17, 19, 24, 26, 35, 36, 41, 45, 50, 53, 56].

We define a digital signature scheme as proposed by Goldwasser et al. [32]. A digital signature scheme consists of the following polynomial-time algorithms: a key generation algorithm KeyGen, a signing algorithm Sign, and a verification algorithm Verify. KeyGen takes as input the security parameter λ and outputs a pair of keys (pk, sk), where sk is the secret key and pk is the corresponding public key. Algorithm Sign takes a message m from the message space $\mathcal{M}$ and the secret key sk as input and outputs a signature σ. Algorithm Verify takes as input the public key pk, a message m and a signature σ, and outputs `accept` or `reject` depending upon whether the signature is valid or not. Any of these algorithms can be probabilistic in nature. A digital signature scheme has the following properties:

1. *Correctness*: Algorithm Verify always accepts a signature generated by an honest signer, that is,

$$\Pr[\text{Verify}(pk, m, \text{Sign}(sk, m)) = \texttt{accept}] = 1.$$

2. *Security*: Let $\text{Sign}_{sk}(\cdot)$ be the signing oracle and $\mathcal{A}$ be any probabilistic polynomial-time adversary with an oracle access to $\text{Sign}_{sk}(\cdot)$. The adversary $\mathcal{A}$ makes polynomial number of sign queries to $\text{Sign}_{sk}(\cdot)$ for different messages and gets back the signatures on those messages. The signature scheme is secure if $\mathcal{A}$ cannot produce, except with some probability negligible in λ, a valid signature on a message not queried previously, that is, for any probabilistic polynomial-time adversary $\mathcal{A}^{\text{Sign}_{sk}(\cdot)}$, the following probability

$$\Pr[(m, \sigma) \leftarrow \mathcal{A}^{\text{Sign}_{sk}(\cdot)}(1^\lambda) : m \notin Q \wedge \text{Verify}(pk, m, \sigma) = \texttt{accept}]$$

is negligible in λ, where Q is the set of sign queries made by $\mathcal{A}$ to $\text{Sign}_{sk}(\cdot)$.

As a concrete example, we mention the algorithms of the BLS signature proposed by Boneh, Lynn, and Shacham [11]. Let the algorithm BLSetup(1^λ) output (p, g, G, G_T, e) as the parameters of a bilinear map, where G and G_T are multiplicative cyclic groups of prime order p, g is a generator of G and $e : G \times G \to G_T$ (see Sect. 11.2.3). KeyGen chooses $sk \xleftarrow{R} \mathbb{Z}_p$ as the secret key, and the public key is set to be $pk = g^{sk}$. The algorithm Sign uses a full-domain hash $H : \{0, 1\}^* \to G$, and it generates a signature $\sigma = H(m)^{sk}$ on a message $m \in \{0, 1\}^*$. Given a message-signature pair (m, σ), the algorithm Verify checks $e(\sigma, g) \stackrel{?}{=} e(H(m), pk)$. Verify outputs `accept` if and only if the equality holds.

11.2.5 Erasure Code

An $(n, f, d)_\Sigma$ erasure code is a forward error-correcting code [44] that consists of an encoding algorithm Enc: $\Sigma^f \rightarrow \Sigma^n$ (encodes a message consisting of f symbols into a longer codeword consisting of n symbols) and a decoding algorithm Dec: $\Sigma^n \rightarrow \Sigma^f$ (decodes a codeword to a message), where Σ is a finite alphabet and d is the minimum distance (Hamming distance between any two codewords is at least d) of the code. The quantity $\frac{f}{n}$ is called the rate of the code. An $(n, f, d)_\Sigma$ erasure code can tolerate up to $d - 1$ erasures. If $d = n - f + 1$, we call the code a maximum distance separable (MDS) code. For an MDS code, the original message can be reconstructed from any f out of n symbols of the codeword [46]. Reed-Solomon codes [54] and their extensions are examples of nontrivial MDS codes. We give a simple example, from [44], of a Reed-Solomon code below.

Let us consider the finite field $\mathbb{F}_{2^2} = \{0, 1, \alpha, \gamma = \alpha^2\}$ with $\alpha^2 + \alpha + 1 = 0$. A $(3, 2, 2)$ Reed-Solomon code over $\mathbb{F}_{2^2}$ consists of 16 codewords:

$$
\begin{array}{cccc}
000 & 1\alpha 0 & \gamma 0\alpha & \gamma\alpha 1 \\
01\alpha & \alpha\gamma 0 & 10\gamma & 111 \\
0\alpha\gamma & \gamma 10 & 1\gamma\alpha & \alpha\alpha\alpha \\
0\gamma 1 & \alpha 01 & \alpha 1\gamma & \gamma\gamma\gamma.
\end{array}
$$

This code can correct a single erasure ($d - 1 = 1$). For example, $1 * \gamma$ ("$*$" denotes the erasure) can be decoded uniquely to 10γ. In other words, a partially erased codeword can be reconstructed from the other two symbols available.

11.2.6 Oblivious RAM

Goldreich and Ostrovsky introduce the notion of oblivious RAM (ORAM) [31]. In a RAM (random access memory) model, there is a CPU and a memory module. Anyone can intercept the communications between the CPU and the memory module and observe the memory access patterns. Oblivious RAM (ORAM) is a probabilistic RAM where the access pattern is independent of the address input to the memory module.

ORAM involves a hierarchical data structure which allows hiding memory access patterns. This data structure consists of hash tables of different lengths at different levels. The number of levels is $O(\log n)$. An element of a hash table contains an (*address, value*) pair. When an address is searched for a read operation, the address is first hashed and the hash value is matched with the hash table at the top level. If a match is not found, the address is hashed again and matched with the hash table in the next level, and so on. If a match is found, random locations are searched in the hash tables in the subsequent levels. This is continued until the last level. If an address is found more than once, ORAM returns the most updated value residing at the topmost level. For a write operation, the new value is inserted into the hash table of the top level. As each address search is associated with hash tables in every level of the hierarchical data structure, an adversary cannot gain any knowledge about the pattern of the search. For the same reason, ORAM takes time polynomial in $\log n$ for each read or write operation as all the hash tables need to be consulted to hide the actual access pattern. There is a "rebuild" phase which is executed periodically to rebuild the levels (due to too many insertions). Recent works on ORAM include [33, 37, 52, 59, 62, 64, 67].

11.2.7 Proofs of Retrievability

A client uploads a file to the cloud server. However, the client needs a guarantee that *all* her data are stored in the server untampered. Proofs-of-retrievability (POR) schemes make the client be assured that her data are stored intact in the server. Juels and Kaliski introduce proofs of retrievability for static data [38]. Static data mostly include archival data which the client does not modify after she uploads the file to the server. However, some of the POR schemes deal with dynamic data where the client modifies her data. We provide a brief idea about the building blocks of POR schemes. We discuss them in detail in Sects. 11.3 and 11.4.

In the setup phase, the client preprocesses her file F_0. The preprocessing step involves encoding the file F_0 with an erasure code to form another file F. Then an authenticator is attached to each of the blocks of F (for checking the integrity of the blocks later). Finally, the client uploads F along with the authenticators to the server. We consider the file F as a collection of n blocks or segments where each block is an element of $\mathbb{Z}_p$. The client can read data from the file she has outsourced. She performs audits to check the integrity of her data. An audit comprises of two algorithms for proof generation and proof verification. During an audit, the client generates a random challenge and sends it to the server which acts as a prover. Upon receiving the challenge, the server responds to the client with a proof. The client then verifies the integrity of the data by checking the validity of the proof. If the proof is valid, the verification algorithm outputs 1; otherwise, it outputs 0. For dynamic POR schemes, the client can issue write operations along with read operations. The basic operations are illustrated in Fig. 11.1.

POR schemes satisfy two properties: correctness and soundness. The correctness property demands that the proof generated by an honest server always makes the verification algorithm output 1. The soundness property of POR schemes is formalized by the existence of an extractor algorithm that extracts F after interacting with a malicious server which passes an audit (i.e., the verification algorithm outputs 1) with any probability nonnegligible in the security parameter λ.

There are two types of POR schemes: *privately verifiable* and *publicly verifiable*. In private verification schemes, only the client can perform audits as the verification of a proof requires some secret information. On the other hand, in publicly verifiable schemes, anyone can verify the proof supplied by the server. In privacy-preserving

Fig. 11.1 Basics of a proofs-of-retrievability scheme

auditing, the verifier (any verifier other than the client) cannot gain any knowledge about the data outsourced to the server [66].

11.3 Proofs of Retrievability for Static Data

In the static setting, the client does not modify her data once they are outsourced to the cloud server. We discuss two POR schemes for static data below. However, there are other POR schemes related to static data. We mention some of them in Sect. 11.5.

11.3.1 POR Scheme by Juels and Kaliski

Juels and Kaliski [38] propose the first POR scheme for static data. A similar scheme for online memory checking is given by Naor and Rothblum [47]. Though the basic idea is the same for both of the schemes, the first one uses *sentinels* (random strings that are independent of the file's content) and the latter scheme uses MACs for authentication. Here, we describe the MAC-based solution and make a brief note about the sentinel-based solution.

The client selects $k \xleftarrow{R} \mathcal{K}$ as her secret key, where $\mathcal{K}$ is the key space for a MAC. Let the client have a file F_0 with f blocks or segments which she wants to upload to the cloud server. The client encodes F_0 with an erasure code to form a file F with n segments. Let each segment of the file F be an element of $\mathbb{Z}_p$, that is, $F[i] \in \mathbb{Z}_p$ for all $1 \leq i \leq n$. The client computes $\sigma_i = \text{MAC}_k(i||F[i])$ for all $1 \leq i \leq n$ and uploads the file F along with the tags $\{\sigma_i\}_{1 \leq i \leq n}$ to the server.

During an audit, the client generates a random challenge $Q = \{i\}$ and sends it to the server which acts as a prover. Upon receiving Q, the prover responds to the client with $\{(F[i], \sigma_i)\}_{i \in Q}$. The verification algorithm, for each $i \in Q$, checks if

$$\sigma_i \stackrel{?}{=} \mathrm{MAC}_k(i||F[i]),$$

and outputs 1 if the equality holds for each $i \in Q$; it outputs 0, otherwise. If the MAC scheme is secure, then the server cannot produce a valid MAC on a message of its choice without knowing the secret key k. Now, the client can get a fraction (say, ρ) of the data blocks of F by interacting with a server which passes an audit with some probability, nonnegligible in the security parameter λ. Since the initial file F_0 has been encoded to form F, all the blocks of F_0 can be retrieved from ρ-fraction of blocks of F.

The scheme mentioned above is privately verifiable as only the client (having the knowledge of the secret key k) can verify the integrity of her data. However, this scheme can be turned into a publicly verifiable scheme if MACs are replaced by digital signatures.

In the original scheme proposed by Juels and Kaliski [38], the blocks of the encoded file F are encrypted, and a large number of random elements (sentinels) are inserted in random locations of F. The server cannot distinguish between the encrypted blocks of F and the sentinels. During an audit, the verifier (only the client can be the verifier) checks the authenticity of several sentinels at different positions. If the server modifies a considerable fraction of the blocks, a similar fraction of sentinels are modified as well (as the sentinels are inserted in random locations of F). The server cannot selectively delete non-sentinel blocks as it cannot distinguish them from sentinels. Thus, with high probability, the server cannot pass the audit. On the other hand, once the client challenges for some sentinel locations, they are revealed to the server. Therefore, the future challenges must not include these locations. This makes the number of audits that can be performed in this scheme bounded.

11.3.2 POR Schemes by Shacham and Waters

Shacham and Waters propose two short and efficient homomorphic authenticators in their POR schemes for static data [57, 58]. The first one, based on pseudorandom functions, provides a POR scheme which is privately verifiable (i.e., only the client can verify a proof) and secure in the standard model[1]; the second one, based on BLS signatures (see Sect. 11.2.4), gives a POR scheme which is publicly verifiable (i.e., anyone can verify a proof) and secure in the random oracle model[2] [8].

As mentioned by Shacham and Waters, Reed-Solomon codes are necessary against adversarial erasures where the server can delete blocks selectively. One

[1] Standard model is a model of computation where the security of a cryptographic scheme is derived from some complexity assumptions (e.g., hardness of factoring large integers [70] or hardness of finding discrete logarithm of an element of a finite group [68].)

[2] Random oracle model is a model of computation where the security of a cryptographic scheme is proven assuming a cryptographic hash function used in the scheme as a truly random function.

drawback of these codes is the complexity of encoding and decoding is $O(n^2)$, where n is the number of blocks of the file uploaded to the server. We can employ codes with linear decoding time instead of Reed-Solomon codes. However, these codes are secure against random erasures only. Shacham and Waters discuss a solution to this problem strictly for the privately verifiable scheme. We briefly describe the schemes below.

11.3.2.1 POR Scheme with Private Verification

The client chooses (α, k) as her secret key, where $\alpha \xleftarrow{R} \mathbb{Z}_p$ and $k \xleftarrow{R} \mathcal{K}$ ($\mathcal{K}$ is the key space for a pseudorandom function). Let $h : \mathcal{K} \times \{0,1\}^* \to \mathbb{Z}_p$ be a pseudorandom function [28, 39, 42]. Let the client have a file F_0 with f blocks or segments which she wants to upload to the cloud server. The client encodes F_0 with an erasure code to form a file F with n segments. Let each segment of the file F be an element of $\mathbb{Z}_p$, that is, $F[i] \in \mathbb{Z}_p$ for all $1 \le i \le n$. The client computes $\sigma_i = h_k(i) + \alpha F[i] \mod p$ for all $1 \le i \le n$ and uploads the file F along with the tags $\{\sigma_i\}_{1 \le i \le n}$ to the server.

During an audit, the client generates a random query $Q = \{(i, \nu_i)\}$ and sends it to the server which acts as a prover. Upon receiving Q, the prover computes $\sigma = \sum_{(i,\nu_i)\in Q} \nu_i \sigma_i \mod p$ and $\mu = \sum_{(i,\nu_i)\in Q} \nu_i F[i] \mod p$. The prover responds to the client with (σ, μ). Then the client verifies the integrity of her data by checking the verification equation

$$\sigma \stackrel{?}{=} \left(\alpha\mu + \sum_{(i,\nu_i)\in Q} \nu_i h_k(i) \right) \mod p,$$

and outputs 1 or 0 depending on whether the equality holds or not. As discussed in Sect. 11.2.7, a POR scheme is correct if the verifier always outputs 1 when the proof is supplied by an honest server. The correctness of the scheme can be proved as below:

$$\begin{aligned} \text{Correctness :} \quad \sigma &\cong \sum_{(i,\nu_i)\in Q} \nu_i \sigma_i \\ &\cong \sum_{(i,\nu_i)\in Q} \nu_i \left(h_k(i) + \alpha F[i] \right) \\ &\cong \alpha \sum_{(i,\nu_i)\in Q} \nu_i F[i] + \sum_{(i,\nu_i)\in Q} \nu_i h_k(i) \\ &\cong \left(\alpha\mu + \sum_{(i,\nu_i)\in Q} \nu_i h_k(i) \right) \mod p \end{aligned}$$

In this privately verifiable scheme, only the client can perform the verification as the verification algorithm requires the knowledge of the secret key (α, k).

11.3.2.2 POR Scheme with Public Verification

Let there be an algorithm BLSetup(1^λ) that outputs (p, g, G, G_T, e) as the parameters of a bilinear map, where G and G_T are multiplicative cyclic groups of prime order $p = \Theta(\lambda)$, g is a generator of G and $e : G \times G \rightarrow G_T$ (see Sect. 11.2.3). The client chooses $x \overset{R}{\leftarrow} \mathbb{Z}_p$ as her secret key. The public key of the client is $v = g^x$. Let $\alpha \overset{R}{\leftarrow} G$ be another generator of G and $H : \{0, 1\}^* \rightarrow G$ be the BLS hash (see Sect. 11.2.4). Let the client have a file F_0 with f blocks or segments which she wants to upload to the cloud server. The client encodes F_0 with an erasure code to form a file F with n segments. Let each segment of the file F be an element of $\mathbb{Z}_p$, that is, $F[i] \in \mathbb{Z}_p$ for all $1 \leq i \leq n$. The client computes $\sigma_i = (H(i) \cdot \alpha^{F[i]})^x$ for all $1 \leq i \leq n$ and uploads the file F along with the tags $\{\sigma_i\}_{1 \leq i \leq n}$ to the server.

During an audit, the verifier generates a random query $Q = \{(i, \nu_i)\}$ and sends it to the server which acts as a prover. Upon receiving Q, the prover computes $\sigma = \prod_{(i,\nu_i)\in Q} {\sigma_i}^{\nu_i}$ and $\mu = \sum_{(i,\nu_i)\in Q} \nu_i F[i] \mod p$. The prover responds to the verifier with (σ, μ). Then the verifier verifies the integrity of client's data by checking the verification equation

$$e(\sigma, g) \stackrel{?}{=} e\left(\prod_{(i,\nu_i)\in Q} H(i)^{\nu_i} \cdot \alpha^{\mu}, v \right),$$

and outputs 1 or 0 depending on whether the equality holds or not. The correctness of the scheme can be proved as below:

$$\begin{aligned}
\text{Correctness}: \qquad \sigma &= \prod_{(i,\nu_i)\in Q} \sigma_i^{\nu_i} \\
&= \prod_{(i,\nu_i)\in Q} (H(i) \cdot \alpha^{F[i]})^{\nu_i x} \\
&= \left(\prod_{(i,\nu_i)\in Q} H(i)^{\nu_i} \cdot \prod_{(i,\nu_i)\in Q} \alpha^{\nu_i F[i]} \right)^x \\
&= \left(\prod_{(i,\nu_i)\in Q} H(i)^{\nu_i} \cdot \alpha^{\sum_{(i,\nu_i)\in Q} \nu_i F[i]} \right)^x \\
&= \left(\prod_{(i,\nu_i)\in Q} H(i)^{\nu_i} \cdot \alpha^{\mu} \right)^x
\end{aligned}$$

In this publicly verifiable scheme, the verifier does not need the secret key x to verify the response from the prover; knowledge of the public key pk would suffice for that purpose. Due to this reason, any third-party auditor (TPA) can perform audits on behalf of the client (owner of the data). In privacy preserving auditing, there is an additional requirement that the TPA should not learn the data on which the audits are being performed. For example, Wang et al. use the publicly verifiable scheme of Shacham and Waters, and they achieve privacy-preserving auditing using a technique called random masking [66].

11.4 Proofs of Retrievability for Dynamic Data

In the previous section, we have described some POR schemes for static data which the clients do not modify once they are uploaded in the cloud server. A natural question comes if any POR schemes are available for dynamic data where the clients modify their outsourced data "efficiently." In this section, we discuss about the difficulties of modification of the uploaded data. Then, we will mention two POR schemes for dynamic data.

To maintain the retrievability of the whole file, erasure coding has been employed on the file. The blocks of the file are encoded in such a way that the file can be retrieved from a fraction of blocks of the encoded file. The content of each block is now distributed in other $O(n)$ blocks. Therefore, to actually delete a block, the server has to delete all the related blocks. This restricts the server from deleting or modifying a block maliciously and still passing the verification with nonnegligible probability in λ. However, this advantage comes with some drawbacks. If the client wants to update a single block, she has to update all the related blocks as well. This makes the update process inefficient as n can be very large.

Cash et al. [16] discuss about two failed attempts to provide a solution of the problem mentioned above. In the first case, a possible solution might be to encode the file locally. Now, each codeword consists of a small number of blocks. Therefore, an update of a single block requires an update of a few blocks within that particular codeword. However, a malicious server can gain the knowledge of this small set of blocks (within a codeword) whenever the client updates a single block. Thus, the server can delete this small set of blocks without being noticed during an audit. In the second attempt, after encoding the file locally, all of the n blocks are permuted in a pseudorandom fashion. Apparently, the server cannot get any information about the blocks in a codeword. However, during an update, the server can identify the related blocks in a codeword. Therefore, the server can again delete these blocks and pass the verification during an audit.

Due to the issues discussed above, only a few POR schemes for dynamic data are available in the literature. Now, we briefly mention two of these schemes below. The first scheme [16] exploits oblivious RAM for hiding data access patterns. The second scheme [60] uses an incremental code to reduce the amortized cost for updates.

11.4.1 POR Scheme by Cash, Küpçü and Wichs

Cash et al. [16] propose a POR scheme for dynamic data using ORAM (see Sect. 11.2.6). They proceed as the first attempt mentioned in Sect. 11.4. That is, the data is divided into several chunks where each chunk contains a few blocks in it. Then, the blocks in each chunk are encoded "locally" using an erasure code to form a codeword. Thus, an update on a single block requires updating only related blocks of that particular codeword. This makes the update process much more efficient than that when all the blocks of the data are encoded to form a single large codeword. However, this solution comes with a drawback that the malicious server can now identify all the related blocks and delete these blocks selectively. As the number of blocks in a codeword is small, the server has a considerable chance to get through an audit.

Cash et al. introduce ORAM as a solution for the problem mentioned above, still keeping the update-complexity low. Small chunks are encoded to form small codewords to make the updates efficient. However, the challenge is to hide the access patterns from the server so that the server cannot identify the blocks in a codeword. ORAM lets the client read from the outsourced data in a pseudorandom fashion (using ORAM-Read protocol). It also provides a privacy-preserving way to write the blocks of a codeword (using ORAM-Write protocol). We give a high-level overview of the scheme as follows.

In the setup phase, data blocks are divided into chunks and chunks are encoded to form codewords. In this phase, the ORAM protocol is initiated as well. For a read operation, the exact location of the block is found from the chunk address (*add_ch*) and the offset (*add_off*), and this address is fed into ORAM-Read. For a write operation, *add_ch* and *add_off* are calculated first. Then, the codeword corresponding to *add_ch* is obtained (using ORAM-Read) and decoded. The exact block is located (using *add_off*) and modified accordingly. The new chunk is now encoded again and updated in the server using ORAM-Write. To run the audit protocol, a set of random locations are read using ORAM-Read, and their authenticity is checked. The verifier outputs 1 if and only if the data integrity is preserved.

11.4.2 POR Scheme by Shi, Stefanov, and Papamanthou

The privacy of the access patterns is achieved by the scheme proposed by Cash et al. [16]. However, Shi et al. [60] argue that a POR scheme need not hide the access patterns and it must satisfy only two properties: authenticated storage (the client needs an assurance about the authenticity of her data) and retrievability (the client can extract her data at any point of time). Shi et al. propose another dynamic POR scheme where the scheme satisfies these two properties, and it is more efficient (in terms of the computation cost or communication bandwidth required for the basic operations) than the scheme by Cash et al. as the additional cost for hiding access patterns is now eliminated. Here, we describe the basic construction of the scheme briefly.

The main challenge is to reduce the write cost since an update in a single block is followed by updates on other $O(n)$ blocks. In this scheme, the encoded copy is not updated for every write operation. Instead, it is updated (or rebuilt) only when sufficient updates are done on the data file. Thus, the amortized cost for writes is reduced dramatically. However, between two such rebuilds, this encoded copy stores stale data. Therefore, they introduce a temporary hierarchical log structure which stores values for these intermediate writes. During an audit, $O(\lambda)$ random locations of the encoded data file as well as the hierarchical log structure are checked for authenticity. The scheme involves three data structures: an uncoded buffer U which is updated after every write and reads are performed on this buffer only, an encoded (using an erasure code) buffer C which is updated after every n writes, and an encoded log structure H which accommodates every update between two rebuilds of C.

The buffer U contains an up-to-date copy of the data file. Reads and writes are performed directly on the required locations of U. Merkle hash tree [45, 71] is used for U to check the authenticity of the read block. Reads and writes are never performed directly on the buffer C. After n write operations, the buffer U is encoded using an erasure code (see Sect. 11.2.5) to form a new copy of C, and the existing copy of C is replaced by this new one. The log structure H consists of $\log n + 1$ levels and stores the intermediate updates temporarily. The l-th level consists of an encoded copy of 2^l blocks using a $(2^{l+1}, 2^l, 2^l)$-erasure code for each $0 \leq l \leq \log n + 1$. When a block is updated, it is written in the topmost level ($l = 0$). If the top l levels are already full, a rebuild is performed to accommodate all the blocks up to l-th level as well as the new block in the $(l + 1)$-th level and to make all the levels up to l-th level empty. Shi et al. employ a fast incrementally constructible code based on fast Fourier transform [69]. Using this code, the rebuild cost of l-th level takes $O(\beta \cdot 2^l)$ time, where β is the block size. The l-th level is rebuild after 2^l writes. Therefore, the amortized cost for rebuilding is $O(\beta \log n)$ per write operation. This improves the earlier scheme of Cash et al. [16] which requires $O(\beta\lambda(\log n)^2)$. Each rebuild of C is followed by making H empty. To perform an audit, the verifier chooses $O(\lambda)$ random locations of the encoded buffer C and $O(\lambda)$ random locations of each full level of the hierarchical log structure H and check for authenticity. The verification algorithm outputs 1 if all the blocks are authentic; it outputs 0, otherwise.

Shi et al. [60] improve this basic construction by using homomorphic checksums. In this improved construction, the cost of communication bandwidth and the cost of client computation are further reduced to $\beta + O(\lambda \log n)$. However, the server computation remains the same, that is, $O(\beta \log n)$.

11.5 Conclusion

In this chapter, we have given a brief overview of proofs-of-retrievability (POR), and we have discussed some POR schemes. There are several POR schemes in the literature which we have not covered in this chapter. Interested readers may take a look at these works [2, 12, 13, 18, 22, 51, 63].

11.6 Review Questions

1. What is the difference between provable data possession (PDP) and proofs of retrievability (POR)?
2. What is an erasure code? How are the erasure codes used to achieve proofs of retrievability (POR)?
3. Describe the challenges for constructing dynamic POR schemes. How can they be solved?

References

1. Amazon: Amazon S3. http://aws.amazon.com/s3/
2. Armknecht F, Bohli J, Karame GO, Liu Z, Reuter CA (2014) Outsourced proofs of retrievability. In: Proceedings of the 2014 ACM conference on computer and communications security, Scottsdale, 3–7 Nov 2014, pp 831–843
3. Arora S, Barak B (2009) Computational complexity – a modern approach. Cambridge University Press, New York
4. Ateniese G, Burns R, Curtmola R, Herring J, Khan O, Kissner L, Peterson Z, Song D (2011) Remote data checking using provable data possession. ACM Trans Inf Syst Secur 14(1):12:1–12:34
5. Ateniese G, Burns RC, Curtmola R, Herring J, Kissner L, Peterson ZNJ, Song DX (2007) Provable data possession at untrusted stores. In: Proceedings of the 2007 ACM conference on computer and communications security, CCS 2007, Alexandria, pp 598–609
6. Ateniese G, Pietro RD, Mancini LV, Tsudik G (2008) Scalable and efficient provable data possession. In: 4th international ICST conference on security and privacy in communication networks, SECURECOMM 2008, Istanbul, p 9
7. Bellare M, Guérin R, Rogaway P (1995) XOR MACs: new methods for message authentication using finite pseudorandom functions. In: Advances in cryptology – CRYPTO 1995, Santa Barbara, pp 15–28
8. Bellare M, Rogaway P (1993) Random oracles are practical: a paradigm for designing efficient protocols. In: Proceedings of the 1993 ACM conference on computer and communications security, CCS 1993, New York. ACM, pp 62–73
9. Boneh D, Boyen X, Shacham H (2004) Short group signatures. In: Franklin M (ed) Advances in cryptology – CRYPTO 2004. Lecture notes in computer science, vol 3152. Springer, Berlin/Heidelberg, pp 41–55
10. Boneh D, Gentry C, Lynn B, Shacham H (2003) Aggregate and verifiably encrypted signatures from bilinear maps. In: Biham E (ed) Advances in cryptology – EUROCRYPT 2003. Lecture notes in computer science, vol 2656. Springer, Berlin/Heidelberg, pp 416–432
11. Boneh D, Lynn B, Shacham H (2004) Short signatures from the Weil pairing. J Cryptol 17(4):297–319

12. Bowers KD, Juels A, Oprea A (2009) HAIL: a high-availability and integrity layer for cloud storage. In: Proceedings of the 2009 ACM conference on computer and communications security, CCS 2009, Chicago, 9–13 Nov 2009, pp 187–198
13. Bowers KD, Juels A, Oprea A (2009) Proofs of retrievability: theory and implementation. In: Proceedings of the first ACM cloud computing security workshop, CCSW 2009, Chicago, 13 Nov 2009, pp 43–54
14. Camenisch J, Hohenberger S, Pedersen M.Ø (2012) Batch verification of short signatures. J Cryptol 25(4):723–747
15. Camenisch J, Lysyanskaya A (2004) Signature schemes and anonymous credentials from bilinear maps. In: Franklin M (ed) Advances in cryptology – CRYPTO 2004. Lecture notes in computer science, vol 3152. Springer, Berlin/Heidelberg, pp 56–72
16. Cash D, Küpçü A, Wichs D (2013) Dynamic proofs of retrievability via oblivious RAM. In: Johansson T, Nguyen P (eds) Advances in cryptology – EUROCRYPT 2013. Lecture notes in computer science, vol 7881. Springer, Berlin/Heidelberg, pp 279–295
17. Cha JC, Cheon JH (2003) An identity-based signature from gap Diffie-Hellman groups. In: Desmedt Y (ed) Public key cryptography – PKC 2003. Lecture notes in computer science, vol 2567. Springer, Berlin/Heidelberg, pp 18–30
18. Chandran N, Kanukurthi B, Ostrovsky R (2014) Locally updatable and locally decodable codes. In: Proceedings of theory of cryptography – 11th theory of cryptography conference, TCC 2014, San Diego, 24–26 Feb 2014, pp 489–514
19. Chow SSM, Yiu S, Hui LCK (2005) Efficient identity based ring signature. In: Ioannidis J, Keromytis A, Yung M (eds) Applied cryptography and network security – ACNS 2005. Lecture notes in computer science, vol 3531. Springer, Berlin/Heidelberg, pp 499–512
20. Curtmola R, Khan O, Burns RC, Ateniese G (2008) MR-PDP: multiple-replica provable data possession. In: 28th IEEE international conference on distributed computing systems (ICDCS 2008), Beijing, pp 411–420
21. Diffie W, Hellman M (2006) New directions in cryptography. IEEE Trans Inf Theory 22(6):644–654
22. Dodis Y, Vadhan SP, Wichs D (2009) Proofs of retrievability via hardness amplification. In: Theory of cryptography, 6th theory of cryptography conference, TCC 2009, San Francisco, pp 109–127
23. Dropbox: Dropbox. https://www.dropbox.com/
24. ElGamal T (1985) A public key cryptosystem and a signature scheme based on discrete logarithms. In: Blakley G, Chaum D (eds) Advances in cryptology – CRYPTO 1984. Lecture notes in computer science, vol 196. Springer, Berlin/Heidelberg, pp 10–18
25. Erway CC, Küpçü A, Papamanthou C, Tamassia R (2009) Dynamic provable data possession. In: Proceedings of the 2009 ACM conference on computer and communications security, CCS 2009, Chicago, pp 213–222
26. Fiat A, Shamir A (1987) How to prove yourself: practical solutions to identification and signature problems. In: Odlyzko A (ed) Advances in cryptology – CRYPTO 1986. Lecture notes in computer science, vol 263. Springer, Berlin/Heidelberg, pp 186–194
27. Galbraith SD, Paterson KG, Smart NP (2008) Pairings for cryptographers. Discret Appl Math 156(16):3113–3121
28. Goldreich O (2001) The foundations of cryptography – volume 1, basic techniques. Cambridge University Press, Cambridge/New York
29. Goldreich O (2004) The foundations of cryptography – volume 2, basic applications. Cambridge University Press, New York
30. Goldreich O (2008) Computational complexity – a conceptual perspective. Cambridge University Press, Cambridge/New York
31. Goldreich O, Ostrovsky R (1996) Software protection and simulation on oblivious RAMs. J ACM 43(3):431–473
32. Goldwasser S, Micali S, Rivest RL (1988) A digital signature scheme secure against adaptive chosen-message attacks. SIAM J Comput 17(2):281–308

33. Goodrich MT, Mitzenmacher M (2011) Privacy-preserving access of outsourced data via oblivious RAM simulation. In: Automata, languages and programming – 38th international colloquium, ICALP 2011, Zurich, part II, pp 576–587
34. Google: Google Drive. https://www.google.com/drive/
35. Hess F (2002) Efficient identity based signature schemes based on pairings. In: Nyberg K, Heys H (eds) Selected areas in cryptography – SAC 2002. Lecture notes in computer science, vol 2595. Springer, Berlin/Heidelberg, pp 310–324
36. Johnson D, Menezes A, Vanstone S (2001) The elliptic curve digital signature algorithm (ECDSA). Int J Inf Secur 1(1):36–63
37. Jr., JLD, Stefanov E, Shi E (2014) Burst ORAM: minimizing ORAM response times for bursty access patterns. In: Proceedings of the 23rd USENIX security symposium, San Diego, pp 749–764
38. Juels A, Kaliski Jr. BS (2007) PORs: proofs of retrievability for large files. In: Proceedings of the 2007 ACM conference on computer and communications security, CCS 2007, New York. ACM, pp 584–597
39. Katz J, Lindell Y (2007) Introduction to modern cryptography. Chapman and Hall/CRC, Boca Raton
40. Koblitz N, Menezes A (2005) Pairing-based cryptography at high security levels. In: Smart N (ed) Cryptography and coding. Lecture notes in computer science, vol 3796. Springer, Berlin/Heidelberg, pp 13–36
41. Lamport L (1979) Constructing digital signatures from a one-way function. Technical report, Computer Science Laboratory, SRI International (Oct 1979)
42. Luby M, Rackoff C (1988) How to construct pseudorandom permutations from pseudorandom functions. SIAM J Comput 17(2):373–386
43. Lynn B (2007) On the implementation of pairing-based cryptosystems. PhD thesis, Stanford University (June 2007). https://crypto.stanford.edu/pbc/thesis.pdf
44. MacWilliams FJ, Sloane NJA (1977) The theory of error-correcting codes. North-Holland Publishing Company, Amsterdam/New York
45. Merkle R (1990) A certified digital signature. In: Brassard G (ed) Advances in cryptology – CRYPTO 1989. Lecture notes in computer science, vol 435. Springer, New York, pp 218–238
46. Mitzenmacher M (2004) Digital fountains: a survey and look forward. In: Proceedings of ITW 2004, San Antonio, pp 271–276
47. Naor M, Rothblum GN (2009) The complexity of online memory checking. J ACM 56(1):2:1–2:46
48. NIST: Recommendation for block cipher modes of operation: the CMAC mode for authentication (May 2005). http://csrc.nist.gov/publications/nistpubs/800-38B/SP_800-38B.pdf
49. NIST: The keyed-hash message authentication code (HMAC) (July 2008). http://csrc.nist.gov/publications/fips/fips198-1/FIPS-198-1_final.pdf
50. NIST: Digital Signature Standard (DSS) (July 2013). http://nvlpubs.nist.gov/nistpubs/FIPS/NIST.FIPS.186-4.pdf
51. Paterson MB, Stinson DR, Upadhyay J (2013) A coding theory foundation for the analysis of general unconditionally secure proof-of-retrievability schemes for cloud storage. J Math Cryptol 7(3):183–216
52. Pinkas B, Reinman T (2010) Oblivious RAM revisited. In: Advances in cryptology – CRYPTO 2010, Santa Barbara, pp 502–519
53. Rabin MO (1979) Digitalized signatures and public-key functions as intractable as factorization. Technical report, Massachusetts Institute of Technology, Cambridge
54. Reed IS, Solomon G (1960) Polynomial codes over certain finite fields. J Soc Ind Appl Math 8(2):300–304
55. Rivest RL, Shamir A, Adleman L (1978) A method for obtaining digital signatures and public-key cryptosystems. Commun ACM 21(2):120–126
56. Schnorr C (1991) Efficient signature generation by smart cards. J Cryptol 4(3):161–174
57. Shacham H, Waters B (2008) Compact proofs of retrievability. In: Advances in cryptology – ASIACRYPT 2008, Melbourne, pp 90–107

58. Shacham H, Waters B (2013) Compact proofs of retrievability. J Cryptol 26(3):442–483
59. Shi E, Chan TH, Stefanov E, Li M (2011) Oblivious RAM with $O((\log N)^3)$ worst-case cost. In: Advances in cryptology – ASIACRYPT 2011, Seoul, pp 197–214
60. Shi E, Stefanov E, Papamanthou C (2013) Practical dynamic proofs of retrievability. In: Proceedings of the 2013 ACM conference on computer and communications security, CCS 2013, New York. ACM, pp 325–336
61. Sipser M (1997) Introduction to the theory of computation. PWS Publishing Company, Boston
62. Stefanov E, Shi E, Song DX (2012) Towards practical oblivious RAM. In: 19th annual network and distributed system security symposium, NDSS 2012, San Diego
63. Stefanov E, van Dijk M, Juels A, Oprea A (2012) Iris: a scalable cloud file system with efficient integrity checks. In: 28th annual computer security applications conference, ACSAC 2012, Orlando, pp 229–238
64. Stefanov E, van Dijk M, Shi E, Fletcher CW, Ren L, Yu X, Devadas S (2013) Path ORAM: an extremely simple oblivious RAM protocol. In: 2013 ACM conference on computer and communications security, CCS 2013, Berlin, pp 299–310
65. Stinson DR (2006) Cryptography – theory and practice. Discrete mathematics and its applications series. Chapman and Hall/CRC, Boca Raton
66. Wang C, Chow SSM, Wang Q, Ren K, Lou W (2013) Privacy-preserving public auditing for secure cloud storage. IEEE Trans Comput 62(2):362–375
67. Wang XS, Huang Y, Chan TH, Shelat A, Shi E (2014) SCORAM: Oblivious RAM for secure computation. In: Proceedings of the 2014 ACM conference on computer and communications security, CCS 2014, Scottsdale, pp 191–202
68. Wikipedia: Discrete logarithm. https://en.wikipedia.org/wiki/Discrete_logarithm
69. Wikipedia: Fast fourier transform. https://en.wikipedia.org/wiki/Fast_Fourier_transform
70. Wikipedia: Integer factorization. https://en.wikipedia.org/wiki/Integer_factorization
71. Wikipedia: Merkle tree. https://en.wikipedia.org/wiki/Merkle_tree

Binanda Sengupta received his BE and MS degrees in Computer Science and Engineering from Jadavpur University, Kolkata, and Indian Institute of Technology Kharagpur, India, respectively. His broad research area includes cryptology, coding theory, and computational number theory. Currently, he is a PhD student in Indian Statistical Institute, Kolkata, India, and he is pursuing his research on efficient cryptographic protocols for distributed storage towards his PhD thesis.

Sushmita Ruj received her B.E. degree in Computer Science from Bengal Engineering and Science University, Shibpur, India, in 2004, and Masters and PhD in Computer Science from Indian Statistical Institute, India, in 2006 and 2010, respectively. She was an Erasmus Mundus Post Doctoral Fellow at Lund University, Sweden, and Post Doctoral Fellow at University of Ottawa, Canada. She is currently an Assistant Professor at Indian Statistical Institute, Indore, India. Prior to this, she was an Assistant Professor at IIT, Indore. She was a visiting researcher at INRIA, France; University of Wollongong, Australia; Kyushu University, Japan; and Microsoft Research Labs, India. Her research interests are in applied cryptography, security, combinatorics, and complex network analysis. She works actively in mobile ad hoc networks, vehicular networks, cloud security, and security in smart grids. She has served as program cochair of IEEE ICCC (P&S Track), IEEE ICDCS, IEEE ICC, etc., and served on many TPCs. She won a Samsung GRO award in 2014.

Vehicular Cloud Networks: Architecture and Security 12

Farhan Ahmad, Muhammad Kazim, and Asma Adnane

Abstract

Cloud computing has been widely adopted across the IT industry due to its scalable, cost-effective, and efficient services. It has many applications in areas such as healthcare, mobile cloud computing (MCC), and vehicular ad hoc networks (VANET). Vehicular cloud networks (VCN) is another application of cloud computing which is a combination of cloud and VANET technologies. It is composed of three clouds named vehicular cloud, infrastructure cloud, and traditional IT cloud. In this chapter, the three clouds involved in VCN are presented using a three-tier architecture, and the security issues related to each tier are described in detail. After describing the detailed architecture of VANET, their components, and their important characteristics, this chapter presents the architecture of VCN. It is followed by the detailed analysis of the threats to which each tier-cloud of VCN is vulnerable.

Keywords

Cloud computing • Vehicular ad hoc networks • Vehicular cloud networks • Three-tier architecture • Security • Threats

12.1 Cloud Computing

Cloud computing is a model that enables users to access resources such as infrastructure (hardware, processing, memory, network, and services), platform (custom applications), and software through Internet according to their requirements. This

---

F. Ahmad (✉) • M. Kazim • A. Adnane
Department of Computing and Mathematics, College of Engineering and Technology, University of Derby, Derby, UK
e-mail: f.ahmad@derby.ac.uk; m.kazim@derby.ac.uk; a.adnane@derby.ac.uk

S.Y. Zhu et al. (eds.), *Guide to Security Assurance for Cloud Computing*,
Computer Communications and Networks, DOI 10.1007/978-3-319-25988-8_12

helps the businesses to reduce costs by enabling them to pay only for the services they use and saves them from investing heavily on IT infrastructure. Cloud has been widely adopted in IT industry across the world during the last decade. The major advantages that cloud provides are easy access to information and resources, less personnel training, ability to scale up or scale down the resources easily, business continuity through backup and recovery, quick deployment, and cost efficiency. As a result, all the major companies including Apple, Samsung, Google, Microsoft, and Amazon are using cloud computing for different applications.

The amount of data being transferred to cloud services such as iCloud, Dropbox, and Google Drive is increasing every day. Along with that, cloud has many applications in various areas where it is used in combination with different technologies. Mobile cloud computing is referred to as an architecture in which data storage and data processing take place outside the mobile device and in the cloud. Users can access data in cloud through wireless Internet. As a result, not only the mobile applications can be used by a large number of cloud customers, but also the mobile devices do not need to have large processing power and storage to process data. Some applications of mobile cloud computing include mobile commerce, mobile learning, mobile healthcare, and mobile gaming [48]. Many health organizations are using cloud computing to store the record of their patients anonymously.

Another application of cloud computing is in vehicular ad hoc networks (VANET). VANET is a technology that uses short-range communication protocols such as wireless local area network (WLAN) technology to create a mobile network among vehicles in an approximately 100 to 300 m distance [45]. All the participating vehicles in VANET act as wireless nodes, and they can exchange different messages among each other and adjacent roadside infrastructure to support traffic safety and make driving experience more comfortable. Some of the messages that can be exchanged between vehicles in VANET are vehicle collision warning, security distance warning, driver assistance, cooperative driving, and dissemination of road information, Internet access, map location, automatic parking, and driverless vehicles [17].

Vehicular cloud networks (VCN) is a promising technology which introduces the concept of merging VANET technology with cloud computing. This provides an unlimited computing resources and storing/downloading VANET data via the Internet. The extension of traditional computing facilities with vehicular computing resources such as storage, processing, and sensing can help drivers in new ways to overcome critical road safety and congestion issues.

Rest of the chapter is organized as follows: Section 12.2 introduces the VANET in detail including its architecture, components, and its different characteristics. Section 12.3 leads to VCN where the three-tier architecture and its operation is explained. Threats in VCN are introduced in Sect. 12.4, where different threats in each tier are explained in detail and the review questions are given in Sect. 12.5.

12.2 Vehicular Ad Hoc Networks (VANET)

VANET are considered as the backbone of intelligent transportation system (ITS) as it ensures traffic safety and traffic assistance. This section introduces the VANET architecture, its different components, and their characteristics in detail.

12.2.1 VANET Architecture

VANET is an emerging technology with its main motivations to ensure life safety and security on the roads. In VANET, the vehicles are equipped with communication interfaces, which enable the transportation of important messages between neighboring vehicles and adjacent infrastructure in the vicinity of communication range [4]. Infrastructure refers to the static entities and is mostly positioned along the roadside. In the context of VANET, this refers to *roadside units (RSUs)*. This includes a speed camera, relay node (RN), or mobile communication base station.

In VANET, the transportation of messages is carried via two modes. These are

1. Vehicle-to-vehicle (V2V) communication
2. Vehicle-to-infrastructure (V2I) communication

In V2V communication, the messages are shared with neighboring vehicles via short-range communication protocols. These include dedicated short-range communication (DSRC) technologies and wireless LAN protocols, i.e., IEEE 802.11. V2V communication results in short-range communication where it ensures communication between neighboring vehicles without any support from infrastructure. On the other hand, V2I communication ensures communication between vehicles and adjacent infrastructure with the help of RN or any mobile communication technologies such as long-term evolution (LTE). V2I communication is used for transporting messages generated by source vehicle over large geographical location.

Figure 12.1 depicts the architecture of VANET in case of an accident. It can be seen that the vehicles close to the vicinity of accident receives messages via V2V communication, while other vehicles receives messages via V2I communication.

12.2.2 Components of VANET

VANET consists of several components, i.e., vehicular user, vehicle, messages, infrastructure, wireless communication network, back-end server, and attackers.

- *Vehicular user:* Vehicular user constitutes the most important entity in VANET. The user privacy including personal data, geographical location, and confidential information must be guaranteed in VANET.
- *Vehicle:* The important assets in vehicle are its on-board unit (OBU) with communication capabilities, application unit (AU) with several applications

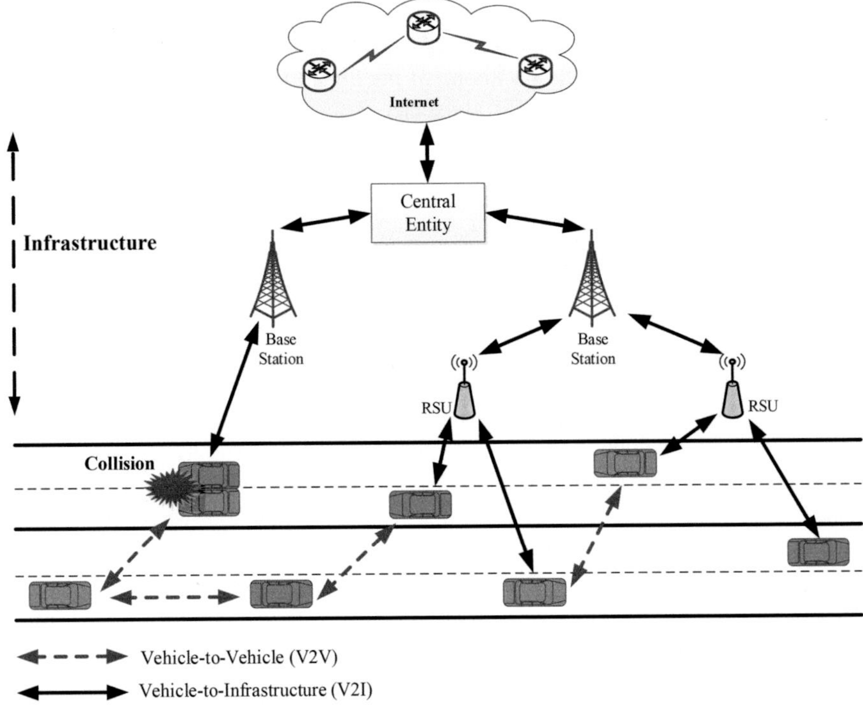

Fig. 12.1 VANET architecture; example of collision of vehicles

like collision avoidance system, and different sensors which collect information from surroundings.

- *Messages:* Messages contain various important information which are exchanged between vehicles and adjacent RSU. This contains accident warning, driver and vehicular passenger information, confidential data, weather and road traffic information, etc.
- *Infrastructure:* Infrastructure acts as a bridge for exchanging messages between vehicles and back-end server. Infrastructure also enables the messages to be transmitted over a large geographical location. This includes adjacent RSUs, speed camera, and RNs.
- *Wireless communication network:* It provides the air interface to transmit the important messages to neighboring vehicles and RSUs. In VANET, there are three types of communication.

1. In-vehicle communication between OBU and sensors via internal high-speed buses
2. Communication between two vehicles via DSRC technologies
3. Communication between vehicle and RSU via mobile communication such as LTE and RN

- *Back-end server:* Back-end server lies in the Internet domain containing the application server such as collision avoidance application server. The messages received on server are transmitted via RSU to vehicles on large geographical location.
- *Attacker:* Attacker is a temporary component in VANET; it is usually active for a short period of time. The main motivation of attacker is to manipulate the information and modify the information and vehicular network for his own benefits. The attacker must be identified and eliminated from the network intelligently.

12.2.3 Important Characteristics of VANET

VANET is designed to provide a safe and comfortable journey to the vehicular user on the road. VANET is also useful in fleet management where different vehicles have identical destination address [5, 6]. However, VANET relies on applications which depend on the availability of different vehicles and RSUs in the vicinity of source vehicle to transport the messages. These generated messages must arrive at the destination without any alteration from an attacker as this can lead to a drastic impact on the overall network operation and performance. Therefore, from security point of view, integrity of the information is one of the important aspects in VANET [7, 8].

VANET possess different unique properties which makes them different from other ad hoc networks. These are as follows:

12.2.3.1 Decentralized Systems

One of the main characteristics of VANET is the distributed and decentralized system since the occurrence of fixed infrastructure is not guaranteed in VANET. This lack of central entity poses different challenges such as secure message routing and QoS [9].

12.2.3.2 High-Speed Mobility and Dynamic Topology

VANET involves high-speed vehicles which are mostly randomly dispersed in the network. According to [10], two vehicles meet each other for a very short span of time which makes the network highly dynamic with constantly changing topology. Therefore, the availability of messages for this randomly changing topology must be ensured.

12.2.3.3 Cooperative Message Routing

Since VANET lacks centralized routing entity, the cooperation between two vehicles is necessary for message routing. Due to high-speed mobility of vehicles, the routing table cannot be maintained and updated all the time. Researchers have proposed different routing protocols in VANET which are grouped in six categories: topology-based routing, geo-cast routing, broadcast-based routing, position-based routing, infrastructure-based routing, and cluster-based routing [10–12].

12.2.3.4 Real-Time Processing

Real-time processing of information in VANET is of great importance since any delay in the important life-saving situation might affect the network severely. The information in VANET must ensure the security requirements, i.e., confidentiality, availability, authenticity, and integrity, and must ensure to process the safety messages in real-time environment [13].

12.2.3.5 User and Data Privacy

Vehicular user constitutes the most vital entity in VANET. Privacy of the vehicular user's information such as name, address, and geo-location must be secured from the malicious attacker [14].

12.3 Vehicular Cloud Networking (VCN)

VANET usually involves vehicles equipped with different communication interfaces which enable the vehicles to communicate with others via dedicated short-range communication (DSRC) or mobile communication such as long-term evolution (LTE) [15, 16]. Each vehicle posses some storage and computation resources. Due to fixed size hardware limitations of vehicles, these storage and computation resources are limited in nature. In the future, the bandwidth hungry applications such as vehicular user multimedia applications and social networking applications may not be supported by the vehicle itself. Therefore, different vehicles must cooperate together to share their resources, resulting in a newly emerging vehicular technology, called vehicular-based cloud networks (VCN).

In recent years, different research projects have been carried out which merge VANET with cloud computing. The concept of VCN was first introduced by the authors in [17] in the form of autonomous vehicular clouds (AVC). In AVC, the computing and communication resources are assigned dynamically to the users. In [18], the authors have taken a step further where they introduced a platform as a service (PaaS) model to provide multiple services to users in a highly dynamic environment. Hussain et al. proposed an architecture with multiple clouds such as vehicular cloud (VC), vehicles using clouds (VuCs), and hybrid clouds (HCs) [19]. The authors in [20] proposed a hierarchical structure of cloud computing in vehicular networks. However, security aspect of VCN is missing in existing literature. The main contribution of this chapter is twofold: Firstly, it presents a 3-tier architecture of cloud-based vehicular networks, and, secondly, it identifies threats in each tier of the architecture.

12.3.1 Vehicular-Based Cloud Networking (VCN) Architecture

The hierarchical architecture of VCN is depicted in Fig. 12.2. It is a three-tier architecture which consists of following levels:

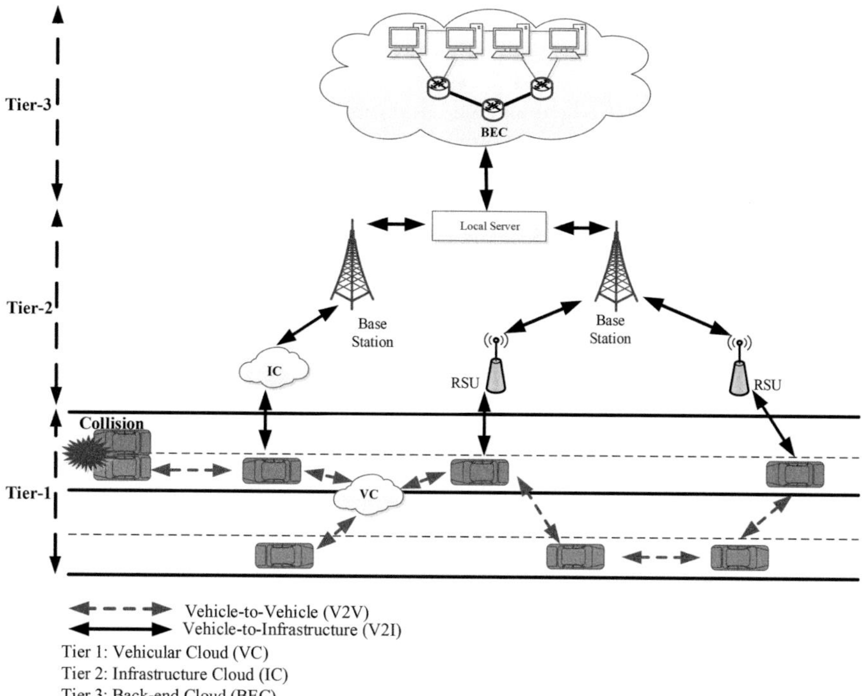

Fig. 12.2 Vehicular-based cloud networking architecture

1. Tier-1 cloud: vehicular cloud (VC)
2. Tier-2 cloud: infrastructure cloud (IC)
3. Tier-3 cloud: back-end cloud (BEC)

1. ***Vehicular cloud (VC):*** In VC, the physical resources (storage and computation) of vehicles are shared between group of vehicles only. This results in high overall efficiency of the network. The scope of VC is local in the context of VANET where information is shared between vehicles via V2V communication. Due to high mobility and dispersed distribution of vehicles in the network, the formation of VC is technically very difficult. The best example to implement VC is for fleet vehicles where the start and destination of the vehicles are mostly similar. These fleet vehicles can share their resources, resulting in a VC which can be used to serve different applications such as road information, weather information, etc.
2. ***Infrastructure cloud (IC):*** IC is initiated by adjacent RSU along the road where other vehicles request to access the services provided by the cloud. The scope of this cloud is local to small geographical area where RSU is located. Communication between two different ICs is carried out through dedicated local servers. The technically difficulty of formation of this cloud varies in different scenarios. If an extensive amount of RSU is available in a region, then different

vehicles and RSUs can share their resources resulting in IC. However, despite the fact that VCN mostly faces high-speed mobility of vehicles in the network, IC is technically formed for a very short span of time.

3. ***Back-end cloud (BEC):*** Back-end cloud is the largest cloud in vehicular environment which exists in the Internet domain. BEC has more resources which can be used by vehicles for extensive data storage and high computation [20]. The scope of BEC is spread over the large geographical area to serve the vehicles.

12.3.2 Vehicular-Based Cloud Networking (VCN) Operation

To create and initiate a cloud in vehicular networks, it needs a cloud leader. If leader is a vehicle and no RSU participates in its cloud formation, then the cloud created is VC. However, if the request for cloud is initiated by RSU, then it forms IC, where other vehicles can access the resources of cloud.

The cloud leader invites other vehicles and RSUs in its vicinity by transmitting the resource request messages (REQs) to form a cloud. Any vehicle wishes to join the cloud responds back to the cloud leader with resource reply messages (REPs) where these vehicles act as cloud members [21]. When cloud leader receives the confirmation via REP messages, it keeps its members' ID and assigns different tasks to them. The members communicate constantly with its cloud leader. Based on the permission from cloud leader, the members can publish and share the content received from leader with other vehicles.

Cloud leader is responsible to maintain the cloud it created. However, if any member wishes to leave, the cloud sends the resource, leaving message to the cloud leader. In that case, the cloud leader releases that specific member and recruits new members by broadcasting REQ messages. However, in case a cloud leader no longer wants to keep the cloud, it broadcasts the cloud release message.

12.4 Threats in Vehicular-Based Cloud Networking

VCN extends the list of assets explained in Sect. 12.2.2 by adding assets related to cloud itself. This includes data, custom, and user-defined applications and infrastructure. This section introduces different threats to 3-tier structure of VCN.

12.4.1 Threats to Tier-1 and Tier-2 Clouds

The threats in this category are specific to tier-1 and tier-2 clouds of VCN. The threats lie to the vehicles, adjacent infrastructure, messages, wireless communication, and the resources which vehicles and RSU share among them. The threats can be exploited as:

12.4.1.1 Vehicle

Usually, VCN involves highly mobile vehicles, and the two vehicles communicate with each other for a very short span of time to form VC. However, there are still some threats to vehicles and its different components. The attacker can plan to access the OBU or AU of vehicle and sensors. The threat also includes the software running on AU and sensors where the strong aim of attackers is to introduce malware. Firmware updates are also one of the targets where the attacker injects malicious code inside the in-vehicle network via CAN. This can lead to drastic results, e.g., the attacker can misconfigure the sensor with its malicious code [22, 23].

12.4.1.2 Adjacent Infrastructure

Infrastructure includes the static entity called RSU. As these are not mobile, the major threats lie to its hardware. Usually, physical security to RSU hardware is provided via CCTV. Other threats to infrastructure include illegal access of attacker to its software platform and DoS attack.

12.4.1.3 Wireless Communication

Wireless communication is a medium, responsible for exchanging messages with other vehicles. This includes both V2V and V2I communication. As this wireless medium is exposed to different vulnerabilities, if offers several opportunities to an attacker to exploit it for its own benefits. The threats to wireless communication include denial of service (DoS), tempering and alteration of the messages en route and jamming the wireless communication channel, etc.

- *Denial of service (DoS):* DoS attack is one of the critical attacks in ad hoc networks, and in case of VCN, it can leave a severe impact on the network. In this attack, the attacker blocks the communication channel by refusing other cloud members to forward important messages to the cloud, other vehicles, and RSU in the vicinity.
- *Data tempering:* The main motivation of the attacker is to alter and modify the messages en route to vehicles, RSU, IC, and VC in this attack [24].
- *Jamming the wireless communication channel:* This type of attack results in the complete jamming of wireless medium responsible to carry the messages. Jamming of the wireless medium is the result of DoS attack most of the time.

12.4.1.4 Messages

Messages contain important information about a particular event, which is usually exchanged among the vehicles and adjacent RSUs during V2V and V2I communication. Threats to these messages always exist where the main interest of the attacker is to compromise its confidentiality, integrity, and authenticity (CIA). The threats to information can be exploited in the following different security aspects.

- *Threats to confidentiality of message:* Confidentiality is a significant security aspect which provides secrecy by limiting access of attacker to the message.

The threat caused by this aspect is the illegal monitoring transmitted in V2V and V2I communication.

- *Threats to authenticity of message:* The routing of accurate and authentic message should be ensured in VCN as it involves several life-saving contexts. The source and destination of messages must be known and verifiable. The threat which lies to messages from this perspective is the ID theft of vehicular user from an attacker. This can lead to severe and drastic results in VCN, especially during the event of an accident.
- *Threats to integrity of message:* Message transmitted from source should arrive at the destination without any alteration to its content. The threat from this aspect is that the message can be tempered, modified, or deleted from attacker in transit while carrying the transmission of message between two vehicles [25]. Therefore, integrity of message in both modes of communication, i.e., V2V and V2I, should be ensured.
- *Threat to availability of message:* Since the main aim of vehicular network is to provide drivers safety, it should be ensured that the message transmitted from any vehicle and tier-1 and tier-2 cloud regarding any particular context is available to other neighboring vehicles and adjacent RSU.
- *Non-repudiation:* Non-repudiation ensures the message generated from sender and receiver is verifiable by the authorities [26]. Therefore, the senders should be responsible for the messages generated. The threat from this category is the denial of message produced by sender or denial of message reception by receiver through the clouds.

12.4.1.5 Vehicular Cloud

As VC is the result of sharing of computation and storage resources of vehicles, therefore, the main threats lie to the cloud platform itself. An adversary may attack the cloud by injecting malware into the cloud platform. Threat also lies to the important messages, as these are communicated between the vehicles through this cloud. Privacy is also one of the important security aspects which aim to ensure that the identity of the vehicular user is kept secret from an unauthorized person [27]. The threats in this regard include revealing the vehicular user identity, its geographical location, and sensitive information.

12.4.1.6 Infrastructure Cloud

Since both static and mobile entities are involved in IC, the threats lie to both cloud platform and the messages. The attacker may prevent the static RSU to exchange messages with other members by implementing DoS attack. Threats also exist to the messages which are communicated via infrastructure cloud. The possible scenario is the rouge cloud member, which becomes part of the cloud to steal important information via spoofing. This can produce threat to the privacy of the user information. This rouge cloud member must be identified and cleverly removed from the cloud.

12.4.2 Threats to Tier-3 Cloud

In this section, we focus on the threats that can be used to launch attacks on the tier-3 cloud. These attacks can be launched on the vehicular data once it has been transferred to a traditional IT cloud. We do not consider the attacks on the vehicular cloud which is temporarily formed among vehicles in local area to share their data and processing.

12.4.2.1 Data Breaches

Data breach in infrastructure cloud is the leakage of vehicular data to an unauthorized entity who does not have the legal right to see that data. Data breach is a very common attack, and Cloud Security Alliance (CSA) [28] has mentioned it as the most critical threat in cloud. According to CSA, 91 % of cloud tenants consider it as a significant threat in cloud computing. It can result in the loss of data security properties of confidentiality and integrity.

Data breaches in infrastructure cloud mostly occur due to flaws in application designing, operational issues, insider attackers, and insufficiency of authentication, authorization, and audit controls. Moreover, virtual machine (VM) escape attack [29] can be used to breach vehicular data of other users in a cloud environment. To launch a VM escape attack, an attacker leases a VM in cloud to run a script through which he can break out of his VM and access the code of Virtual Machine Manager (VMM). Having access to the code of VMM provides root privileges to the attacker who can access the data from services processing vehicular data on cloud. Similarly, attacker will also be able to access the vehicular data if it is stored in cloud or being processed by any application.

12.4.2.2 Data Loss

Data loss is referred to the loss of vehicular data in infrastructure cloud. Data life cycle in cloud has five main stages, namely, creation, transfer, processing, storage, and destruction. Once the vehicular data has been transferred to the cloud, it will be processed by applications and stored in the cloud storage. Data loss in cloud occurs during data transfer to and from cloud, during processing by applications or in cloud storage [30]. CSA in their survey have listed data loss is the second most significant threat in cloud computing with almost 91 % of cloud tenants considering it as a significant threat [28]. Data loss mostly occurs due to insider attacks which include data deletion, data corruption, and loss of data encryption key and other issues such as faults in storage system and natural disasters.

12.4.2.3 Account or Service Hijacking

Account or service hijacking is a term referred to an attack in which attacker steals the credentials of victims to access their data and services in cloud [31]. This not only results in loss of confidentiality, integrity, and availability of data, but attacker can also use these credentials to launch attacks from victims' account. Account or service hijacking of vehicular data can be done by the network attacks such as phishing, SQL injection, cross-site scripting (XSS), botnets, and software vulnerabilities such as buffer overflow. In phishing attacker usually sends an email that seems to come from a legitimate authority to the user with the purpose of stealing his identity such as login credentials. XSS is done by compromising the web application to contain a malicious script which maybe a JavaScript, HTML, or flash and sending it to a benign user, while botnet is a network of interconnected computers over the Internet that can perform automated tasks such as distributed denial of service attack.

12.4.2.4 Denial of Service

Denial of service (DOS) attacks can be launched from cloud services or from outside the cloud that consume the resources including data, storage, virtual machines, and network bandwidth. This results in the unavailability of these resources to the legitimate users due to which vehicular services running on infrastructure cloud will be unable to respond to user requests. DOS attacks are very common in cloud computing, and 81 % of cloud tenants consider it as a relevant threat [28]. Another variant of DOS attack is distributed denial of service (DDOS) attack in which more than one sources are used to launch this attack [32]. Some attack sources in DDOS attack are legitimate users who are compromised by network attack such as Trojan which makes the DDOS hard to detect. Other ways of launching DOS attack include exploiting the vulnerabilities in web server, databases, and applications, resulting in unavailability of resources.

12.4.2.5 Insecure Interfaces and APIs

Application programming interfaces (APIs) is a set of rules that governs how applications communicate with each other and the underlying operating systems or libraries. All the cloud service models including IaaS, PaaS, and SaaS have standard and custom APIs for their applications. Different applications can be integrated into the cloud using APIs, and cloud providers have introduced APIs for their platforms. Some of the widely used APIs are Amazon Web Service (AWS) API, Google Compute Engine, VMware vCloud API, and OpenStack API [33]. The security of an application in cloud depends on the security of its APIs. Insecure APIs on vehicular services can result in the violation of authentication and access control principles. Moreover, the attacker having access to data can lead to the loss of data confidentiality or integrity.

12.4.2.6 Malicious Insider

Malicious insider is an employee of the cloud organization with access to its resources and assets such as data, but he misuses his privileges to perform unauthorized actions. CSA has defined malicious insider as the employee whose actions result in the loss of security properties of confidentiality, integrity, or availability of organization's information or information systems. Having malicious insiders is a critical threat in cloud with 88 % of cloud users considering it as a relevant issue [28]. Malicious insiders can also be hobbyist attacker who exploits organizations' resources weaknesses just for fun. Moreover, lack of security measures for vehicular applications protection in cloud can also be exploited by the malicious insiders.

12.4.2.7 Abuse of Cloud Services

Abuse of cloud services in VCN is referred to the tenants who misuse the vehicular cloud services they have purchased. Misuse includes the illegal or unethical use of services by tenants that violate their contract with service provider which is called service-level agreement (SLA) [34]. Abuse of cloud services was the most common threat in cloud computing in 2010, but different security measures were introduced to prevent it, and now it is the seventh most critical threat in cloud computing. Cloud services have been used to launch different attacks over the years. A botnet attack was launched in 2009 using Amazon's EC2 services as the command and control servers for that attack [35]. Similarly, the unlimited computation power of cloud can be used to launch password-cracking attacks such as brute force, performing DOS attacks and others such as cross-site scripting.

12.4.2.8 Shared Technology Vulnerabilities

Cloud service provider's provision shared resources such as computation, network, and storage resources to different users. However, the sharing of resources such as hard disk, RAM, and GPUs might not offer perfect isolation. If isolation is not properly implemented, a malicious attacker can get unauthorized access to cloud resources, VMs, customer's data, and sensitive vehicular data. Almost 82 % of users consider shared technology vulnerabilities as a relevant threat in cloud that can have impact on IaaS, PaaS, and SaaS services models [28]. XEN is an open-source virtualization platform for cloud that has a XEN hypervisor with API toolstack and other features [36]. A vulnerability of local privilege escalation was found in XEN that can be used to launch guest to host virtual machine escape attack.

12.5 Review Questions

1. What are the main characteristics of the modes of transporting messages in VANET?
2. Identify different key infrastructure components in VANET and explain their main purpose.
3. How important is real-time processing in context of VANET?
4. What are the key differences between the clouds in three-tier architecture of VCN?
5. To which attacks is the wireless communication in VCN most vulnerable?
6. What is the difference between the threats to the authenticity of message and non-repudiation in VCN?
7. What are the main stages in data life cycle in cloud? In which stages can data loss occur?
8. Name the attacks that can be launched in tier-three cloud network to hack accounts or services.
9. How can the tier-three cloud services be misused by tenants?
10. Which shared technology vulnerability was discovered in XEN virtualization platform?

References

1. Dinh HT, Lee C, Niyato D, Wang P (2013) A survey of mobile cloud computing: architecture, applications, and approaches. Wirel Commun Mob Comput 13(18):1587–1611
2. Chandrasekaran G (2008) VANETs: the networking platform for future vehicular applications. Department of Computer Science, Rutgers University
3. Boukerche A, Oliveira HA, Nakamura EF, Loureiro AA (2008) Vehicular ad hoc networks: a new challenge for localization-based systems. Comput Commun 31(12):2838–2849
4. Ahmad F, Adnane A (2015) Design of trust based context aware routing protocol in vehicular networks. In: Ninth IFIP WG 11.11 international conference on trust management (IFIPTM'15), Hamburg
5. Ahmad F, Marwat SNK, Zaki Y, Goerg C (2014) Tailoring LTE-advanced for M2M communication using wireless inband relay node. In: Proceedings of world telecommunications congress 2014 (WTC'14). VDE, Berlin, Germany, pp 1–3
6. Ahmad F, Marwat SNK, Zaki Y, Mehmood Y, Cörg C (2014) Machine-to-machine sensor data multiplexing using LTE-advanced relay node for logistics. In: 4th international conference on dynamics in logistics (LDIC'14), Bremen
7. Mármol FG, Kuhnen MQ (2013) Reputation-based web service orchestration in cloud computing: a survey. Concurr Comput Pract Exp. doi: 10.1002/cpe.3177
8. Alriyami Q, Adnane A, Kim Smith A (2014) Evaluation criteria for trust management in vehicular ad-hoc networks (VANETs). In: The 3rd international conference on connected vehicles & expo (ICCVE 2014), Vienna. IEEE
9. Raya M, Hubaux J-P (2007) Securing vehicular ad-hoc networks. J Comput Secur 15(1):39–68
10. Li F, Wang Y, Routing in vehicular ad-hoc networks: a survey. IEEE Veh Technol Mag
11. Lin Y-W, Chen Y-S, Lee S (2010) Routing protocols in vehicular ad hoc networks: a survey and future perspectives. J Inf Sci Eng 26(3):913–932
12. Benamar M, Benamar N, Singh KD, El Ouadghiri D (2013) Recent study of routing protocols in VANET: survey and taxonomy. In: WVNT 2013: 1st international workshop on vehicular networks and telematics, Marrakech
13. Al-kahtani M (2012) Survey on security attacks in vehicular ad hoc networks(VANETs). In: 6th international conference on signal processing and communication systems (ICSPCS), Gold Coast, pp 1–9
14. Wex P, Breuer J, Held A, Leinmuller T, Delgrossi L (2008) Trust issues for vehicular ad-hoc networks. In: Vehicular technology conference, 2008. VTC Spring 2008, Singapore. IEEE, pp 2800–2804
15. Grassi G, Pesavento D, Wang L, Pau G, Vuyyuru R, Wakikawa R, Zhang L (2013) Acm hotmobile 2013 poster: vehicular inter-networking via named data. ACM SIGMOBILE Mob Comput Commun Rev 17(3):23–24
16. Grassi G, Pesavento D, Pau G, Vuyyuru R, Wakikawa R, Zhang L (2014) VANET via named data networking. In: IEEE conference on computer communications workshops (INFOCOM WKSHPS), Toronto. IEEE, pp 410–415
17. Olariu S, Eltoweissy M, Younis M (2011) Towards autonomous vehicular clouds. EAI Endorsed ICST Trans Mob Commun Appl 11:e2
18. Bernstein D, Vidovic N, Modi S (2010) A cloud PAAS for high scale, function, and velocity mobile applications-with reference application as the fully connected car. In: Proceedings of the 2010 fifth international conference on systems and networks communications (ICSNC), Nice. IEEE Computer Society, pp 117–123
19. Son J, Eun H, Oh H, Kim S, Hussain R (2012) Rethinking vehicular communications: merging vanet with cloud computing. In: Proceedings of the 2012 IEEE 4th international conference on cloud computing technology and science (CloudCom), Taipei. IEEE Computer Society, pp 606–609
20. Yu R, Zhang Y, Gjessing S, Xia W, Yang K (2013) Toward cloud-based vehicular networks with efficient resource management. IEEE Netw 27:48–55

21. Lee E, Lee E-K, Gerla M, Oh S (2014) Vehicular cloud networking: architecture and design principles. IEEE Commun Mag 52:148–155
22. Nilsson DK, Larson UE (2008) Combining physical and digital evidence in vehicle environments. In: Third international workshop on systematic approaches to digital forensic engineering (SADFE'08), Berkeley. IEEE, pp 10–14
23. Nilsson DK, Larson UE (2008) Conducting forensic investigations of cyber attacks on automobile in-vehicle networks. In: Proceedings of the 1st ACM international conference on forensic applications and techniques in telecommunications, information, and multimedia, Adelaide
24. Yan G, Rawat D, Bista B (2012) Towards secure vehicular clouds. In: Sixth international conference on complex, intelligent and software intensive systems (CISIS), Palermo, pp 370–375
25. Plossl K, Nowey T, Mletzko C (2006) Towards a security architecture for vehicular adhoc networks. In: IEEE first international conference on availability, reliability and security (ARES), Vienna
26. Mejri MN, Ben-Othman J, Hamdi M (2014) Survey on VANET security challenges and possible cryptographic solutions. Veh Commun 1:53–66
27. Grover J, Gaur MS, Laxmi V (2013) Trust establishment techniques in VANET. In: Wireless network security, signals and communication technology. Springer, Berlin, pp 273–301
28. Group TTW et al (2013) The notorious nine: cloud computing top threats in 2013. In: Cloud security alliance, 2013, San Francisco
29. Kortchinsky K (2009) Cloudburst: A VMware guest to host escape story. In: Black Hat USA, Las Vegas
30. Armbrust M, Fox A, Griffith R, Joseph AD, Katz R, Konwinski A, Lee G, Patterson D, Rabkin A, Stoica I et al (2010) A view of cloud computing. Commun ACM 53(4):50–58
31. Choubey R, Dubey R, Bhattacharjee J (2011) A survey on cloud computing security, challenges and threats. Int J Comput Sci Eng (IJCSE) 3(3):1227–1231
32. Kazim M, Zhu SY (2015) A survey on top security threats in cloud computing. Int J Adv Comput Sci Appl (IJACSA) 6(3):109–113
33. Zafar MS, Ahmad F (2014) A study on personalization and customization mechanisms of vehicular cloud platform. In: IEEE/ACM 7th international conference on utility and cloud computing (UCC), London, pp 812–817
34. Patel P, Ranabahu AH, Sheth AP (2009) Service level agreement in cloud computing. In: International conference on Object-Oriented Programming, Systems, Languages and Applications (OOPSLA), Orlando, USA
35. Whitney L (2009) Amazon EC2 cloud service hit by botnet, outage. CNET News, vol 11
36. Matthews JN, Dow EM, Deshane T, Hu W, Bongio J, Wilbur PF, Johnson B (2008) Running xen: a hands-on guide to the art of virtualization. Prentice Hall PTR, Upper Saddle River

Farhan Ahmad received his B.Sc. degree in Electronics Engineering at COMSATS Institute of Information Technology, Abbottabad, Pakistan, in 2009 and M.Sc. degree in Communication and Information Technology at University of Bremen, Germany, in 2014. He developed his M.Sc. thesis in the domain of M2M communication and LTE-Advanced Networks. He is currently pursuing his PhD studies at the College of Engineering and Technology, University of Derby, UK, where his current research focuses on security and trust in vehicular networks, mobile communications, and information centric networking.

Muhammad Kazim is a PhD student at the University of Derby, UK. His research area in PhD is cloud computing security. Before starting his PhD, he completed his masters degree in Computer and Communication Security from the National University of Sciences and Technology, Islamabad, Pakistan, in 2014. Earlier, he completed his bachelor's degree in Information and Communication Systems Engineering also from the National University of Sciences and Technology in 2011. Other research areas of his interest are computer networks, computer security, and communication systems.

Asma Adnane joined the University of Derby as a full-time senior lecturer in Networks and Security from the University of Leicester, where she was Knowledge Transfer Partnership associate with CrowdLab as their database and security expert. Asma has a PhD in Computer Science and has published several papers on ad hoc network security and trust management. She was aso a research associate/lecturer in France at the University of Rennes, University of Nantes, and ENSI-Bourges.

Index

S.Y. Zhu et al. (eds.), *Guide to Security Assurance for Cloud Computing*, Computer Communications and Networks, DOI 10.1007/978-3-319-25988-8